FBI Diary
Profiles of Evil

Peter M Klismet Jr

The author has tried to accurately recreate events, locales, and conversations from his memories of them. The views and opinions expressed in this book are solely those of the author. In order to maintain anonymity, in some instances the author may have changed the names of individuals and places. The author may have changed some identifying characteristics and details such as physical properties, occupations, and places of residence.

Published by Fountain Blue Publishing of California.
http://www.fountainbluepublishing.com

First Publishing: March 2016

Book design by Fountain Blue Publishing

Editing by:
Kris Franklin
www.krisfranklin.com

10 9 8 7 6 5 4 3 2 1

DISCLAIMER

The views and opinions expressed in this book are those of the author, and do not represent the views and opinions of the FBI. This book is meant to accurately portray the life and times of the people in it; however, some creative license has been taken to keep the flow of the story vital, clear, and intact. Historical people are mentioned by name; most other characters carry fictitious names that may represent a composite of more than one person, or exaggerated traits to emphasize a point. The same holds true for conversations, alleged quotes, classroom lectures, interviews, and interrogations that take place throughout the book. Together, I hope they create an entertaining, and informative excursion into a dimension of our world which very few people have had an opportunity to see. Any errors of fact in the book are mine, alone.

DEDICATION

This book could not have been completed without the patience of my family members during the course of thirty years in law enforcement. It's not easy to endure the long hours, trips out of town, and other demands of a career this long. It's taken me many years to understand this, and I am appreciative of what you had to tolerate, particularly my former spouse, Mary Ann, who passed away in February of 2013.

I would also like to dedicate this book to the victims and families of victims whose cases are enumerated within the pages of this work, and to the families and friends of all those who have met their fate at the hand(s) of violent sexual predators. Hopefully, we can get better at identifying these people before they start their killing careers, and in this process to determine better ways to deal with them before they strike. I'll say a few prayers for that to occur someday.

Last but not least would be my two editors. My wife, the amazing Miss Nancy, read page after page to me from a computer screen as we drove on trips, and made changes as we rolled along the highway. She is truly a trooper, an extraordinarily bright and articulate woman and she knows I love her dearly.

The overall editor for this book was the diligent and resourceful Robin Widmar. She constantly held my feet to the fire, and would never allow me to think about uttering the words, "That's good enough." She was amazingly patient with me as we went through this second edition. What she did was to turn this into a much better book than the first edition.

ACKNOWLEDGMENTS

Dave Bundy, Editor of the *Lincoln Star Journal*, was kind enough to approve the use of their research and incredible articles on the Helen Wilson case. Thank you Dave, Catharine Huddle, and the other top-notch reporters from the *Star* who did their best to bring an incredible injustice to the attention of the public. The work you did was, and remains, a sterling example of thoroughly-researched investigative reporting.

For Supervisory Special Agents Bob Ressler and Roy Hazelwood, both retired from the Behavioral Sciences Unit at the FBI Academy in Quantico, Virginia, I reserve my very special thanks. Each of you was instrumental in kindling a fire within me that has burned for thirty years. I continue to appreciate your mentorship and friendship. Regrettably, between the first edition of this book being released and the present edition going to the publisher, Bob Ressler has passed away. There are few people around who truly understand and appreciate the contributions Bob made to understanding and fighting violent crime. They can't be measured in words. As you will see from the chapters that involve him inside this book, I had and always will have the greatest respect for Bob. He was a true icon and we will all miss him greatly.

Finally, I would like to recognize the many dedicated officers, deputies, and agents who give so willingly of their time and lives, and whose friendship and professionalism I will always remember. Few understand how hard you work daily for our safety.

CHAPTER ONE

Comes Now the Unicorn!

Medieval knowledge of the legendary creature stemmed from biblical accounts and ancient sources. In fable, it was variously described as a wild ass, a goat, or a horse, and sometimes a combination of all three. Most often, the beast was thought to be a horse, but a most unusual one, with a huge spiraling horn projecting from its forehead toward the sky. In some stories, it is described as having a goat's beard and cloven hooves. It was said to be a wild woodland creature, a symbol of purity and grace, which could only be captured by a virgin. Its horn was said to have the power to render poisoned water potable, and to heal sickness. Its powers were thought to extend beyond even these miracles. Despite all evidence to the contrary, there was never a confirmed sighting of the animal. Until the nineteenth century, belief in the creature was widespread among historians, writers, poets, physicians, and theologians. While many wished to believe the unicorn roamed freely, no one could prove its existence, and the legend became the stuff of children's fairy tales.

During my time in the FBI, people would react to my occupation with, "I've never seen one of you, except on television." Or, "You *can't* be an FBI agent. They can't tell anyone what they do." I'd get, "I've never met an FBI agent in my life," and even, "I've heard of you, but I didn't really believe you existed." The most common response was, "Why in the world do we have FBI agents here?" The latter was far and away the most popular, particularly when I was in Iowa and Nebraska. It didn't take long to figure out I was, in fact, a unicorn.

Another question I often fielded was, "What is it like to be an FBI agent?" And yet another was, "What was the most interesting case you ever worked on?" The answer to the question, "What was it *really* like to be an FBI agent?" was the most difficult to answer. In truth, there was no single, correct answer. Because of the popularity of the television show *The FBI*, people had a certain image, if not stereotype, of what an FBI agent was supposed to look and act like. Another comment I frequently heard was, "You don't look like Efrem Zimbalist, Jr."

Well, no kidding.

While some legends fade away, others are born and prosper.

The infancy of an American legend began over one hundred years ago in Washington, D.C., in an institutional rather than mythological sense. Twelve Secret Service agents were assigned to form what was then called the Bureau of Investigation, or BOI. It took many years for that tiny, insignificant organization to grow into the mammoth agency it is today.

Prostitution was the initial focus of the BOI. Agents were tasked with visiting and making surveys of brothels to enforce provisions of the White Slave Act. With such a limited jurisdiction, the BOI grew slowly. But it did grow, and with the jurisdictional focus on prostitution it was not a surprise that corruption was rampant, even involving the first director, Stanley Finch. Hardly the things of which legends are made.

Finally, it became clear that changes had to be instituted. In 1924, President Calvin Coolidge appointed a young Department of Justice attorney, John Edgar Hoover, as the sixth director of the BOI. When he took over the bureau, it had approximately 650 employees, 441 of which were Special Agents. In 1935, Hoover was instrumental in changing the name of the organization to the Federal Bureau of Investigation. During his forty-eight year reign, which ended with his death in 1972, Hoover built the FBI into a large and efficient crime-fighting agency. Many innovations, including a national crime laboratory and a centralized fingerprint file, began under his watch. Many others would follow. And the legend grew.

But Hoover was also known to be somewhat capricious in his leadership. He frequently fired FBI agents if he thought they didn't convey the image he sought. He relocated agents who displeased him into career-ending assignments and locations such as Butte, Montana, and later Alaska. Hoover wanted to be the face of the FBI, and wanted his agents to be nameless and to labor in anonymity. One such agent, Melvin Purvis, was a prime example. Dedicated, incorruptible, and hard-working, Purvis was one of Hoover's most effective agents in capturing and breaking up gangs in the 1930s. It was Purvis who set the trap in which the notorious John Dillinger was killed in Chicago. For this high-profile case, Purvis received substantial local and even national acclaim. In no time, a jealous Hoover forced him out of the bureau. Purvis would later commit suicide, and most people felt his unfortunate demise resulted from his treatment by Hoover.

Relatively little was known about the FBI until a highly acclaimed documentary/drama, *The FBI Story*, hit movie screens in 1959. Starring in the squeaky-clean movie was James Stewart, and the film portrayed the FBI in the most positive light possible. The FBI had total control over the production, with J. Edgar Hoover acting as a co-producer of sorts, approving every frame of the film and having a pivotal role in selecting the cast for various roles. Hoover even made a brief cameo appearance. Each member of the cast, and those later involved in a television show, had to undergo exhaustive FBI background checks. Hoover did not want anyone involved with his publicity coups to tarnish the reputation of the bureau. With the growing popularity of television shows in the 1960s, Hoover found a vehicle to further publicize his growing organization. In 1965, *The FBI* premiered on prime time Sunday nights and was an immediate hit. A relatively unknown actor, Efrem Zimbalist, Jr., became the new face of the FBI. Personally selected by Hoover, Zimbalist's striking good looks perfectly depicted the image Hoover desperately wanted to convey to the American public. The show portrayed Zimbalist as Inspector Lewis Erskine, whose calm, methodical demeanor became iconic to the image Hoover wanted his agents to portray. And for Hoover, it was all about *image*. A veritable propaganda machine, he wanted the American public to believe his organization was invincible. And that's exactly what the public came to believe, until a whirlpool of controversy enveloped the agency in the late 1960s.

Hoover parlayed the popularity of the show, presented spurious statistics to Congress, and sought new federal violations for the FBI to enforce. The agency grew yearly, and is presently comprised of nearly 35,000 employees with approximately 15,000 as Special Agents. It's less an organization than an institution in modern society. But the standards established by Hoover continue in place, with only slight modifications. While he, alone, was allowed to address the media during his reign, that task has since been delegated to the Special Agents in Charge who supervise what is now fifty-six Field Offices across the country, including Alaska, Hawaii, and even Puerto Rico. But the people who do the field work, the Special Agents, continue to remain faceless.

If you were an FBI agent in the 1930s, you were poorly trained and out-gunned, but expected to battle the likes of John Dillinger, "Baby Face" Nelson, "Pretty Boy" Floyd, not to mention Bonnie and Clyde. In the 1940s, it was all about identifying potential spies in the war effort. In the 1950s, you were probably trying to identify communists because Senator Joe McCarthy made that a priority. The 1960s ushered in a new emphasis on the Mafia, which had been a plague on society for many years, but hadn't been immediately identified by the director. Instead, Hoover was preoccupied with *problems* such as the Ku Klux Klan, and civil rights activist Martin Luther King, Jr., one of Hoover's avowed enemies. And then, of course, there were the radical and violent student groups and the Black Panthers, among others. It was perhaps the most turbulent time in the history of the FBI.

As the 1970s dawned, the Vietnam War became the most controversial issue of the times. Mr. Hoover made anti-war protestors and other dissidents his highest priority, even authorizing illegal wiretaps and searches. The 1980s, under a different director, focused on violent crime and drugs, which largely continued into the 1990s.

When I entered on duty with the FBI in 1979, the easy answer to "What was it like?" depended on which of

the then fifty-nine field divisions you worked in, a
which squad you were assigned to. Later, in Los Angeles
in the 1980s, I was assigned to an Organized Crime
squad. Back then, it meant my squad was in a fight with
the Mafia. It was all about gambling, prostitution, and
control of the pornography industry, as well as a variety
of other criminal activities. We had several undercover
operations going, one of which was setting up a
pornography distribution business in the San Fernando
Valley. Much to our surprise, five Mafia members showed
up one day to muscle in on our operation, and we wound
up taking out the entire Mafia family in Los Angeles.
They were prime candidates for "Stupid Criminal"
recognition. It's not usually a good idea to threaten to
extort the FBI. Other squads in Los Angeles were
dedicated to bank robberies, foreign counterintelligence,
white-collar crime, and a myriad of other federal
violations.

Bank robberies in Los Angeles were a plague in the
'80s, and continue to be. On Christmas Eve of the first
year I was in Los Angeles, we had twenty-four, which
was then a national record. It's probably been long-since
eclipsed.

While I enjoyed my job in Los Angeles, everything
other than my work was incredibly stressful. My day
would start at 5:00 a.m. when I'd wake up and
immediately shower, shave, and, if I was lucky, have a
cup of coffee. I'd drive several miles, park my car, and
meet my carpool at six. We'd leave Thousand Oaks,
which was about thirty-five miles from our office, and
hope to be at the office by 7:30 a.m. The traffic to the
office was bumper-to-bumper, and fraught with heavy,
choking smog as we got further into the city. I wondered
why my eyes were burning so badly in the first few
weeks, and then I realized it was the smog. I'd race out
of the office at five o'clock, meet my carpool, and pray
we'd make it home by seven-thirty. They were extremely
long days. It was not only exhausting, but nerve-
wracking, and was turning me into a weekend alcoholic.
Something had to change. It was driving me nuts.

I was fortunate enough to work on some great
investigations during my two years in Los Angeles, and
then was lucky to get me and my family out of there. It
had to be fate. One of my buddies and I were on the

elevator headed for lunch when we stopped on the floor below. Two agents on our squad got aboard. One was looking at a routing slip from FBI Headquarters and said, "Who in the hell would ever want to go to the Omaha Division?" He crumpled the paper up and threw it into the trash can. I thought about it for a few seconds, and retrieved it. FBIHQ was seeking an agent with organized crime experience to volunteer for an undercover assignment in, of all places, Burlington, Iowa. I considered it, talked to my family, and applied. And, as the great Paul Harvey used to say, "That's the rest of the story."

CHAPTER TWO

Culture Shock: L.A. to Cedar Rapids, Iowa

Each city in the United States has its own distinct rhythm and identity. It's a life pulse that springs from the people and the land. Embedded in the DNA of Cedar Rapids, Iowa, is an agriculturally based work ethic that is partially summed up in the town's nickname, "The City of Five Seasons." The fifth season gave you an opportunity to enjoy the other four. For some it was nicknamed "The City of Five Smells," and Cedar Rapids does, in fact, have a unique odor, noticeable as one drives within several miles of the outskirts of town. A blend of scents from corn-based manufacturing plants, soy bean processing centers, meat packing houses, and a huge Quaker Oats cereal plant all contribute to the unique, but not unpleasant, odor. Once you've been to Cedar Rapids, you'll never forget it.

With its agricultural emphasis, rain is important to the entire state of Iowa, and it is also critical to all of the farming states in the Midwest. Abundant snow during the harsh winters insulates the rich soil, and in the spring melts off and provides huge, moist fields where crops are planted and thrive with the help of the warm sun and natural humidity. Few places enjoy the fertile soil and ideal growing conditions of Iowa and much of the Midwest.

In the early summer of 2008, a so-called "five-hundred-year flood" engulfed a sizeable part of Cedar Rapids. A torrent of flood waters from a heavy snow melt in Minnesota and northern Iowa submerged a good part of the city, inundating downtown businesses, many homes, and anything else which found itself to be within reach of the deluge. The city of Cedar Rapids was turned into Lake Cedar Rapids, and the fate of the town would be mentioned, infamously, in the national news for weeks. It was a completely unexpected natural disaster of epic proportions, perhaps rivaling that of Hurricane Katrina several years earlier, but without the extreme loss of life. While moisture is a critically important resource for Iowa farming, *that much* moisture flowing south to join the Mississippi River was simply too rapid, completely saturated the ground, and proved devastating. Friday, June 13th, was an apocryphal day for Cedar Rapids in more ways than simply being Friday the 13th. Floodwaters of the Cedar River crested at the highest level ever recorded, forever changing the thriving and industrious town of nearly 125,000 souls. While the town is often confused with the better-known Grand Rapids, Michigan, Cedar Rapids, Iowa, is an important link in the agricultural and technological chain of America.

The similarities are noteworthy in that both towns prosper largely as the result of the agricultural industries at their core, which in turn draw other businesses to both cities. In Cedar Rapids, one of the largest employers is Rockwell-Collins, which manufactures high-tech electronic instrumentation for NASA flights, the Space Shuttle, and most of the major aircraft companies. If you fly on a commercial airline, you can thank workers in Cedar Rapids for your safe departure and arrival, and probably for avoiding other planes flying around in the sky.

The surging waters overtook neighborhoods no one ever dreamed would flood. They raced through every downtown business and most public buildings, displacing city and county services. The County Court building and Linn County Sheriff's Office were among several county offices built on an island in the middle of the Cedar River. Perhaps a clever idea when built, these offices were nearly submerged and did not function during the emergency. The city of Cedar Rapids is still in a long recovery process.

Luckily I wasn't in Cedar Rapids in 2008. But equally lucky for me I *was* there some years before. It turned out to be eleven of the best and most interesting years of my life. Yes, in Iowa!

The then fifty-nine FBI field offices were scattered throughout the fifty states and Puerto Rico. I'd arrived in the Omaha Division, which covered the states of Iowa and Nebraska, after completing an undercover assignment in southeastern Iowa. Following the undercover assignment, I was assigned to the Cedar Rapids Resident Agency of the Omaha Division. The office was allotted slots for three Special Agents and one secretary at that time. When I arrived in October, I was the third agent and, of course, I had the least seniority. Which was certainly not a good thing, because I got all the nuisance work, the so-called "One Shot Leads," background checks, and old-dog cases that had been sitting around collecting dust for many years. Had I been there in 2008, my office on the second floor of the United States Courthouse and Federal Building would probably have been under a few feet of water.

Cedar Rapids was my second FBI assignment, plus I'd been a cop in Ventura, California, for almost ten years. So while I wasn't exactly wet behind the ears, I had only two years of experience in the bureau when I arrived in Cedar Rapids.

One agent in the office, Jerry Geiger, worked strictly on what were then called "Foreign Counter Intelligence" cases, and are probably called "Terrorism" cases today. I was surprised to hear that when I got there, but I eventually discovered a good part of Geiger's work revolved around the University of Iowa, about twenty-five miles down Interstate 380. Numerous students and scholars from foreign countries attended or taught at the university and other colleges in the area. The bureau apparently had some responsibility to watch over their activities, in the event they were subversives or wanted to steal technology. Or something else. I had no clue why we were concerned about them. My first thought about stealing our ideas was, *what're they gonna steal? The formula for a rootworm insecticide? Who cares?* The work Geiger did seemed to be highly secretive, yet I didn't find myself even slightly interested in learning about it. Frankly, I was glad someone else was doing it.

Jim Whalen was the Senior Resident Agent. He'd been there for nearly ten years when I arrived, and in fact had been my "Contact Agent" on the undercover assignment. After Whalen discovered I worked hard and did very thorough and complete paperwork, he implored the bosses in Omaha to have me fill the third, then empty, slot when my current assignment was over. He probably figured I would be better than getting a brand-new, clueless "baby agent" straight out of the FBI Academy. And he was probably right.

There were two common questions I heard from people in Iowa. The first usually was, "Why do we have the FBI in Iowa?" Most admitted they didn't even know we had an office in Cedar Rapids. So I'd explain why. And the second most frequent question was, "I'll bet it was culture shock to come here from Los Angeles." I probably heard that one a hundred times or more. While it was more of a statement, I guessed it was supposed to be framed as a question. Thus, my answers to the second question became pretty standard. "I really wanted to see what a snow blower and zero-degree temperatures were all about." Or, "Yeah, I really miss the smog. In fact, I got sort of addicted to it. But I solved that by starting my bureau car in the morning, going back to the exhaust pipe, and sniffing the fumes for a of couple minutes. Then I'm good to go."

I probably had about fifty "One Shot Leads" and the dreaded "Applicant" cases re-assigned from Jim Whalen to me as soon as I arrived. Some were at least six months old. Whalen didn't like doing them, and they shouldn't have been his bailiwick. Since he was a more senior, experienced agent, he was expected to develop more complex investigations. Which he did, and didn't really have time to be bothered by the annoying stuff. So a ton of it had accumulated and sat undone until I arrived. It was fairly simple work that a newer agent could do and learn from. All of the offices around the bureau would have cases that might have a lead to interview someone, or to conduct some type of investigation in our territory. Our job would be to cover the lead and send a communication back to the originating office with the report of the interview or investigation. For example, if the Los Angeles FBI office was doing a background investigation on an applicant for a government job, and the person listed a former employer, school, or a reference in eastern Iowa, they'd send an "Airtel" or teletype to us, explain what the lead was, and it was our job to conduct the necessary investigation and interviews. Once those were accomplished, we reported back to the "O.O." (Office of

Origin) at a specified time. This is what we had sitting around in the office for months before I arrived, and many of them were well behind the deadline.

Applicant work was a horse of a different flavor, and Whalen simply hated doing background checks on government applicants. As did everyone with more than a year in the bureau. Simply put, it was a pain in the ass, but J. Edgar Hoover once said, "It's the most important work in the bureau." Even though Hoover died many years before I signed up, a new agent was loathe to bitch about having to do it, lest he or she incur the wrath of superiors, many of whom were, as we called them, "Hooverites." They had come into the bureau during Hoover's reign, and still operated on the same principles he'd imbued in the bureau after so many years as director. But all of them had hated doing the applicant work as young agents. It was something like a vicious cycle, and once they'd risen in bureau ranks, they quickly forgot about how annoying applicant work could be. With the University of Iowa just down the road, we got plenty of it.

If an applicant for a job as an FBI agent or support employee, for example, grew up in Cedar Rapids, Dubuque, or Iowa City, or went to one of the many other colleges in our territory, then we'd have the job of conducting the entire investigation and setting out leads for other offices to cover. It was easy work, but tedious, and often required a lot of driving around in our territory since the bureau didn't like the interviews done over the phone. It was to my advantage that my first assignment at the Los Angeles FBI office was to the Applicant Squad for six months before I was rotated into Organized Crime. Thus, when I arrived in Cedar Rapids, applicant work and the various reports involved weren't something foreign to me and I could handle them efficiently and properly. I hit the ground running, and I found there was an endless supply generated out of Iowa City because of the size of the University of Iowa. I know my prowess impressed Whalen and the supervisors in Omaha.

But it wasn't all about applicant work. All sorts of criminal cases had leads to be covered, interviews to be done, and investigations to be completed for offices around the country. Fugitive cases were a good example. An office would have a person under indictment for federal charges, but the person didn't show up for court and was then considered a fugitive. The FBI had a classification for what we called "UFAPs," meaning Unlawful Flight to Avoid Prosecution cases. I doggedly tracked down more than a few of them, or scraped up some information from relatives or friends that eventually led to their capture. One arrest I made on a lead from Los Angeles was a woman who'd been involved in a serious stabbing at a bar. The police had secured a warrant for her arrest but couldn't find her, so they contacted their local FBI office. That generated a federal arrest warrant for UFAP, and Los Angeles sent out leads all over the country, which was a pretty routine thing. I found the woman at her mother's house, arrested her, and she copped out to everything she'd done. That single lead produced two trips to sunny L.A.: the first to testify at her preliminary hearing, and the second to testify at her trial. Both times I went to L.A. were during Iowa winters. It was a nice opportunity to warm up for a few days. So it was worth digging a little harder to find a fugitive, because it could lead to better things down the line.

While I was in Iowa, I first discovered how close to being a unicorn I was. Most people in rural Iowa led fairly simple and uncomplicated lives, and that's exactly how they liked it. The specter of violent crime, or crime of any type, was rarely an issue for them.

One fall afternoon I was racing around covering a bunch of different leads, and decided to drop by a farm near Tama, Iowa. I knocked on the front door and an older lady, probably in her early seventies, opened it.

"Good afternoon, ma'am," I said. "I'm Special Agent Pete Klismet from the FBI and I'm looking for a fugitive you might have seen around here." At the same moment, to properly identify myself, I flipped open my credentials, which she stared at intently. No surprise there. Most people had never seen a set of FBI "creds."

I was unfolding the fugitive's picture to show her when she looked up from my creds and said, "No sir, never saw him, but he looks like a pretty bad character, all right." The picture she was looking at was, of course, me.

It was hard to keep from laughing, but I finally got the picture of the fugitive out and showed it to her.

Unfortunately, she hadn't seen him, either. My eyes were watering from laughing when I left, and over the years I got plenty of laughs telling that story—probably more than any other experience in my long bureau career.

CHAPTER THREE

First Letter of Censure

Hey Pete!" Jim Whalen sounded uncharacteristically excited as he plopped down in my office one afternoon while I was dictating a report. "What're you working on?"

"Oh, nothing important, really. Just this report." I quickly switched off my recorder and looked up at him. "I've got a bunch of other stuff to organize and get out of here the rest of the week. And more next week, I suppose. Why, you got something in mind?"

"I know you've been busting your butt and knocking out the work left and right, but here's something I just found out about. I got a call from the sheriff down in Johnson County. He wanted to see if we could help with a case they've got started down there. It looks like they've got an informant telling them about a gambling operation in Iowa City. Apparently there's a bar involved where they're taking bets on games, and some guy by the name of Denny Anderson is running the whole show. Anderson's girlfriend is involved somehow, but I don't know much more than that. Don't know her name or anything about her. But I suspect you can find out pretty quick. How's it sound to you?"

"Sounds interesting to me." In those days, the FBI worked Interstate Gambling cases, if there was a connection with organized crime. The truth was, *all* gambling cases back then, even though they might be local, had a connection with Las Vegas, and thus the organized crime figures who essentially ran Las Vegas. In this case, the problem was we didn't have that connection. But maybe we could make it and work the case.

"I don't know anything about gambling, do you?" Jim asked.

"Well, I *guess* I do. When I was in L.A. working on the Organized Crime squad, I got involved in a gambling case with San Diego, Las Vegas, and somewhere else. Philadelphia, I think. Anyhow, it was a bunch of Mob guys, so we wound up getting wiretap approval. I ran the whole show in L.A., even though I barely had a clue what I was doing. Some of the old guys helped me out, so I guess the answer is 'yes,' I do know something about it."

"Then you're the right man for the job." Jim sounded pretty enthusiastic. "You've done a great job of getting all of this junk done and out of the office, but there comes a point where you have to start developing some substantive cases. Know what I mean?"

"Pretty much. But I haven't really had time with all of this crap to whittle down to size."

"I completely understand what you're saying, and you're right. You've done a hell of a job, but the way I see it, some agents are 'lead coverers,' and some others can never progress to the point where they're 'case agents'—developing real cases with some substance. That's where I want you to get. And I think you're ready for it. This might be the case to put your teeth into."

"Sounds all right to me. What do you want me to do?"

"Get a hold of the sheriff down there and see who he wants you to pair up with. It could turn into something good."

"Okay, will do," I said. "I'll give him a call first thing in the morning. I assume it's not a crisis that can't wait. I've gotta get these reports done and outta here. And my kids have parent-teacher conferences tonight, so I'm going to head home, have a bite to eat, and then my wife and I are going to run over and visit with the kids' teachers."

"Everything going okay?" Jim was always concerned that everyone was happy and doing fine at home.

"Oh, yeah. They've had some problems adjusting since we moved here from California. Well, not them so much, but the kids who grew up here have teased them a little and don't seem to want to let them join the group, so to speak. So it's been a bit of a struggle at times."

"Well, that's kids, I suppose. It'll get better."

We spent several months working with an informant in the Iowa City area. We had him place bets, make payoffs to Anderson and his girlfriend, and eventually I was able to get arrest warrants for ten people, and search warrants for several houses, a couple of bars, and an insurance office in the small town of Solon. Since the center of the operation was at Anderson's house, I served the search warrant there, accompanied by several sheriff's deputies and police officers. When we arrived, Anderson came to the door while on the phone. I showed him my creds and got a different response than I received from the farm lady.

"Oh shit," he said. "I was wondering when you guys would show up." I told him to give me the phone and I put the cuffs on him.

I told my search team to start their search of the house and sat Anderson down in the dining room to talk with him. And the phone kept ringing. And ringing. It was a Saturday morning during football season, so that made sense. Every time it rang, he'd look knowingly at me. Finally, I had an officer take him out to a car, and when the phone rang, I started answering it.

"This is Code 22. I've got five hundred on Michigan with the points, and a thousand on Nebraska over Colorado straight up."

"Okay, got it," I replied, furiously writing down all of the info.

"Hey," the man said. "Who the hell is this? Where's Denny?"

"Oh, sorry, Denny had an emergency in the family (which was basically true), so I told him I'd take the calls for a while (which was also true). This is Pete...sort of a friend of Denny's (not so true)."

"Okay, Pete. I'll have a little more action coming in later."

"Sounds good. Talk to you then. Over and out."

Over the course of the next hour, I took about fifty thousand dollars in bets on college football games. I don't recall anyone using their full name, except for a guy who'd always identify himself as "Brian." The investigation progressed quickly, because Denny was nice enough to have taped most of his phone calls, probably for his own protection. So we spent hours and hours listening to tapes and eventually collected enough evidence to indict Denny and nine others at the Federal Grand Jury a few months later. Down the line, everyone pled guilty. Denny got a couple years' full-ride scholarship to one of the federal penitentiaries. When he entered his plea in court, he told the judge he considered himself to be something of a "Community Recreation Director." The judge wasn't real excited about that explanation, and told him so as he meted out the specifics of his "scholarship."

The story had several other interesting developments. While they were not indicted on federal charges, we developed evidence on approximately a hundred more people who had placed numerous bets with the organization over a period of several years. Prominent among them was a former Iowa basketball coach. That information somehow was "leaked" to the media (not by me) and produced a huge article run in the *Cedar Rapids Gazette* and *Des Moines Register*. The coach later admitted to his involvement. We eventually submitted a ton of evidence and names of bettors to the Johnson County Attorney, but since they were all non-federal misdemeanors, he declined to prosecute. It was an election year! One of our defendants did a post-plea briefing, and told us about the entire scope of the operation, identifying yet more gamblers.

As a final highlight of the case, I did something no one else in the bureau probably ever has done. Or had done to them. The investigation garnered me a "Quality Step Increase," which meant I went from a GS-10 to an 11 about two years early. And, I got a brand-new bureau car from that year's fleet, which didn't please some of the senior agents in the division. But where good lies, bad may also loom. I received the dreaded "Letter of Censure" from my Special Agent in Charge. The letter was because I didn't 'properly document' some of the money used by the informant. I parceled it out to the informant rather than give him the total amount I'd received as 'buy money.' Seemed to me like the right thing to do, but apparently my SAC didn't like the way I did it. Thus, "The Letter." So the last two things in the file were a commendation and a censure letter. Lucky for me, this is the only Letter of Censure I'd ever receive. Such are the ways of the bureau!

CHAPTER FOUR

$300,000 in Stolen Student Loan Checks

How would you like your first criminal case to be a big splash and ready for ten slam-dunk guilty pleas?" I asked.

"That sounds pretty good. Tell me whatcha got."

I'd placed a call from my office to the newest Assistant U.S. Attorney (AUSA) in Des Moines, Rick Rooney. I hadn't met him yet, but I knew he was brand-new and a former Deputy D.A. for Polk County, Iowa, so I figured he'd be the one to call about a newly-minted case I'd dug up. I needed a hot-running AUSA with virtually nothing on his plate to work this one with me.

"Rick, do you know me?"

"Only by reputation," he said.

"Uh-oh, is that good or bad?"

"Good, so far. I've talked to a couple of guys here who have mentioned you as doing some very good work for them."

"Glad to hear that and now I've got something to run by you that is one of the more interesting cases I've been involved in so far.

"Alright, tell me more."

"The case involves a woman who was working in the Financial Aid office at the University of Iowa. She's got this boyfriend who talks her into stealing financial aid checks and then he takes them over to Chicago. He has a bunch of friends in Chicago who get fake IDs and cash the checks at banks all over the city. I've got everybody identified and tons of pictures of them cashing checks at the bank. And even more. Sound interesting enough to make a trip over to see you?"

For purposes of Federal Courts, Iowa is split right down the middle, with Interstate 80 being the dividing line. Everything south of I-80 is in the Southern District of Iowa, and everything north is in a completely different jurisdiction for federal crimes. As luck would have it, Iowa City is south of I-80 by a few miles, so virtually all of my cases had to be prosecuted in Des Moines, which is about 130 miles from Cedar Rapids.

"When can you come over?" Rooney asked.

"How's tomorrow sound?"

"See you here at what time?"

"I should be there around ten. It's a two-hour drive from here."

"Oh." He paused. "How much money are we talking about here, and what are your federal violations?"

I thought for a moment. "I've got a little over three hundred thousand dollars in checks taken. For starters, I think we've got Interstate Transportation of Stolen Property and Wire Fraud. I'm sure we can dig up some more if we need to, but those will work pretty well."

"Three hundred thousand bucks? You're kidding me."

"Nope. She swiped about one hundred checks at an average of three thousand dollars each."

"How about you make it here at nine and we'll go out for breakfast? No phones ringing there and we can get a lot more accomplished. Sounds like we're gonna need to spend some serious time talking."

"Yes we are. Maybe the whole day. I'll just get going a bit earlier. See you then."

While it was good to have the meeting with Rooney set up, I had more than a few other things on my plate. It seemed like every time I managed to whittle the pile down to manageable proportions, even more would come in the mail from Omaha. When I left Los Angeles, I would never have had the slightest inkling how busy agents could be in a resident agency. Foolishly, I thought they'd be out playing golf or goofing off in some other way. It wasn't taking me a whole lot of time to realize quite the opposite was true. I didn't feel resentful of Jim Whalen at all. He'd put in his time, and he had enough experience to work on developing bigger and more important cases. Just like he said he wanted me to do. With my results on the gambling case, it was like a shark smelling blood in the water. The stolen check case could result in another ten. My thinking was, *why spend all sorts of time on a case with a single indictment and conviction, when you can develop cases that provided multiple convictions? Good cases though.* Ten was a good number, but I also knew that wasn't going to happen on every case I got my teeth into. I also didn't know how many of those multiple indictment cases were in my future.

CHAPTER FIVE

Fried Eggs and Pabst Blue Ribbon Beer?

I arrived at the U.S. Attorney's office at nine o'clock sharp. During the gambling investigation, which was also prosecuted in Des Moines, I'd made so many trips to the capitol city of Iowa that my gleaming new bureau car practically knew the way by itself. But I'd also learned that the two-hour drive could be very productive in terms of getting work done. So I'd bring some paperwork with me, turn on my tape recorder and dictate investigative reports as I sailed along I-80. Made the trip seem like a breeze.

Rooney came out to greet me in the reception room. He was a huge guy, about six-foot-six, and probably just under three hundred pounds, with a dark handlebar moustache that would make Marshal Matt Dillon proud. With a booming voice and a ready laugh, I could immediately tell that AUSA Rick Rooney was going to be a fun guy to work with. Little did I know that we'd become close friends for years.

"Let's take my bureau car," I said. He managed to fold his legs into the passenger seat and pushed the lever to put the seat back as far as it would go. "Okay, where are we heading?"

Rooney went to law school at Drake University in Des Moines, so he knew all sorts of places to eat. He appeared to be a guy who'd done plenty of it. "There's this place right over by the campus where they've got the best breakfasts in town. Everyone goes there. You'll see students and some old farmers slopping down PBRs with their breakfast. Hop on University and head south."

"Beer and eggs?" I was cringing.

"You bet. Nuthin' better."

Must be an Iowa thing, I thought.

Grease permeated the air when we walked in the front door. "My kinda place," I said, but didn't really mean it. I was always up for something new, and this would prove to be quite an experience. Sure enough, there were several older guys at the counter having breakfast with bottles of Pabst Blue Ribbon sitting beside their plates. We took a table and a waitress whose big hair made her look like a refugee from the 1960s took our orders. Rooney wanted a PBR. I was good with skim milk. *I'm not opposed to drinking beer, but with breakfast?*

"Time to go to work." Rooney kicked off the business part of the meeting. "What've you got for me?"

I'd brought several copies of checks and some other documentary evidence with me, so I opened my briefcase and started pulling them out to show Rooney. "Here's how it went." I showed him a picture of a driver's license photo. "This gal is sorta the ringleader. And this guy is her boyfriend. He's the brains of the outfit, if there are any brains involved." The woman, Diane Miller, was white, hefty, and not particularly attractive. Her boyfriend, Terrell Johnson, was black, decent-looking, tall, and muscular in build.

"He a basketball player or something?" Rooney asked. I wasn't surprised at his comment, because Iowa City was a lily-white town, and if someone saw a young black male, the assumption was he was either a football or basketball player at the university.

"Nope. Didn't even go to school there."

I pulled out several checks and handed them to him. "These are copies of some of the checks. What they did was to get Diane to snatch some student loan checks after hours. She'd stay late and act like she was working on something. She's talked to me and admitted the whole thing."

"How about him?"

"Told me to go screw myself."

"Figures. So how did their little scheme work?"

"Her job was to get checks that looked like they were made out to black people. Her words, not mine."

"How in the hell do you do that?" Rooney asked. "I don't see any pictures on the checks. Do any have 'em?"

"Nope. She said he told her to look for '*black people's names*.' Jones, Washington, Johnson, Jackson, whatever. Names like that."

"Oh, okay, I got it now. So after they got the checks, what happened next?"

"Once our boy Terrell got 'em, he'd hop in his car and head over to Chicago."

"Is he from there?"

"Yep," I replied. "Tons of friends, too. Homeboy from the south side. Cabrini Green projects, I believe."

"Figures." Rooney continued looking at checks. "How old?"

"He's twenty-five, she's almost thirty."

"Nice couple, huh?"

"Oh yeah, a modern version of Romeo and Juliet. It was his job to put the checks in his homeboy's hands. Their job was to get a false ID to match the name on the check. Apparently that wasn't too hard to do in Chicago. After they cashed the checks, Terrell and Diane got one half of the profit."

"Did *he* cash any?"

"Oh yeah. Quite a few, actually. I've got a file on everyone who cashed one. Photos, the original check, copies, IDs – you name it."

"How many potential defendants do we have?" Rooney asked.

"Including Diane and Terrell, we're at ten right now."

"Will it go any higher?"

"I don't think so. I've made one trip over there to work with the Postal Inspectors. They're the ones who came up with the information and ran with it. So most everything I've got, I've gotten from them."

Rooney took a good-sized drink from his bottle and asked, "Why didn't they handle the case over there?"

"Couple of reasons. One, the amount of money involved is below the guidelines for the U.S. Attorney in Chicago. Two, the whole scheme originated in Iowa, so they thought they'd let us have the case."

"So you've been over there?"

"Yep. Spent almost a week with the Inspectors. Crazy bunch of guys. It's some sort of an undercover squad and when they're all together in their squad room it looks like the bar scene out of *Star Wars*. But don't get me wrong, they're a bunch of great guys. A little motley, but good guys," I said.

"Did they take you down to Rush Street?"

"Oh yeah. Went down there one night after we knocked off and...well, it was pretty ugly."

"So how did they come up with the case?" Rooney held up his bottle as a signal for the waitress to bring him another one. *I think I'm going to barf. Maybe not. I've been known to put a fried egg on top of a piece of chocolate cake. Maybe beer with eggs isn't any worse than that...yeah it is!*

"One of their undercover guys got wind of some guy selling stolen checks. So they set up a deal with him and bought a few."

"For what?" he asked.

"I think he paid something like ten percent of face value."

"Then if the check was about three thousand bucks, he'd pay three hundred, right?"

"Exactly. And most of the checks were a little more than three thousand apiece."

"Screwed up a lot of people's efforts to get a degree, didn't it?" Rooney didn't sound too happy about that, and it was clear from the expression on his face, too. *Or maybe the beer this early in the morning is getting to his digestive juices. No way I could do it so early in the day.*

"Sure did. I guess they've got a real mess on their hands at the college. I have no clue what they're going to do."

"I'll bet," he said as our breakfasts arrived. They looked as greasy as the place smelled. The eggs were oily enough that if I tilted the plate about one degree, they'd slide right off onto the table. Awful looking stuff. I put the eggs on top of my hash browns and chopped them up to avoid that from happening.

"Oh yeah...great stuff," Rooney said, practically drooling over what didn't look like one of the tastiest breakfasts I'd ever seen. "Now all I need is another PBR." And he ordered one.

We talked a bit as we ate, and I discovered Rooney was a huge Iowa Hawkeye fan. "Grew up one, even though I was from a town much closer to Iowa State," he said. "Mom and Dad both graduated from the University of Iowa, so I've been a fan all my life.

Well, I thought, *that might explain why he isn't too*

happy about this caper. Do they drink beer with breakfast?

"Ever been to a football game there?" I asked.

"A few over the years, but none in the recent past since Coach Fry got there."

"My partner in the office has some pretty good contacts for tickets. I've gone to quite a few games. Great fun."

"Hard to get, though, aren't they?"

"Well, yeah, but Jim might be able to scratch some up if you let me know when. I think Michigan's coming to town this Saturday. Wanna go?"

"I'd love to go!"

"I'll ask him when I get back. I have no idea where they'll be located, but my theory is, you're inside the stadium, and a lot of people aren't."

"Good point. Speaking of which, when do you have to go back? I'm thinking we've got some work to do." Rooney seemed to be enjoying the toxic mixture in front of him.

"I can stick around for a few days if you can carve out the time," I said.

"My plate is pretty empty right now, so it's a great week for me to get off to a good start. I think the U.S. Attorney will love this case. He's an Iowa law school grad, you know."

"I did know that. I wound up doing his entire background investigation before he was appointed."

"You're kidding."

"Nope, just another one of my duties. We do background checks on you guys and even federal judges. Actually, your boss must be a pretty crazy guy. When I was doing interviews, I remember a lawyer telling me that he's 'one of the greatest legal minds of the seventh century.'"

Rooney laughed and almost spit out a bite of food. "That is a great statement. Yeah, he's a piece of work, all right. Old school lawyer. Thinks he's Melvin Belli or something. Runs around like a chicken with his head cut off half the time. Yelling and screaming at his chief assistant. They're quite a pair. Kinda like ol' Hoover and Clyde Tolson. Been together for years. George is kind of like his whipping boy. They are a couple of big drinkers. By the end of the day, both of 'em are about half in the bag. I think they both keep a good supply of whiskey or something in their offices."

"Aren't political appointments great?"

"You can say that again. But if not for him, I wouldn't have this job."

We paid our bill and headed back to the office. I had his undivided attention for the entire day, and when we were getting close to calling it a day he asked me, "Are you spending the night here or driving back?"

"I've already got a room at the Holiday Inn down by the river. Stay there all the time."

"Well, why don't we do this? My place isn't too far away, down on the southeast side. Let me check with my wife and see if she can throw something extra on for dinner. You up for that?"

"Sure. Love to. Sounds like a great idea."

And so began a friendship that would endure for years. I discovered that Rick was not only a huge fan of Iowa sports, but a serious connoisseur of quality beer. And most other adult beverages, as well. He was also a legitimate, talented singer and thespian with many theater appearances behind him and many to come in future years. All of which worked well with me, since I'd become a major Hawkeye fan, had always loved live theater, and was known to hoist the occasional beer or slop down a few vodka-tonics myself.

CHAPTER SIX

Price Fixing School Buses in Iowa and Nebraska

The University of Iowa check fraud case produced ten felony convictions and another Quality Step Increase for me, so I'd gone from a GS-10 to a GS-12 with just over four years in the bureau. Way ahead of schedule. The big, multi-indictment cases were working out pretty well. And if it seems like I was getting to handle one case at a time, nothing could be further from the truth. Usually I was juggling another twenty or twenty-five at any given time, which included good ole one-shot leads and applicant cases. But I liked to be busy, and it seemed the more I had to do, the more I did.

Then along came another big case out of the clear blue sky. Or so it seemed. A man called the office one day when I just happened to be there getting some paperwork done.

"Sir, I want to report a case of price-fixing," he said.

"Price fixing? On what?" I said, anxious to get back to my dictating and thinking he was probably some crackpot wanting to complain about different prices at gas stations in town, and how they *coincidentally* seem to go up and down at exactly the same time. Or on hamburger price similarities at McDonalds and Burger King. I'd gotten more than a few of those, too.

"On school buses."

"School buses?" I had heard of bid rigging before, but I had no clue what to do if I was assigned to work such a case. Well, I'd soon learn.

"Yes, sir. I was working as a school bus salesman and I couldn't make a sale."

"So you weren't a good salesman?"

"That wasn't it at all. I was new in the school bus business, but I couldn't break in and make a single sale

because everyone had these agreements between
themselves. They'd carved up the state and they'd
agreed to bid higher or lower depending on whether or
not they were scheduled to win the school district. Every
year they'd jack up the prices a little bit and make more
of a profit."

"Are you kidding me?"

"No sir, I'm not," he said. "And it's been going on
for over twenty years in Iowa and Nebraska."

At this point, I'm thinking, *Oh my God, what do I do
now? Can this really be happening to our school districts
in Iowa where education is a top priority? They're taking
money away from little kids if what this guy is saying is
true.*

"Can you come down here and talk to me about
this?" I asked him.

"You bet. Tell me when and I'll be there."

"How about tomorrow morning at about nine?"

"That'll work. I'll be there at nine sharp." And we
both hung up.

My brain was going about fifty miles an hour, but I
figured I'd sit down with him and discover it was more
about his poor sales tactics than some type of fraud. I
couldn't imagine people doing something like this for so
many years without someone figuring it out. My head
had a million thoughts running through it. *Could there be
kickbacks to the school board? County supervisors?
That's some serious stuff there. What on earth is going
on here? Is this guy full of it?*

The man, who I ultimately cultivated as an
informant, laid out most of the scheme for me and even
showed me some documentation explaining how the
process occurred. We talked for a couple of hours, and I
still had a funny feeling about it. After he left, I sat at
my desk looking at the wall, wondering, *what in the hell
am I supposed to do now?*

I dug out one of the bureau manuals, which I rarely
looked at, and tried to figure out what sort of a federal
violation I might be dealing with. I was clueless. *Maybe
it's mail fraud if some of the documents were mailed to
schools. Could be wire fraud if phone calls were made.
Both probably were.* I kept flipping through, and then I
came to Section Sixty of the Manual of Investigative and
Operational Guidelines (also known as the MIOG). In

short, the violation from the standpoint of the FBI was called "Anti-Trust Violations." So I paged through those investigative guidelines to see if I could figure out what I was supposed to do next. The most important part I found was, in summary, "When and if a Special Agent of the FBI is made aware of possible Anti-Trust violations, the U.S. Department of Justice, Anti-Trust Division in Washington, D.C., must immediately be notified."

Immediately? Oh my God, what have I walked into? Last thing I wanted to do was talk to someone in D.C.

Jim Whalen had left for a week's vacation. We had a new baby agent in the office from Quantico, straight out of the academy. He'd be more clueless than me. Our agent who had worked FCI cases had been transferred several years before.

So how in the hell do I get a hold of these guys? "Immediately" sounds like "now" to me. If I don't call them now, am I going to find myself in deep trouble? Another Letter of Censure? I knew I didn't need many of those in my file. I was really getting stressed out, so I decided to do what the manual told me.

When you call FBI Headquarters or the U.S. Department of Justice, I'd heard you can usually expect to get transferred a minimum of, oh I don't know, maybe five times. And that's on a good day. I found the number for DOJ and called the main number, half scared to death to talk with one of the Deputy Attorney Generals. It sounded like pretty heady stuff to me. Never done it before. These guys are important, I think.

The operator connected me directly to the Anti-Trust Division. The attorney who answered the phone was pretty patient with me, and could probably tell I was nervous.

"Okay, here's what I'm going to do," he said after I told him everything I knew. "If the violations are occurring in Iowa or Nebraska, that's going to fall under our Chicago field office. I'm going to give them a call right after we hang up. You should be hearing from someone there in the next few days or so. I don't know how much they've got going right now, so it may be up to a week."

Since the word "immediately" had me more than a little intimidated, I decided the next best thing to do was call my boss in Des Moines, who actually supervised all

of the resident agencies in Iowa. After listening to what
had transpired over the past two days, he said, "I think
you've done everything fine so far. These are pretty
technical, document-intensive cases, and you probably
need to wait to hear from the guys in Chicago to see if
we're going to open a case or not." That was comforting,
so I figured I'd wait until I found out what the 'big boys'
wanted me to do.

No sooner had I hung up the phone with my
supervisor and taken a deep breath than the phone
rang. "Can I speak to Special Agent Pete Klismet,
please?" a man's voice said.

"This is Pete."

And off we went into the veritable wild blue yonder.
The attorney who called was a Deputy Attorney General
with the Anti-Trust Division in Chicago. And he sounded
like he was *very* interested in the case. I readily told him
I'd never worked an anti-trust case before, and that
didn't seem to bother him a bit. "I'm going to check with
my bosses here, and we may be out there pretty soon.
Do you think your informant will talk with us?"

"I don't see why that'd be a problem," I said. "I'll
call him and tell him. I'm sure he'll be more than anxious
to talk to you." After a little more conversation, we hung
up.

A half hour later the phone rang again. Same
Deputy AG calling from Chicago. "Can you meet two of
us at the Cedar Rapids Airport tomorrow at ten a.m.?"

"Sure." *Damn, these guys are fast.*

"Can you call your informant and have him meet us
at your office?"

"No problem. Will do. See you in the morning."

This was all happening a little too fast. I called my
supervisor back and told him I had two Deputy AG's
coming tomorrow.

"You work fast," he said.

"I think I work out of fear," I replied.

The next morning, I met Deputy Attorney Generals
Alonzo Brady and Mark Preston at the Cedar Rapids
Municipal Airport. They were carrying briefcases, were
dressed in dark suits, and looked very important. I think
I was still a little intimidated. Mr. Preston asked what
time the informant was coming in.

"Eleven o'clock," I answered. "Unless you guys want

to grab a bite to eat first and I can change the time."

"Nope. Eleven will work fine."

We drove to my office in silence, aside from me giving them a little running tour of the city. *This is still happening too fast to suit me,* I thought. But the snowball seemed to be rolling down the hill, gaining more momentum, and adding more snow as it rolled. Little did I know how much snow it would gather in the next couple of years.

Within a week I was feeling like Butch Cassidy when he and the Sundance Kid were being chased by the posse. Butch turned to Sundance and asked, "Who are these guys?" We'd talked to the informant and the AGs were confident we had enough facts to open up a full-blown anti-trust investigation. And so I did.

A couple of days went by, and I received a huge envelope by certified mail that contained a stack of grand jury subpoenas higher than I'd ever seen in my life. Before I knew what hit me, I was running all over Iowa serving the subpoenas on companies and people. It was like a whirlpool: I was in it and I couldn't get out.

But then the waters began to ebb and the case seemed to grind to a halt. And that turned out to work to my benefit.

CHAPTER SEVEN

Psychological Profiling? What's That?

In roughly one billion years, give or take a week, the ever-rotating axis of the earth is doomed to grind to a halt. When that happens, the mechanic who is responsible for maintaining the gears which turn the axis will quickly leap on the first available elevator and go deep inside the earth where the main gear is located so he can fix things up. People will be getting very confused and even mad because they want either daylight or darkness. That's what they're used to.

When the mechanic arrives at the last floor down, he'll walk over to the gear room, open the door, and peer inside. There he will find an attorney sitting at his desk, grinding out one legal motion after another. And most of them will be for "Discovery." You cannot disprove this theory, so you must accept and believe it. An attorney will eventually grind the earth to a complete halt.

The school bus bid rigging investigation began like the start of the Indy 500, and then it was like the starter threw up the "*caution*" flag after a few laps and told the drivers they could only go ten miles per hour for the rest of the race. Or less. A lot happened early on, and then it was like we hit a wall. The subpoenas I served produced more company records than I'd ever imagined could be found on the planet. All of the distributors were required to produce records of their sales for the previous ten years, which was the statute of limitations on Anti-Trust violations. I testified at several sessions of the Grand Jury to acknowledge receiving the documents. But we only had one session per month in Cedar Rapids, where the case was to be prosecuted. Which tended to slow the process down even more.

Alonzo Brady called me early one Friday morning. "Pete, we're having daily contact with the companies and distributors. They all have tons of records, and we're trying to figure out a place to store all of 'em."

"Well, how many are we talking about?" I was thinking a couple of banker's boxes could easily fit in the large walk-in safe that we used to store evidence.

"Right now we're up to one hundred and sixty-three large banker's boxes."

"Oh my God. Do we need a barn or an auditorium?" I could only imagine getting a guy with a forklift to move all of these things around, and the words "right now" were the operative part of Brady's answer. I was wondering how fat this pig was going to become.

"Pretty close," he laughed. Brady was a serious guy, but he did have a fairly well-developed sense of humor, when required. "We don't have enough room here in Chicago at our office, and I was wondering if you might know a place where we could store them."

"Is there some central place you were thinking of?"

"Cedar Rapids is about as central as anyplace I can think of. That way the attorneys from the companies in Iowa and western Nebraska can make the trip in no more than five hours. But we also need to have someone act as the custodian of the records."

"What does that mean?" I could already see Brady's eyes focusing on me as the "custodian."

"Basically, the person needs to be on call when the attorneys and potential defendants want to come over and review the documents. We're in what we call the 'document review' phase of the case. We want to give them this opportunity before we decide who and what we're going to indict down the line."

"Who or *what*?"

"Correct. With what we've been reviewing, we expect to indict at least six companies, and maybe up to eight people. That's for starters. It's going to get worse."

This was starting to get even more serious than I ever anticipated. "Well, Mr. Brady, here's the deal from my standpoint. There is no way I can be at the beck and call of defense attorneys seven days a week, twenty-four hours a day. For you guys I can be, but I've got a ton of other cases I'm working on, and my supervisor has told me I have to manage this case right along with the rest of 'em. So I guess we need to figure something out."

"Okay, we'll figure that part out. I understand what you're saying. Don't worry about it. But the thing I'd like you to look for is a place to store all of this stuff. Any ideas?"

"Not sure." My mind was turning quickly, trying to decide if there was a space large enough in the Federal Building I worked out of. I knew there was a basement and thought there might be a couple of vacant spaces down there, but I'd have to check. "Let me check with the building manager here and see if he's got some space available. I'll get back to you as soon as I talk to him."

"All right, that'll work. And thanks for everything you've handled, Pete. You've done a great job and we really appreciate it."

"You're welcome. Let me do some checking and I'll let you know right after I do."

While the case was languishing, I had more than enough to do. All of the indictments and convictions I'd generated caused the main office in Omaha to think we had work to do in Cedar Rapids. Meanwhile, Jim Whalen was working on several drug cases with local agencies, and they were taking off like Saturn rockets. So the Omaha headquarters office wound up assigning us a few brand-new agents within a couple of months. That was a good thing for me, because it was hard to focus on the big cases when you had little gnat cases chewing on your leg all the time.

So there I was, again, one afternoon sitting alone in the office and trying to get something or another organized. It seemed I was never lacking in something to do, and part of that involved training the new people we'd acquired, which wasn't hard, because both of them were quick studies.

The phone rang.

"Pete, this is Tom Moore in Omaha. How're you doin'?"

"Good, Tom. Busy, but good. What's up with you?" Tom was the training coordinator for the Omaha Division. Very important job in the grand scheme of things. He was the guy who set up meetings with our National Academy associates, all of whom are senior police officers and executives who've attended the FBI

National Academy. A very prestigious thing for law enforcement. Tom also coordinated closely with the FBI Academy on upcoming training schools for agents and support staff in the division.

"Hey, look, I've got something to run by you."

"Okay."

"I just talked to the boss and he wants you to be the division coordinator for the new Psychological Profiling program the bureau is starting."

"The *what*?" This was a new one on me.

"It's called Psychological Profiling."

"Never heard of it. Why me?"

"Well, frankly, the SAC likes your background as a cop before you came to the bureau," he said. "So when I asked him who he wanted to send, your name jumped right up. He thinks you've done a hell of a job the last couple of years you've been out there."

"That's a nice compliment, but I don't even know what this is about."

"I suppose that'd help, wouldn't it? The bureau has told all fifty-nine field offices they need to designate one agent per division to attend a two-week school they've put together. As I understand it, they're going to provide training to our guys and have them work with local law enforcement on violent crime. You've obviously done a good job of working with local law enforcement, and I know your background and degrees. So, you're the guy if you want to do it."

"Wow. I guess I should be flattered."

"You're right. This is something very selective. The bureau has told the SACs to send their best agents, not the usual guys they just want to get out of the office for a couple of weeks. You know, the RODs."

"The who?"

"Retired on Duty guys."

"Got it. Well, do I have a day to think it over? I'd like to run it by my wife and kids. And Jim Whalen. There's a good chance he's going to drive in there and kill you, right after he kills me. I don't think he's going to be thrilled to hear I might be gone for a couple weeks. We're both busting our butts out here."

"I've heard that. The boss said you and Jim have generated about a third of the indictments and convictions in the entire division over the past year. And there're over sixty agents in the division. Everyone knows what you're doing out there. You guys are golden."

I was surprised at that comment. "That's nice to know, but I assume it doesn't mean I'll get transferred does it? I've told my wife and kids I want to stay here until the kids finish high school. At least. We really do like it here."

"Oh, no. That's the last thing we want to do. We've *got* to have a coordinator for the division, and that would be you. I know the program is building back there, so there might be an opportunity to go back to the academy at some point. You know, to work in the unit. But not unless you want to go."

"Well thanks, Tom. This sounds like interesting stuff. Let me give you a call back tomorrow."

"I'll look forward to hearing from you."

I particularly liked what Tom said about wanting to keep the coordinator in the division. My kids were both in school and I'd promised them we'd stay in Cedar Rapids as long as possible. At least long enough to enable them to graduate from high school, and there were some great colleges not far away. I didn't want them to be like army brats, moving around the country at the whim of the FBI. This sounded like a pretty good opportunity for me and for my family to stay in a place we really liked.

CHAPTER EIGHT

Submarines in Vietnam?

Agreeing to attend the profiling school at Quantico opened a completely new chapter in my life and my career. I saw it as an opportunity to be on the ground floor of a program that was cutting edge, exciting, and on the cusp of modern law enforcement. I'd read how the field of law enforcement and criminology had gone through two waves, and was now entering the third. The first was pioneered by Scotland Yard, using clues and evidence to both solve cases and convict criminals. The second would be the analysis of crime frequency, or what factors cause crime in some areas but not others, and how predictable crime might be. The third wave was running in parallel to the others: a study of the criminal mind. The fascination with this aspect was probably what drew my interest above anything else.

As I look back on my decision to become one of the first "profilers" in the FBI, I suppose I was probably something of a natural for it. When I was a college undergraduate in the criminal justice program, I was fascinated by the theories of criminology, and studied them intently in the classes I chose. I also took a summer class titled "Criminal Typologies," which ostensibly explained various types of criminal acts. I found that equally fascinating, and composed a term paper which was comprised of original ideas, and which Professor Pat Reed used as part of his lecture for the last class. "You've got a good mind," he once told me, and raved about the ideas I came up with. Plus he was very complimentary to me on my paper and class participation. I actually felt a little embarrassed. In addition to my criminal justice courses, I took a healthy number of psychology and sociology classes, because I decided I wanted to minor in each. If by no process other than osmosis, I think some of it stuck in my thick Polish brain!

But I also learned something practical about *criminal behavior theory*. Cops were very skeptical about it. The words *psychology* and *sociology* were not terms they were interested in hearing. It was a period when the U.S. government had allocated millions of dollars to educate police officers under a program known as the "Omnibus Crime Control Act." Thus, when I was an undergraduate at a brand-new state college in Denver, every class I took had some police officers as students right along with me. Many were in uniform, having just gotten off duty or prior to going on duty. Many departments had implemented educational requirements for promotions. Some, like the one I joined after graduation, required a bachelor's degree.

I wasn't a young, pimple-faced eighteen-year-old freshman when I started college. I'd spent four years in the Navy, serving on two World War II vintage diesel submarines, and had made two Vietnam tours in, as we fondly called it, the "Tonkin Gulf Yacht Club." But it wasn't very yacht-like. In fact, as I look back, it was horrible duty. One hundred men confined in a space suited for far fewer, working in filthy bilges with diesel oil spewing all over as you were trying to repair a motor. Or crawling around in one of the two huge battery compartments, watering the batteries with distilled water every three days, hoping to avoid touching the metal ceiling and a battery post at the same time. I have no clue how many times I got zapped by 250 volts of DC current. The job wasn't a lot of fun. Submarine service, while quite selective and a source of pride to be a member of, was not good duty. But I was young enough to not really care.

In two tours in the Tonkin Gulf, we did shore recon and mapping at night. We couldn't surface because we were too close to the shoreline and would be quickly attacked by Vietnamese gunboats. Or worse. And "worse" occasionally showed up. So we did our recon by periscope.

During our first deployment we stayed submerged for forty days in the Gulf on one occasion. We were the very first sub in the Gulf after two destroyers, the U.S.S.

Turner Joy and the U.S.S. *Maddox*, were attacked by Vietnamese gunboats. That turned out not to be one of the brighter ideas by the Viet Cong, since the two destroyers sank the gunboats and everything else the V.C. mustered up to attack us with. This single incident was significant because that, alone, escalated the Vietnam War to epic proportions. And we were right in the middle of it all.

When we finally surfaced, I was the first one through the conning tower and onto the bridge to stand watch, which in itself was a bit dangerous if enemy gunboats happened to be in the area. Lucky for me, they weren't because we had gone far enough into international waters that they didn't deign to pay us a visit. But what I do most remember was getting my first smell of the fresh air. After forty days of smelling disgusting body odors, diesel oil permeating the ship, and every other nasty thing one could imagine, my reaction to the *fresh air* was to immediately barf all over the side of the bridge.

We had several dicey moments during our cruises in the Gulf of Tonkin. I was lying in my bunk reading one night when I started hearing a strange pinging noise. I looked around trying to see if some moron was messing with me, when a low voice came over the ship's speakers. It was the Captain. "Gentlemen," he whispered, "we are being tracked by what we believe is a Russian destroyer. We're going to dive below test depth to get below temperature gradients. And, I want everyone to rig for 'silent running.' That is all. Carry on." "Silent running" meant keeping onboard noise to a minimum; that is, don't even think about talking beyond a whisper. And so I laid in my bunk for several hours reading and not saying a word to anyone.

For a sub, temperature gradients are a significant factor in hiding from enemy ships on the surface. Water in the ocean has different temperatures at different depths, somewhat like layers on a cake. In theory, at least, if a submarine was below enough gradients, the sonar of a surface ship wouldn't be able to penetrate to it. So it would follow that the more gradients you were under, the better the odds of hiding. To "run silent and run deep" was one of the catch phrases of the sub service.

The pinging continued as we went silently down to a depth over four hundred feet. I distinctly remember thinking back to some of the old World War II movies I'd seen and how the American destroyers would roll fifty-five gallon drums of explosives called "ash cans" over the stern of the ship to sink German subs. And I also remember thinking, *I'm nineteen years old, and this is where I'll die.* But the Russian ship must have lost us, and everyone on the boat breathed a collective sigh of relief. However, it wasn't the first one to come after us. I never got used to it. Being below four hundred feet was scary enough without thinking you might go a lot lower if one of the ash cans hit its mark.

Another of our important duties was rescuing downed pilots. If an F-4 was hit by an enemy missile, the pilot's job was to head for the Tonkin Gulf, if possible, and ditch in the ocean. All pilots had a deployable raft inside the plane, and our job was to locate and recover the pilot before the Viet Cong found him. We recovered quite a few grateful pilots during our tour.

We also met with aircraft carriers several times and took on Underwater Demolition Teams, now known as SEALs. Then we'd sneak as close to the coast as we safely could, fill the torpedo tubes and essentially shoot them and their equipment out so they could stealthily approach the shore. On one occasion we deployed a team, and we learned that one of the UDT members had somehow gotten caught in the ship's current, came backwards and was chopped up by the propellers. Hearing about this was a very solemn moment on the ship, because we'd all gotten to know the team members in the few days they were with us. And it was to me the most horrible experience of my life to think about what had happened to that highly-trained and courageous man.

I enjoyed the Navy in many ways, but I was glad when my discharge day arrived and I could go back to Colorado. The Navy waved several intriguing offers in front of me before I was discharged. First was a so-called "Variable Re-Enlistment Bonus," which was ten thousand dollars. A lot of money back then, when you could buy a brand-new Ford Mustang for about fifteen hundred bucks. And, because my test scores were fairly high when I took them in boot camp, they offered me a full-ride scholarship to the Naval Academy. The latter came with a six-year commitment after the Academy. But I turned it down because I had saved plenty of money, and knew I was going to college when I got out. Which I ultimately did, and finished my bachelor's degree in three years.

The driving force behind my desire to attend college was unquestionably my mother. While she and dad were awaiting his discharge following WWII, they were in New Orleans. She enrolled in and attended Tulane University, and I was always impressed by that, even though she didn't finish her degree. My dad had finished the eighth grade, which was the standard at the time. When he was fourteen, he went to work on a still for Al Capone's bootlegging operation, although he wasn't aware of whose still it was at the time. Eventually, he gave up that lucrative occupation and got into the Civilian Conservation Corps, learning the trade of masonry at a state park near Superior, Wisconsin. There he met my mother at a weekly dance.

My dad and Uncle Phil, who also had joined the corps, eventually branched off and started a brick laying and contracting business in Stevens Point, Wisconsin, when dad was eighteen or so. At some point, that got my dad to take off on his own. He was drafted into the Army and started a family after he was discharged from the service. Once he was out, he got the travel bug to support his new wife and growing family. I was born in Stevens Point and was the oldest of what would become five children. My mom had lost a baby who would have been born before me, so I never had an older brother or sister. We moved to Michigan, Louisiana, Texas, Iowa, and eventually to Denver by the time I was four years old, because that was where the work was. Denver was the new "boom town" in the United States.

But all was not rosy for the family. Dad had a serious drinking problem, and was also abusive toward my mom and younger brother. Not so much me, probably because I was the oldest and something of the "fair-haired boy" in the family. While dad made decent money, I certainly didn't grow up with the proverbial *silver spoon* in my mouth. Rather, I'd describe our upbringing as lower middle class. But because we were

Catholic, we went to Catholic schools at a minimal price, and I think that gave me a better foundation for my education than most kids got in public schools. The nuns were not inclined to put up with much crap and they held my feet to the fire. I'm glad they did, because it certainly didn't happen when I went to public school. I remember Sister Barbara, who set what I believe is still the Olympic record for breaking three-foot wooden rulers over my back. Three in one year! I was a bit ornery, mouthy, probably harbored some incipient anger due to the situation at home, and if it had been diagnosable at the time, suffered from ADD. But those diagnoses didn't exist back then.

My dad had always wanted to own a bar, a somewhat logical occupation for a person who enjoyed drinking as much as he did. So he gave up bricklaying and bought a bar in a pretty tough part of town. We lived in a dungeon-like basement with the bar above us. From the bar, I unwittingly got a great education in human behavior, although I was only eight when dad and mom started running the place, which dad re-named "The Quench Bar." It was a 3.2 beer joint, which in Colorado during those years meant if you were eighteen or older, you could drink that percent of beer. Hard liquor wasn't allowed, but the patrons still got hammered pretty well. Which meant problems. As in fights. However, my dad had been the U.S. Army heavyweight boxing champion of the South Pacific during his years in the service, so he didn't need to hire a bouncer. For entertainment on Friday and Saturday nights, my best friend and I would climb a tree and sit there, waiting for the side door to fly open and to see my dad throwing out a drunk. If the drunk made the mistake of challenging Dad, the fight was over pretty quickly. That gave me yet more opportunities to learn about the human condition.

In the tenth grade, I transferred to Englewood High School in a neighboring Denver suburb, because it was apparent I was not going to ever become the starting quarterback on the J.K. Mullen Catholic High School football team, even though I'd gone there on a partial scholarship. The guy ahead of me went on to be a second team All-American quarterback at the University of Wyoming. He was better than me – a lot better! And I didn't make the basketball team in my freshman year, because the coach wanted players with speed, and that wasn't my strong point. Shooting, yes; speed, no. For a combination of reasons I fell into the "wrong crowd" after I transferred to Englewood High School. I quit sports, except for baseball in the summers, and the baseball crowd turned out not to be the best choice for friends, either. But I was only fifteen and was glad to have some friends, since acceptance at that age is critically important.

I pretty much goofed off after my sophomore year, and in the second semester of my junior year I quit school. I was ditching so much with the gang I hung out with that there wasn't much purpose to even trying. But then I made a decision which would positively impact the rest of my life. One of my buddies, coincidentally named "Bud," decided to get out of town and enlist in the Navy. That didn't work well for Bud, since he was kicked out of boot camp and was home in about a month. We teased him unmercifully for being a queer or a misfit. Notwithstanding Bud's poor experience with the Navy, my best friend Jerry Woodhead and I decided we'd give it a try ourselves. So at seventeen years and two months of age, I was off to San Diego and boot camp.

Boot camp was a veritable breeze. I was named Assistant Petty Officer in Charge of my company, which worked for a while, until I came down with a case of pneumonia that almost killed me. After three weeks in Balboa Naval Hospital, I was re-cycled to another company and graduated. From there it was home for a few weeks' leave, and then on to submarine school. Going to sub school was voluntary rather than mandatory. We'd had a brief presentation about sub service in boot camp, and the sailor who talked about subs talked about how "elite" and difficult to get in it was. He said sub sailors were "the best of the best" in the Navy, although I'd probably have to differ with that now. The SEALs are the most elite, but subs are a close second. I was excited to be joining what I thought was the best. Trying to be *the best* was something that would follow and guide me for the rest of my life.

And so about four years later, there I was, a Navy and twice-over Vietnam vet, sitting in a Criminology class at Metropolitan State College in Denver. Seated to my right was a crusty old Denver police officer, who always came to class in his wrinkled and rumpled dark blue uniform. He always had the stub of a huge, unlit but stinky as hell cigar in his mouth. He was grossly overweight with a huge belly hanging over his Sam Browne belt, and he barely fit on the chair in the classroom. We nicknamed him "The Whale" because he was about the same size as one of those denizens of the deep. But we never told him we called him that. We were young, but we weren't stupid, and we valued our lives.

Dr. Tom Johnson was one of our professors. A somewhat typical academic, Johnson had gone straight from high school to Michigan State, where he went right through, receiving his bachelor's, master's, and doctorate in Criminology without ever so much as stepping outside of academia. That night in class, he was espousing on a theory of criminology, and The Whale, with the ever-present cigar in the side of his mouth, suddenly blurted out, "that's a bunch of fuckin' bullshit."

I didn't know what to do. I was scared to turn my head, and I certainly wasn't going to *say* anything for fear of getting my head cracked open by his nightstick. My immediate thought was, *you can't talk that way to a college professor*. So I sat there and did nothing. As did everyone else in the class.

Professor Johnson obviously didn't know what to say, so he didn't. The Whale didn't say another word, but did light his cigar and no one said a word, including the professor. Huge plumes of blue smoke filled the room, and no one protested. It was a very different era. Finally, after a pregnant pause of several tense minutes, class resumed with Johnson continuing to talk about theories he basically knew nothing about.

I got a clear message from that little event—maybe several messages. First, I learned the old timers out on the street were probably the guys who could give you the straight scoop on why people committed the crimes they did. I also discovered, from The Whale and others, that the explanation for crime often involved the word "assholes." Or "scrotes." And sometimes "scumbags." The other important thing I learned was to never speak unless you truly knew what you were talking about. If you read it out of a book, that didn't mean you knew everything about it. And that if I ever decided to become a college professor, which eventually occurred, I would never teach a class that I hadn't dealt with in the 'real world' of law enforcement.

From my college experience, and time on the streets with the Ventura Police Department, I learned most veteran officers were skeptical, or even afraid, of new things – things they thought were "hocus pocus," or anything different than what was in their comfort zone. And that should have given me a major clue as to the resistance I would eventually be confronted with in trying to promote a concept such as "Psychological Profiling." The word *psychological* scared the hell out of everybody, except for those with pretty open minds. And cops weren't often numbered in that group.

CHAPTER NINE

The FBI Academy's Most Select Class, Ever

Good morning ladies and gentlemen and welcome to the very first class of Psychological Profiling ever held at the FBI Academy. And, for that matter, probably the world. I can't begin to tell you how excited we all are to see you here and to see this moment finally arrive. It's been in the planning stages for years. If you don't know me, and many of you may not, my name is Roger Depue and I'm the Unit Chief of the Behavioral Science Unit here at the academy."

The speaker, who I *didn't* know, was an average-sized guy, probably about six feet tall and a very solid two hundred pounds. Or slightly more. His dark suit fit his obviously muscular physique perfectly, and he was shaped something like a V, with broad shoulders and narrow hips, clearly someone who made more than an occasional visit to the weight room. With dark, well-trimmed hair parted on the right and combed over to the side in a slicked-back look, he resembled a former Marine Corps officer—which it turns out he was. Not being familiar with the rank structure at FBI Headquarters or the FBI Academy, I wasn't sure how I would ultimately address him. I'd figure that out in due course.

He continued. "I think it's important for you to understand *why* you're here. We think you are the best of the best."

Whoa, wait a minute, seemed like I'd heard this before. And the last time I heard it I wound up on a stinky submarine off the coast of Vietnam.

"We specifically told your SACs to choose the best agent in his division he could give us. Several SACs didn't send us what we wanted, and we told them to either send someone else or not participate in this program. We believe this class is the most important the bureau has ever offered, and it is, without doubt, the most outstanding group we've ever had attend an in-service at the FBI Academy."

I was starting to like this guy. His voice was very slow, calm and measured, something of a monotone, and he spoke in a straightforward, no-nonsense but poised manner. And the guy *looked like* an FBI agent. If he'd been in a lineup and someone was asked to pick out the FBI Agent, Dr. Depue would get picked nine times out of ten. Maybe all ten.

"We've checked your in-service packets, and this is easily the most highly-educated class we've ever had at the academy." He paused and looked out at the class. "You may not realize why that's important, but what it tells me is we have a lot of people in this room who have open minds." Another pause. He spoke very slowly. "And you will discover in the next two weeks that is the most important tool you will have. Now, I think it's important for you to understand who's sitting around you." He once more looked around the classroom. "We have seven attorneys in the class." He paused again, then dead-panned, "I'm not so sure that's such a good thing." The class roared. Attorneys and accountants were all J. Edgar Hoover, the former director of the FBI, would hire for years. Most agents in the bureau found them to be over-analytical and decision-impaired as agents, generally a pain in the ass—with some exceptions. My partner in Cedar Rapids, Jim Whalen, was definitely one of the exceptions. Best agent I'd ever worked with.

"In this group we have twenty-four people with master's degrees," Depue continued. I could see several people nodding positively. "And one person with two master's degrees. Unfortunately, one of those doesn't *count*—"he heavily emphasized the word "count" "—because it's from the University of Southern California." Some chuckles from the class. "I went to UCLA." That got a good laugh. "Where is that person in the room?" He looked around. So did I to see if anyone was going to raise a hand to acknowledge having attended UCLA's primary rival.

"*Where* is that person?" He smiled.

I raised my hand sheepishly, then glanced around

at my classmates with something of a hangdog look,
arms out and palms raised as if to say, "Sorry, guys."
More chuckles.

"Do they still have a football team there?" Depue
knew the answer to *that* question. USC was a
powerhouse and had won several recent national
championships, so I could see where this was heading.

"No sir," I said. "They had to drop it because UCLA
was too good for them." That got a good round of
applause and laughter.

He looked at the nametag on the front of my desk.
"Mr. Klismet, it would appear you're destined to do good
things here."

"Thank you, sir. I hope so, sir."

"Don't call me 'sir.'"

"No, sir." More laughter.

This august group of agents and scholars was
seated in the largest lecture hall at the FBI Academy.
Semi-circular in shape and cantilever-tiered from the
front to the back, I guessed it could easily accommodate
one hundred people. It was at least twice as big as the
classroom I'd sat in four years earlier when I was a New
Agent trainee. Depue was standing behind a podium that
had a huge FBI seal on the front. Seated around him, on
both sides, were several men, but the only one I knew
was Dr. Jim Reese, who had taught a four-hour session
on stress management in my academy class. I thought
Reese was the best instructor I'd ever had during that
class. A graduate of the University of Arkansas, he had
no sign of a southern drawl, and probably had some of
the fastest quips and jokes I'd ever heard. The guy could
easily drop his job and go on the stage as a stand-up
comedian. Dr. Reese was an outstanding lecturer and a
very funny man.

"Now," Depue continued, "I want to take a few
minutes to tell you *why* you're here. And I want to be
very serious and honest with you about this part." Once
again he stared pointedly and effectively at the crowd.
"We have embarked on a project which is, without a
doubt, the most creative and ambitious the FBI has ever
undertaken. Why? There are thousands of murders in
the United States every year which go unsolved. There
are even more thousands of sexual assaults and cases of
child molestation which are not solved by arrest and

conviction. Ladies and gentlemen, I don't have to tell you these are serious crimes and a blemish on the face of law enforcement, nationwide. The FBI, as you know, has jurisdiction on very few cases of homicide. For example, we preside over offenses committed against Federal officers and Federal judges, and murders on Indian reservations and in national parks.

"What we've discovered is that the homicide rate in this country has gone sky high, and we're starting to see the solution rate go in the opposite direction. In the nineteen sixties and nineteen seventies, law enforcement was solving about eighty-five to ninety percent of the homicides in the country. Now, due in large part to drugs, gangs, and serial killers, the solution rate is continuing to drop. We've decided to do our part and look into the phenomenon of serial murder. While we're not sure, we are inclined to believe there are thirty-five to fifty serial killers in operation at any given time in the country. What we *are* sure of is that we have about five thousand unsolved murders in the United States every year.

"We're going to expect a lot out of you. This is the best in-service you'll ever attend, and we plan to have at least two of them each year. We want to acquaint you with cases we're working on now, and cases we've worked on in the past. We're going to inundate you with hours of the research we've done, and tell you how you're going to help us do even more. You are the most qualified and educated class the FBI ever put together, and that's why we think you will be challenged and interested in what we're presenting. Now, let's get to work."

CHAPTER TEN

Profiling "Boot Camp"- Week One

There could not have been a more stark contrast between two people than what we immediately noticed when Bob Ressler began to talk. While Depue was calm and measured in his brief presentation, Ressler seemed to be the type of guy who was all about shooting straight from the hip. The first thing he did was to introduce everyone sitting at the front of the class. "Starting on your left that would be Dr. Jim Reese. To his left is Dr. Jim Horn, in case anyone is wondering if there is a 'doctor in the house.' As you know, Roger Depue is one, too. Can't swing a dead cat around this place and not hit a doctor."

I wasn't sure if Ressler *looked* like an FBI agent, whatever that means to other people, but he dressed nicely in a well-tailored, dark Brooks Brothers suit with only a slight hint of plaid. Very expensive-looking. His full, thick head of light brown hair was groomed neatly, combed from front to back with slight hints of natural waves, and was perfectly trimmed over his ears. Probably about the same size as Depue, or slightly taller. Big shoulders, but not as muscular appearing in his body shape.

He talked so quickly that we caught the cat joke, but it only produced a murmur from the audience. "And, finally, to my left is Roy Hazelwood, who I think only has his GED. Is that right, Roy?"

Hazelwood, sitting casually in his chair with a slight list to the left armrest, seemingly disinterested, simply nodded his head and grinned. He'd worked with Ressler for years, and by his body language you could immediately tell he found Ressler more than a little annoying.

Ressler added, "In addition to being one of our profilers, Roy has developed considerable expertise in sexual assault profiling. You'll be hearing from him more than several times during the next few weeks."

Ressler didn't seem nervous, but did seem to have something of a hyperactive personality and mind which, as we'd soon learn, jumped from topic to topic at warp speed. He then launched into a general description of what we'd be doing over the next two weeks. "I'll spend quite a bit of time with you going through some of the cases we've worked on here, and filling you in on some of the rather extensive research we've been doing. Just so you don't think we've gotten all of this information out of books, Roy, John Douglas, and I have been out on the road off and on for about two years or so. What we've done is to identify multiple murderers around the country and gone out to interview them. Surprisingly, most of them were quite willing to talk to us. I guess it was like, 'What else do I have to do? Might as well talk to the FBI.' That has proven to be quite successful. So much so that John and Roy are just finishing up a book called *Sexual Homicide, Patterns and Motives*." He looked at Hazelwood. "Is that right? Uh...uh...uh...Did I say that right?"

"Good enough for the girls I go out with." Hazelwood sounded like he had the slightest hint of a southern drawl, but not from the Deep South. We'd later find out he was from Florida. He continued his slump to the left side of his chair, and from first appearances seemed to be a pretty casual, easy-going guy. Dark hair combed back like Ressler's, but with a sharp part on the left side. He was wearing a muted grey suit and a loud, multi-colored tie. Seemed to be pretty small in stature, maybe five-foot-nine and maybe a hundred and fifty pounds if he'd been out in the rain all day in heavy clothes.

Ressler seemed to be one of those people who sprinkled the annoying "uh, uh, uh" into most of his sentences. A simple "uh" was annoying enough, but a constant string of them might be a little hard to deal with. "We have some people coming who are as good as we could get. Dr. Stan Samenow is the author of *Inside the Criminal Mind*, which...uh...uh...uh...came out in print about ten years ago. We use it almost daily as a resource. Great man and speaker. We'll have Dr. Ann Burgess and Dr. Nick Groth here from Salem, Oregon. Ann and Nick have spent years doing research into rapists and serial rapists. They've worked closely with Roy, who is our sexual assault expert, and I think you'll find their profiles to be very interesting and informative. And then...uh...uh...uh..., we have Dr. Park Dietz coming." He gazed over at Hazelwood. "Damn, Roy, everyone around here's a doctor except you and me."

"I'm not sure about you, but I'm not smart enough," Hazelwood chimed in and got a decent laugh. We could already tell we were going to like Roy. Depue had left the room, so Ressler skipped to his next attempt at a joke. "Now Roger told you guys what an outstanding class you are. I want to give you another example of that. Would everyone in the room who's been in the military raise your hands?" Many of us did. "Anyone from the Navy, lower your hand." More, including myself did as instructed. "Army, lower 'em." Most did, and only a few remained. "Coast Guard?" And the remaining hands went down. "Is there anyone in here who was in the Marine Corps?" I looked around, no hands were raised. "See," Ressler said, "that's proof this is the sharpest class we've ever had back here. If it was the snake and lizard eaters from SWAT, or the firearms guys, we'd still have hands in the air. All of those guys were in the Marine Corps or the Rangers, or even the SEAL Team. But none of 'em could think their way out of a paper bag unless they could shoot their way through it first."

As he talked, Ressler was walking from one side of the room to the other, and even partway up the stairs at times. It was like trying to follow a chicken chasing grasshoppers. But without question, he was an extremely brilliant man. We'd find out just how brilliant over the course of the next few weeks.

And then his mind went back to where he was earlier, talking about the plans for the next two weeks. "We are going to have the woman here who was the subject of the book *Sybil*. She's going to talk to you about her ordeal with multiple personalities. What'd she have Roy, twenty or so?"

"Something like that," he replied, nodding his head.

"It's a fascinating case and I think you'll be amazed at her explanation of how all of the different personalities evolved as she was young, and how they influenced her as she got older," Ressler said.

"And a man who is becoming the pre-eminent criminal psychiatrist in the country, Dr. Park Dietz, will spend an entire day with us next week. Let's see, who else?" He looked at Hazelwood, who shrugged his shoulders. "Oh, yeah, Dr. Bob Keppel is the chief investigator on the Green River case, and also worked on the Ted Bundy case. He'll be with us for at least a day. And we've got Sgt. Frank Salerno from the L.A. County Sheriff's Office coming to talk about the case of the Hillside Stranglers. Sound good?" We all nodded. "Let's take a break. There is coffee and tea and some juices down the hall near the reception area. Probably some rolls, as well. I'll see you back here in a half hour and we'll start talking about Mr. Edmund Emil Kemper. See ya' then."

We filed out of the room and walked toward the lavishly appointed reception area. Few of us had met, although some of the guys did seem to have known one another before. Most of the group was a little older than me, in their early- to mid-forties. I was thirty-six and seemed to be one of the younger agents. Which made sense, since I only had about four years in the bureau. Some of the guys had been in over twenty years, I guessed.

Pouring some coffee, I introduced myself to Harry Christensen, who was stationed in the coastal town of Pascagoula, Mississippi, which was a resident agency out of the Jackson Division. Harry was a tall guy in his late forties to early fifties, slender in build, and he seemed to have a friendly southern way about him. "So, whaddya think so far?" he said without even a hint of a southern accent.

"Sounds like very interesting stuff to me," I replied. "Quite a cast of characters. More doctorates than you can swing a stick at."

"Yeah, that's kinda the way it is back here. It's almost like a college campus. These guys get back to Quantico and most of 'em have the time to work on their degrees, unlike us poor slobs in the RAs. You in an RA or headquarters city?"

"Cedar Rapids Resident Agency, Omaha Division. Right in the middle of the cornfields."

"How long you been there?"

"Let's see, about three years. I did a six-month undercover assignment and got transferred straight to the RA after that ended."

"So what was the UC assignment about?"

"Pretty much bullshit. Most fucked up and disorganized thing I'd seen in thirteen years in this business."

"Then I'll assume you must have been a cop before you came into the bureau?"

"Yup. Ten years with a police department in Southern California."

"Nice, good experience to have behind you. You'll be way ahead of the power curve. So what was the deal on the UC case?"

"Well, long story short, the Iowa Division of Criminal Investigation had some red hot information on some supposedly big-time people down in the southeastern corner of the state. Our guys got involved because, as you well know, the bureau was all about having every division cranking up some sort of an undercover case."

"Remember it well. Still stuck on doing 'em, I think."

"Yeah, probably. But that's the last time I'll do one," I growled. "So I came out from L.A. to interview with them and eventually agreed to take the job. In retrospect, the only thing that turned out positive about it all was getting my family out of there. L.A., I mean."

"That would be a good thing for sure," Harry agreed.

"Definitely. Anyhow, we finally figured out these boneheads were probably something big twenty years ago, but all they had left was a reputation and a few memories. And those were as old as the bad guys, who in reality weren't as bad as they were supposed to be. Just a bunch of old, retired men. It was so hokey that I kept pleading with the case agent to shut the damn thing down. We kept it running for about five or six months with no results."

"No shit. Not even close?"

"Well, I thought I was really getting somewhere for a while," I said. "I got to be pretty close with the brother of the main guy. Some character by the name of Buzz Melsheedah. Lived over in Peoria, Illinois. His brother, the supposed main man, was Edanu Melsheedah. He lived in a little town in southeastern Iowa. Fort Madison."

"They Iranians or something? Weird names. Camel jockeys?"

"Something like that. Maybe Lebanese. Yeah, I think that's it."

"So this is starting to sound like a typical bureau UC case. You get some info from an informant who is sucking the case agent dry, and everything he's telling you turns out to be a crock of shit."

"Pretty much. The informant was a bit of a psycho himself. Probably a pathological liar. Why they didn't see it from the get-go, I have no clue. Didn't take me long to figure out the guy was full of shit, and what he was telling us was even worse."

"Why have I heard this song before?" Harry laughed and shook his head a bit.

"That wasn't the half of it. I wind up getting close with this guy Buzz Melsheedah, and he's working me for some stolen goods. He tried to set up a deal with a restaurant guy on another deal involving stolen meat, but that didn't work out. So I checked with the case agent in Omaha, and asked him if maybe we could get some TV sets and I could sell them to him like they were stolen. My idea, of course. Just thought it'd ingratiate me a little more with the guy. Give me some credibility, you know."

"Sounds like a good idea, actually. What happened? No money? Case funds run dry?"

"Oh no, money wasn't the problem. They're kicking this idea all over the place back in headquarters as if it was going to be *real* stolen TVs. Lawyers all over the place, and none of 'em smart enough to understand we were going to buy perfectly good, brand spanking new TV's, and *represent* them as stolen. This is not a difficult concept to understand. At least I didn't think it was until the lawyers got involved."

"So what happened then? This is a hell of a story."

"It took about three weeks of battling it out and they finally agreed to do it. They go over to the Nebraska Furniture Mart in Omaha and use case funds to buy ten TVs at about three hundred a pop. Roughly three thousand bucks, total money. Paid cash. They knew a guy over there pretty well."

"So now you're rockin' and rollin'."

"More or less. They load the TVs into the van our radio techs used all the time. Still had the bureau radio in it when they brought it over. Right in plain sight on the dash. Plain Jane van. My kids coulda made it for a government vehicle, and they're only twelve. I made the radio guy who drove it over take the damn radio off the dashboard. Pissed him off, but c'mon. How stupid can you be?"

"Time out. I think I heard you say your kids are twelve. You got twins?"

"Yep. Boy and a girl. They're a couple of cuties. Great kids."

"All right. Ready-made family. Good for you."

"Thanks. It's really been fun for us. So anyhow, the big day finally arrives. The van's there. TVs are in it. And I'm starting to wonder if I'm going to have any backup with me when I drive over to Peoria with a load of what's supposed to be stolen TV sets. I assumed I would. Seems logical right? I was in charge of our Narcotics Unit when I was with the police department. If we had an undercover officer doing *anything*, we had plenty of backup."

"You're kidding me. I don't even want to hear this, do I?"

"Nope. You know exactly what's coming. The case agent and my contact agent hadn't even thought of it. Backup agents? They're gonna let me fly solo. I came this far from telling 'em to take the whole deal and stick it where the sun don't shine. Take the stupid TVs back and forget about it. But stupid me, I bitch for a while and finally agree to drive over all by my lonely little self. And away I go. Couple of hours later I pull into this American Legion post in Peoria where this guy Buzz was a member, I guess. He races out to meet me in the parking lot and goes running back inside. Next thing I know there are a bunch of old guys flying out the front door and heading to the van. They're grabbing TVs out of the back like a bat outta hell and hauling 'em over to their cars. And no sooner do they throw the TVs in their cars then they're haulin' ass out of the parking lot. Looked like the start of the Indy 500. I mean it was like, 'Gentlemen, start your engines.' Wham bam, thank you ma'am and bag ass."

Harry was laughing so hard some other agents around us noticed. "So how did this little caper finally work out?"

"Buzz thought the sun rose and set over me from then on out. But he couldn't do anything because he was just too old and didn't have any contact with the criminal element. We got together a few times, played golf and that, but nothing. I heard he died of cancer about six months after the UC case was over with."

"Are you saying that was all you got accomplished? You're supposed to be buying stolen property, but you're actually selling it? And it isn't even stolen. That is funnier than hell."

"Yeah, I know," I said. "It's almost embarrassing to admit. But then I came pretty close again, this time to someone totally unconnected with the case. You know working UC cases often means you hang out in bars with a bunch of bottom feeders. Anyhow, one night I get to talking to this guy in a bar, and he wanted to know what I did. I bobbed and weaved around, and eventually told him I was something of a fence for just about anything stolen. He was on that like ugly on an ape."

"That sounds like a pretty good start."

"I thought it was. So we started talking about him having been a long-haul truck driver, and how he could get me pretty much anything I wanted as long as it was hauled by a truck."

"And where did that go?"

"Basically nowhere. Just a big flurry of activity with nothing accomplished all over again. Talk about spinning your wheels for nothing. I stayed in contact with this Bob guy over the next couple of weeks. He was anxious to get it going. Hot to trot. Didn't have a job or anything and needed some money. So he tells me he could get a full truck of frozen meat any time I wanted. Now we're talking some serious money. He knew a driver that he said would work with him on the deal. The guy would drop the load at a pre-arranged place, and Bob would just happen along and steal the whole rig."

"Sounds okay so far. What happened?"

"Well, the guy was ready to rock 'n roll and was barking up my shins to get it done. I'm putting him off, because the bureau and our division's principal legal advisor were trying to figure out if we were entrapping him or not. You know, creating a crime."

"*That* definitely sounds like another crock of shit. Depue was right about what he said in there. Once you start to get lawyers involved in these cases, everything goes to hell in a hand basket. It sounds like this guy came to you with the offer first. Right?"

"That's exactly what happened. So the 'no balls' gang in the legal unit at the puzzle palace in D.C. kicked it around for about a month, intellectualized about every ramification and basically legalized it to death. Paralysis by analysis, you know. I'm sure they ran across the street to talk with some Department of Justice attorney about a dozen times before they finally decided to put the kibosh on the whole thing. Kept 'em busy for a while, I guess."

"Figures, damn lawyers. So what happened then?"

"I had to do some pretty fast talking to this Bob guy."

"What'd you tell him?"

"Well, it seemed like the people who backed me with the big bucks were having some cash flow problems. They got ripped on a big drug deal back east, and they didn't have the money to pull this caper off."

"Plausible answer."

"Yeah, he wasn't real thrilled about the whole thing and he kept calling me. I'd see him out every once in a while, but eventually it died a natural death."

"Such are the ways of the bureau. I haven't done one of 'em myself, but we've got enough crap to deal with where I am. Let's head back inside."

Walking down the hall, I told him the last episode. "I ran into some young guy at a bar one night who was supposedly into drugs. This bozo was an exotic dancer, you know the 'Chippendales' type, right? Anyhow, this guy wanted me to go to work with him on the circuit. I didn't even want to think about running that by anyone. Fat chance that'd head anywhere."

CHAPTER ELEVEN

Serial Killer Ed Gein – "Psycho"

Thus began what I can only describe as the two most shocking weeks of my entire life. I'd been a cop for ten years, so it wasn't like I'd fallen off the turnip truck one day going through town. I'd seen more dead bodies than someone should ever see. Terrible things like decapitations by both a car wreck and by a murderer. Every type of suicide you can imagine. And even the garden-variety stabbings and shootings. They were nothing to compare with this.

I'd never dealt with a serial killer in my life, or with the likes of the creatures we would eventually become intimately familiar with during our initial training. At times I felt like I was watching a horror film over and over again. It was like Freddie Krueger in *Nightmare on Elm Street*, *The Texas Chain Saw Massacre*, and Michael Myers in *Halloween*, all wrapped up together. But it was worse.

Much worse.

It made me wonder if these guys wanted to wash us out of the program with gore and horrifying crime scene pictures in the first couple of days. And if that's what they were trying to do, it worked. Four people told them they couldn't deal with it, and returned to their field offices. Literally, it was *that* bad. No, that's not true. It was even worse than *that*.

After our morning break, I decided to sit beside Harry, since I'd apparently made a friend and knew no one else in the class. Ressler was back in front of the class at the lecture podium. Everyone else in the Behavioral Science Unit had returned to their offices and their normal duties. Whatever they were. The whole program was a mystery to virtually everyone in the bureau. And that included me, who had been fat, dumb, and happy in my little RA working bigger cases than I ever imagined I would. And enjoying every minute of it.

Ressler had seemingly switched to another personality. The difference was palpable. Where he'd been something of a psycho-maniac earlier, running all over the room, interspersing "Uh, uh, uh" in virtually every sentence, everything suddenly changed. He started with some slides, and he wasn't having to be extemporaneous any more. He calmed down and, damn, the guy was *unbelievably* good. As they say with kids, he apparently "needed some structure." And boy did we start to see the structure quickly.

He flashed a slide onto the screen and looked back at it. A picture of a pretty normal, if not nerdy-looking, guy with thick, dark, horn-rimmed glasses appeared on the screen. The man appeared to be in his late thirties or early forties. "Anybody know who this guy is?" Ressler asked. No hands went up. "This character is Harvey Glatman and, back in the fifties, he was one of the first multiple murderers, now called 'serial killers,' we know about. There were some others, but Harvey is where we're going to start."

Ressler left the picture on the screen. "Like all of these killers, Harvey was a very interesting guy. When he was a kid, probably about eleven or twelve, he started having fantasies about committing sadistic acts on women. He fantasized about torturing and killing them. He had, shall we say, an 'odd' relationship with his mother. No dad around. Divorced. It seems his mom, a very promiscuous type, would bring her lovers around to the house, and would make Harvey watch her having sex with the men. She was also very sexually abusive toward Harvey. Liked to give him baths up until he was in his teens, and paid particular attention to washing certain 'parts,' if you get my drift here. She'd wash his little 'schwantz' extra-well with soap. You'll see this same pattern with several more of these people we'll talk about in the coming days. Like Ted Bundy, for example. Same thing." Bob used the word 'schwantz' fairly often, and it was self-explanatory to everyone in the class. I never did figure out where he got it from, though it sounded like a Yiddish word to me.

Ressler switched the slide to another scene. This

shot depicted an attractive woman in a desert-like setting, lying in fine sand beside what looked like a cactus of some sort and a bush that was stripped of its foliage. The woman, who appeared to be in her early twenties, was tied up with a rope, hands behind her back, had a gag in her mouth, and a horrified, pleading look in her eyes.

"This guy, unfortunately, grew up," Ressler continued, flashing several more pictures of attractive women in similar poses on the screen as he talked. "His deal was to make contact with the women by way of either a personal ad in the *L.A. Times,* or an ad for models. Naturally, in the L.A. area you had tons of women dying to become actresses, and this is what Harvey's M.O. was. That's how he'd find them. He'd simply take advantage of their desperation to be 'found.' It wasn't that hard for him to find women.

"We're not sure how many women Glatman killed, but we're sure of at least six. He was an unassuming-looking guy, which, contrary to common belief, most serial killers tend to be. People who can literally hide in plain sight. And, particularly with Glatman, that appearance seemed to instill immediate trust and confidence in his victims. 'He doesn't *look* like a person who'd hurt me.' And, no, he wouldn't hurt them. He'd kill them. Since it seems all of these characters have to have a name, they dubbed Harvey Glatman as 'The Lonely Hearts Killer' after he was arrested."

The screen went blank and Ressler returned to the podium.

"Pierce Brooks is here on staff with us and he'll talk to you more about Glatman and some other cases in the coming days. He'll talk about his investigation into Glatman, and how they finally identified him. He's also got a story about talking to Glatman's mom. She told him about the 'personal baths' she'd give Harvey, and how one time she found him in his bedroom with a string tied onto his 'schwantz' and the other end tied to the closet doorknob. Apparently he wasn't real happy about having a 'schwantz' that was only about an inch long, so he was leaning back trying to make it longer. Which I don't really understand, because a one-inch wiener has always worked pretty well for Roy Hazelwood." That got the first good laugh Ressler had managed all day.

"There have been some great detectives in this country, and Pierce Brooks might have been the best of them all. He solved some cases when he was an LAPD detective that are still legendary in the department. Or in the entire country for that matter. But the other thing Pierce did back then is actually part of the reason we're all here in this classroom today. When he was working on the Glatman case, bodies started turning up. Pierce began to wonder if there were similar killings of women in nearby large towns, since the choice of potential victims was like a buffet in Southern California.

"What Pierce would do was go to the library in downtown L.A. and spend most of a Friday looking at papers from towns like San Diego, Bakersfield, and even Las Vegas, which isn't really that far away from L.A. Pierce was a man who was well ahead of his time, because if you were listening to what Roger had to say this morning, what we're envisioning is a nationwide system to do exactly what Pierce was doing in the library. Make sense?" Some heads in the class were nodding. So was mine. I'd been a detective and never would have thought of such a thing. I thought to myself, *Talk about thinking outside the box.*

"Why did it take so long for someone to come up with this idea?" someone in class asked.

"Good question," Ressler replied. "And what they say about 'there's no such thing as a stupid question' isn't true. There are some, but this isn't one of 'em. I don't know a complete answer to that, other than to say everything happens in its own due time. If you think about it, we didn't have things such as computers back then. Our forms of communication were what, telephone? Teletype? Mail? And that was about it. So the reality of it is, we've finally reached the point where we can start to make those connections. It's all about technology, and we hope it'll even get better in coming years. We're just getting the rocket off the launching pad, and you guys are all about to climb aboard if you stay with us. And we hope you do. That's why you're here. It's a very exciting time for all of us, and I hope you're going to see where this is headed and be as keyed up to make it work as we are back here in the unit."

His gaze swept the room. "Everyone with me so

far?" Another slide appeared on the screen behind him. "Anyone know this character?" He seemed to like the word 'character' quite a bit, and it was an appropriate word to use when describing these people.

A hand went up in the back of the class.

"Yes sir," Bob said. "Who is he?"

"Ed Gein."

"What division are you in?"

"Milwaukee."

"That explains why you might know him. How long have you been there?"

"Almost twenty years."

"And that explains it even better. Now, since you know who he is, what can you tell us about him?"

"Well...he was crazier than hell and he was a grave robber."

"That's good for starters." Ressler used a pointer to highlight the man's face on the screen. "This guy was a certified piece of work, to put it mildly. In fact, he just died a few years ago. Mr. Gein was from Plainfield, Wisconsin, of all places. Somewhere up toward the middle of the state."

I knew where Plainfield was. I was born about fifty miles south in Stevens Point, and my dad's entire family came from there. But the name 'Gein' sounded German, and all of my family was Polish. *Probably not related in any way. Thank God.*

Much like Harvey Glatman, Ed Gein was a very plain, normal-looking man. An ordinary face that was sprinkled with several days' growth of salt and pepper beard, normal eyes, certainly not 'psycho-looking.' Really nothing out of the ordinary about him. He wore what looked like a gabardine-patterned, dark hunting cap with a short bill in front. In fact, with the hat and shirt he had on, he looked like the farmer that he was.

"Anyone ever see the movie *Psycho*?" Most everyone in class raised their hand.

"This guy was actually the model for the movie." Another picture materialized on the screen. The slide depicted a woman's body, decapitated, dressed out and hanging much like a deer would have been after being killed—upside down and by her heels, inside a shed. Ressler told us the shed was beside the man's farmhouse. (Some years later, Gein's crimes served as a template for Jamie Gumb, known as "Buffalo Bill" in *Silence of the Lambs*, proving that truth is much more realistic than fiction!)

"Ed Gein, among other things, was a grave robber," Ressler continued. "In nineteen fifty-seven, while most of the town was out hunting, Ed kidnapped a woman named Bernice Worden from her hardware store in Plainfield." He pointed to the woman's body on the screen. "This was Bernice later that night. Ed had come into the store to make a purchase, and apparently did. Some sort of a record was left showing he was the last customer in the store. When her son returned from the day's hunting trip, he found the back door to the store wide open. He noticed a trail of blood leading from inside the store to the back door and down the steps where it stopped. He called the police immediately. Since Ed had been the last customer, they thought they'd go out to his farm and talk to him to see if he might have seen something. Everyone in town knew Ed. He lived on a farm outside of town and was a bachelor farmer. His mother had died a few years before, so he lived in the house alone. People in town always thought he was a *little odd*, but they really didn't think much of it. He was just Ed.

"When the officers went to his farm later that night, Ed wasn't home, so they went out to the barn and the other outbuildings trying to find him. One of the sheriff's deputies walked into the shed you see on the slide behind me. It was pitch dark as the deputy stepped into the shed and he suddenly bumped into something he thought was a deer carcass. And then he switched on his flashlight and realized it was a body. The deputy let out a blood-curdling scream and the rest of the officers came running with their guns drawn. Luckily, no one got shot."

Ressler put up more slides as he talked. I have no idea how I kept from falling out of my seat. "Everyone there came to look, and I'm guessing it must have been a scene right out of the movie *The Werewolf*. Now, granted, it was the dark ages in terms of law enforcement, but these guys were sharp enough to get a search warrant for the house and the entire farm. When they came back, here's what they found." The slides changed more quickly. "These are ten female heads with the tops sawed off...these are four noses, all of women...both of these are women's skulls on his bedposts at the head of his bed, apparently to improve the décor." His attempt at humor was successful, despite the horror we were seeing in front of our eyes.

"This one is a woman's skull in a paper bag...these are four women's noses in the refrigerator...here is a collection of human bones and fragments they found around the farmhouse...this one is Bernice Worden's freshly-decapitated head in a paper grocery sack." The images kept getting progressively worse. "These are various body organs in the refrigerator...these are nine complete faces of human skin cut off the heads of women. These are bowls he used to eat with, but they aren't really bowls. All of 'em are the tops of human skulls, presumably women's. Here we have a pair of woman's lips attached to a drawstring for a window shade..." He stopped to take a breath. His audience was practically hypnotized by the unimaginable revulsion we were seeing.

"What we have here, and it's a little hard to see, are several chairs. All of them are covered with human skin. He sat on 'em around the dinner table. This one is a lampshade. It's covered with human skin, as well. Had enough?"

I felt like sticking my finger down my throat and barfing on the floor. I'd never heard of this guy or anything like what I was seeing in slightly grainy black and white pictures.

Ressler definitely had our attention. "Now here are a few more interesting facts about Ed Gein. When he was first questioned by a deputy at the sheriff's office, the deputy flat beat the shit out of him and he confessed. It was a different era, guys. Miranda had never been heard of, and the police had some *different techniques* than we use now. Big surprise—the confession wasn't admitted at his trial. Nonetheless, he eventually was found unfit to stand trial, another big surprise there, right? So the court decided the only thing they could do was send him to a mental facility. About ten years later, they yanked him out of there, put him on trial, and convicted him for the murder of Bernice Worden. And then they stuck him right back in the same 'Rubber Ramada' for life. Not a whole lot gained there."

Ressler explained that even though the confession

he gave wasn't used in trial, Gein provided some pretty thought-provoking information. He said he would go into what he called a 'daze,' and when he did he'd head straight for graveyards in the area. Gein said all of these dazed states would happen during a full moon. Some of the time he said he would dig up fresh graves of mostly middle-aged women he thought looked like his mother. He found out about the deaths from the newspapers. He'd open the coffins, remove the bodies, and then he'd take them home where he'd haul them out to the shed and skin the bodies. This went on for about five years. Gein told the officers which graves he'd robbed and in which cemeteries. They eventually went back and exhumed the coffins. No bodies inside. But nobody knows if he told the cops about all of the graves he desecrated.

"And it even gets more interesting," Ressler continued. "Gein said when his mother died, he decided he wanted a sex change, but he didn't know how to go about doing it. So what he did was to begin using the women's skins to create a 'woman suit,' and he'd wear it around so he could pretend to be a female. Apparently that worked out okay for him. During a full moon, he said he'd put on the suit he'd stitched together and then he'd go out and dance around in the front yard. Lucky for him, he didn't have many visitors."

A student in the front row raised his hand, and Ressler acknowledged him. "Yes sir."

"Mr. Ressler, from everything we've seen, this guy had to be crazier than a March hare. Why did they ever put him on trial?" The man had an obvious southern accent.

"That's a great question, and it's something we're going to emphasize over and over while you're here," Ressler responded. "As hard as it may be to believe, this guy wasn't insane. By that I mean legally insane. Was he about four trout short of a full stream? Yeah. Can't argue that. But only a few of these guys we're going to be talking about *were* legally insane."

"Gotta be somethin' wrong with the boy." The student shook his head.

"No question about it, and thanks for the observation." Ressler started to pace back and forth in front of the podium. "If you'll all stick with us and pay attention, the picture will unfold right before your eyes. It's one of the most important points we want you to take from this training. As hard as it may be to believe, these people aren't crazy. They plan what they do, and they know exactly what they're doing. Do they know why they're doing it? Probably not, but that's where we come in, because what we're trying to do is look for the *why*. There is a solution matrix we've all been taught at one time or another. To solve a case, you need to look at who, what, when, where, how and finally *why*. Right?"

There was no response from the class.

"Here's what we want to train you to do," he said. "Yes, you have to consider everything else, but when we do consider all of that, we want you to start looking at the why. In other words, we are going to turn that solution matrix upside down. If we train you to look for the why, we think that may help us to understand the motive. Make sense?"

Not yet, I thought. *But we still have quite a way to go, it appears.*

After wandering around in front of the classroom, Ressler returned to the podium, looked at the slide he had up, and went on. "Now, Ed admitted to the officers that his mother told him all women were 'sinful creatures' and 'despicable whores.' All except her of course. Every day she read passages to him from the Bible which dealt with deaths involving women. He said his mother was rarely pleased with anything he or his brother did as boys, even though he did fairly well in school. She often abused them physically and mentally, telling them they were destined to be just like their father, who was an abusive alcoholic and was rarely employed."

Ressler told us Gein's brother had died several years before the madness began, but it was likely Gein killed his younger brother, who died under very suspicious conditions. Lightning started a grass fire on the farm and his mother sent Ed and his brother out to fight the blaze. When Ed came back, the fire was still raging, but it eventually died out on its own. His brother wasn't with him when he returned, and Ed said he didn't know what happened to him. She beat the tar out of him for not having put the fire out, but she apparently didn't say a word about his brother. After the fire was out, the sheriff found the brother's body in the field, burned to a crisp. Even though they found some head wounds on the body, they ruled it an accidental death.

Ressler asked, "Anybody think they can solve this one?" No hands were raised. It wasn't necessary.

Finally, Ressler began to wind up the session. "All right folks. We've gone a little past lunch, but that's not a bad thing in reality. The chow line should be down to manageable numbers by now." I was trying to figure out a reason to eat anything after seeing all of this gore. "I want to finish this segment by asking you a question. We've gone through two pretty interesting cases. When you present something as an instructor, there needs to be a teaching point. Anyone know what it is?"

A couple of hands went up, and he called on one of the few women in the class, who I'd later learn was Mary Jean O'Dell from the San Francisco Division. Mary Jean eventually went on to great fame as a criminal profiler and has continued to remain active to this day.

Mary Jean said, "Mr. Ressler, I'd have to say both of these men were severely abused by their mothers, and that caused them to commit the crimes they committed. They were simply trying to strike back at their mothers."

"That is a great answer," Ressler replied. "You are absolutely right. And that leads me right into the *teaching point* I was trying to get across. Both of these men chose to do what they did in completely different ways. Yes, I agree their mothers seemed to be a factor in what they became. No question about it. But what we haven't begun to talk about is how, and more importantly, *why* they did what they did. And the manner in which they did it. This afternoon we're going to talk about two typologies we've developed over the past several years. Roy Hazelwood coined the terms 'organized' and 'disorganized' personality types for the killers we've studied. When we look at Harvey Glatman, our research would say he fits into the 'organized' category because of the planning he employed in what he did. Ed Gein is the antithesis of Glatman, and would be the poster boy for the 'disorganized' typology. More spontaneous in what he did, and seemingly driven by a deep psychological loathing for all women. Relatively little planning involved. Most of what he did was impulsive. So we'd say he was more of a 'Mission

Oriented' killer. Make sense? Well, maybe not quite yet."

He looked out at the class. "So, you ready to have some lunch? See you at one-thirty."

I looked at Harry, who was already looking at me, and asked, "You gonna eat?"

"Hell, no, I need something to drink."

"Pretty early to start that, don't you think?"

"I've got a nice jug of Ol' Grandad in my room if you wanna join me," Harry said.

"Let's walk and have a meeting about it. You are a bigger piece of work than these two perverts we just got done talking about."

"Thank you...thank you very much."

"Is that the best Elvis imitation you can do?"

"Probably, but you know what? I went to high school with him."

"You've got to be kidding me."

"Absolutely the truth, swear to God. And of course he's the one who got famous."

"Harry, you are destined for bigger and better things. You sure you're not from Georgia?"

"Nope, Ole Miss all the way, brother."

"Well, you're still a peach."

CHAPTER TWELVE

I've Never Seen or Heard of Anything Like This...

It was a struggle, but I convinced Harry we needed to have lunch before we even started to think about heading over to the Boardroom to slop down some booze.

"Let's wait until after class," I implored.

"What are you, a frickin' Mormon or something?" he retorted.

"Oh, for heaven's sake," I said as we walked to the cafeteria by way of the so-called *gerbil tubes* which connected the maze of buildings at the FBI Academy. "Let's get a bite to eat and we can head to the Boardroom after class."

A few of our classmates joined us as we headed toward the cafeteria.

"You guys okay with this stuff?" one asked.

"Not really," Harry replied, "but it looks like we're here for the duration."

"Same with me," our classmate said. "By the way, I'm Denny Koslowski from Chicago. How about you?"

Harry and I introduced ourselves.

Denny appeared to be about the same age as me. "I thought we already had someone from the Chicago Division here," I said.

"Well, that's right," Denny replied. "They put out the memo and I replied, but one of the females in the division applied, too. So, we wound up getting two slots."

"Figures," Harry said. "It's kinda getting that way in the bureau."

"No kidding." Denny had something of a hangdog look on his face.

We kept walking toward the cafeteria, passing an

area where agents watched TV.

"So Denny, what did you do before you came into the bureau?" I asked.

"I was a cop in Chicago. Spent a couple of years workin' homicides."

"Really?" He sounded like someone with the same pedigree as me, but with experience in a much larger city. Which meant a lot more opportunities than me to deal with these types of cases. "Sounds like we're pretty much cut from the same bolt of cloth," I said. "How many years with the Chicago P.D.?"

"Eight before I joined the bureau."

"About nine here, but I didn't work straight homicide. We were a smaller department, about a hundred officers, so our detectives worked everything. When we'd have a homicide, everybody was in it up to their necks. Not a lot of *who done it* cases though. Mostly smoking gun stuff. And we didn't have any of this."

"It's pretty foreign to me, too," Denny said.

By now we were in the chow line. "Only thing I had close to this was a decapitation," I said as we moved forward. "We're out on patrol one night when one of my guys called me on the radio. 'Sarge,' he said, 'you gotta meet me up on Poli near Rangewood.' I asked him what was up and he just said, 'I'll show you when you get here.' So I meet Dan and he takes me over to a small ravine where a paper grocery bag is lying. 'Okay,' I asked, 'what's in there?' 'Look,' he said, and I did. First decapitated head I'd ever seen. Turned out to be a lovers' triangle situation and we had it solved that night."

Denny said, "I was somewhat involved when John Gacy was killing all the young boys, but his house was in Des Plaines, which is a suburb, and we didn't have *any* jurisdiction. Handled a little work for them, but that was about it."

"What a case that was," Harry chimed in.

"Nothing like it had ever happened in the Chicago area, and nothing quite like it since. Thirty-three victims they know about and something like thirty buried under his house." Denny simply shook his head. "I would like to have been involved in it, but I also probably would've killed the damn guy, myself. The state won't ever put him to death. Frickin' lawyers will make millions and he'll be in jail with appeals for the rest of his life."

"Damn, you two guys have a big leg up on most of us in the class," Harry commented. "Very few of us, myself included, who've been bureau agents all of our careers, have never been involved in a homicide investigation. Everyone out there thinks the FBI gets involved in every homicide, but nothing could be farther from the truth."

"I don't know about a leg up," I replied as we finally got to the buffet of great-looking food selections. "I've never seen anything like what we saw this morning."

Denny agreed, adding, "Somehow, I think it's gonna get a lot worse."

"Ya think?" Harry answered, and we all intuitively seemed to know exactly what he was saying.

CHAPTER THIRTEEN

How Many Unsolved Murders Every Year in the U.S.?

Bob Ressler was pacing back and forth around the podium when we returned from lunch, rarin' to go and ready to roll.

I leaned over and whispered to Harry, "This guy has a lot of energy."

"He certainly does."

Little did I know how much energy and information Ressler had.

"Let me tell you a little about how I got interested in all of this," he began. "Michigan State has one of the best criminology programs in the country, and that's exactly why I went there."

That drew a few boos from several people, drawing a few chuckles. One was from me, since I was a major Iowa Hawkeye fan, and the Spartans were known to kick our butts on occasion. It was a Big Ten thing. My wife got her Master's from Iowa, and both of my kids wound up going there as well. My daughter, Loni, got her bachelor's degree and my son, Kary, eventually wound up getting a law degree. I was the black sheep in the family.

But, being a bit of a weasel, I did enroll for a Spanish class at the University one year to get a student ID. That enabled me to apply for student tickets to basketball games, and we wound up with tickets at half court in the first balcony in the old field house. I thought Jim Whalen, who'd had season tickets for years, was going to kill me when I told him what I pulled off. The Hawkeyes had great teams back then, and we enjoyed the football and basketball games for all the years we were there. I dropped the Spanish class a few days after I got my season tickets. And did the same thing the next year. As the saying goes, "Eagles may soar, but weasels never get sucked into jet engines."

"Yeah, yeah, yeah," Ressler retorted. "Boo Wolverines." That also drew some jeers.

"All right," he continued, "I can see we've got some sports Nazis in the class. Don't hold any of this against me. When I finished my degree through the ROTC program, the Army beckoned, and I decided to go into Army CID. Eventually, I spent about ten years in the Army, and then the FBI summoned me. I was lucky enough to get back here and work with some incredible people. It's almost like a perfect storm in this unit, and the combination of people we've got are starting to produce some amazing results. And you're about to become an important part of that."

Ressler paused for a moment to look around the room. "This program isn't going to be another bright idea by the bureau that goes by the wayside after a couple of years. Like 'Crime Resistance.' Remember that? That's not going to happen. We're here to stay and we have all of the necessary approvals to make sure that's exactly where the profiling program is going. What I want to do now is introduce you to Pierce Brooks, who is going to talk about the brand new VICAP program. For those of you who haven't heard of it, it is the Violent Criminal Apprehension Program."

I hadn't.

An older man with a thick head of tousled hair painfully limped down the steps toward the front of the classroom. He wore dark, horn-rimmed glasses and his face was creased. His hair was salt and pepper in color, but much more salt than pepper. His face was a pasty-white or gray color, showing the ravages of age with prominent wrinkles under his eyes and running down both cheeks. Dressed in a camel sports coat and blue pants with a plain white shirt and no tie, he didn't exactly give the immediate appearance of being the genius behind VICAP. How wrong we were.

We greeted Mr. Brooks with the customary round of applause.

"Pierce is now on staff here in the Behavioral Science Unit as a full-time consultant," said Ressler. "As

I mentioned before, he was formerly a detective with LAPD and retired as a Captain. He consulted with Jack Webb, who produced *Dragnet* on television for a number of years in the 1960s, a very popular show. In fact, Mr. Webb thought so highly of Pierce that they named a character in the show after him. When he left LAPD, Pierce went on to become the first Chief of Police in Lakewood, Colorado. After several years there, he went on to Salem, Oregon, where he eventually retired. But we were lucky enough to get a man who is truly a legendary law enforcement officer."

Brooks and Ressler shook hands and Brooks stepped up to the podium as Ressler walked up the stairs to a seat in the back of the room.

"Good afternoon, ladies and gentlemen." Brooks' voice was very weak and scratchy-sounding, almost a croak. I assumed there had been a problem with throat cancer or something. He adjusted the microphone, looked up, and began his talk.

"I'm going to spend a little time with you this afternoon talking about the VICAP program. We've been working on the concept for a couple of years, and with some bugs worked out and the computers in place, we feel like we're ready to be up and running in a couple of weeks. And that's where all of you come in. We want to get as many unsolved murders into the system as possible for starters." He pushed a button and a schematic of the program appeared on the screen. Using a pointer, he explained how VICAP was designed to work. His voice was difficult to hear despite the microphone, and I think many of us leaned forward in our seats, as if being a foot closer would help.

"In the coming months, we're going to be inputting information on unsolved sexual assaults, both on children and sex crimes related to adults. We know there is a connection between sexual assaults and many of our unsolved murders. The next thing we plan to do is start entering information about missing persons. We know many of them turn out to be victims of serial killers, or killers in general. We simply need to get a handle on that and stop ignoring it like we did for many years.

"In the late nineteen seventies, the murder rate began to skyrocket, and that's when the FBI was tasked to look into the problem. We went from about eight thousand murders in nineteen sixty to over twenty thousand in nineteen eighty. It's come down a little since then, but not much. And that's the bad news. Even worse is we are only solving two-thirds of them, so if you do the math, we've got around seven thousand unsolved *every year*. The question we tried to answer was how many of those murders were *stranger* killings. It wasn't easy to calculate with a dearth of accurate data, but we believe there are several thousand."

My chin nearly hit the counter in front of me. I had no clue we had that many murders in the United States. What a narrow perspective I had of the overall problem. I listened more carefully.

"We can explain some of the rise," Brooks croaked, "by the proliferation of gangs around the country, and by the newly-minted crack cocaine epidemic, which by now has literally spread across the nation. There's a lot of money involved here, not to mention turf wars. So we understand that. But that doesn't explain the rest. Once we carve that number out of the total, we believe about ten percent or more are stranger killings. Maybe higher. We just don't know. But what we do know is there is a high degree of likelihood that many of them are the work of serial killers whom we've yet to identify. We don't know how many are out there, but let me give you an example of how the phenomenon of multiple murders has influenced a particular area.

He scanned the room. "We have agents here from every part of the country. A lot of knowledge and experience in the room. Can anyone tell me what town in the country had the highest per capita murder rate a few years ago?"

Several hands went up.

"New York?"

"Nope."

"Washington, D.C.?"

"Nope. You're barking up the wrong side of the country. *That's a clue.*"

"Los Angeles?"

"Nope, but it seemed that way when I was working there." He croaked more than chuckled, then saw one more hand raised.

"San Francisco?"

"Close. Very close. You're getting warm." He

punched a button to change slides. "Would you believe it was Santa Cruz, California, for several years running?"

A slide appeared that depicted a quite normal-appearing young man with long dark hair and a full mustache. He had a bit of a hippy look to him, but actually was fairly clean-cut. "This guy's name is Herbert Mullin," Brooks said.

Another slide, this time of a very hippy-looking character with a scraggly beard, long hair, and the almost stereotypical headband worn by many of the hippie generation in the late 1960s and 1970s. "This is John Linley Frazier."

He switched the slide to a perfectly normal-appearing younger man, probably in his middle twenties. "And this is Edmund Kemper. We call him 'Big Ed.' He's about six foot nine inches tall and close to three hundred pounds. Now, let me pose this question. Do any of these three guys *look like* serial killers?" No one in the class knew what to say and remained quiet to avoid sounding like an idiot.

"Let me pose another question. What does a serial killer look like?" Again he waited for an answer, but no one volunteered anything. "A serial killer looks just like anyone out there. Your neighbor or your barber. Anyone. But most people, even you in all likelihood, have some preconceived idea that they *have to have* a certain look. Well, they don't, and most of them have the ability to, as we like to say, 'hide in plain sight.' When we've arrested them, most people who know them say something like 'No, it can't possibly be him.' But it is."

He turned off the slides. "All right, folks. It's time for a break and then we're going to come back and talk a little more about VICAP. Just so you know, we believe if we had a VICAP system in place when Ted Bundy was doing his spree of killings in Washington State, Utah, Colorado, and eventually Florida, we might have been able to cut him off at the pass before he did the devastation he managed to bring about. More on that later. See you back here in about a half hour. Have some coffee and avoid the pastries. Take it from an old guy, it's bad for your arteries."

CHAPTER FOURTEEN

Santa Cruz, CA: Murder Capital of America?

Brooks was back at the podium, illustrating his comments with plenty of gory slides. "For many years, we estimate somewhere around ninety percent of the murders that occurred in America were between people who knew one another. Some were naturally domestic incidents, while others involved an altercation of some type between people who were acquainted in some form or fashion. We did a pretty good job of solving them for years, but then that started to change.

"The murders in Santa Cruz in the nineteen seventies certainly defied the pattern we'd become so used to. It started to become much more of a challenge to be a homicide detective. Believe me. I was there and I saw the changes over the years I was with LAPD and the other cities I worked in. We seemed to have many more *who done its* appearing on the radar screen, and our solution rates started going down. It was frustrating. Remember the Manson case? How about the Hillside Stranglers? Stranger killings. Virtually no relationship with the victims they killed. We were at a total loss where to start, unlike what we'd been dealing with for many years. It was a completely different type of investigation and we weren't ready for it. It wasn't what we were used to, and often it just didn't make sense. Agencies were fighting back and forth rather than working together.

"Now, to illustrate that, let's go back to what I was saying about Santa Cruz." New slides of the town and the University of California at Santa Cruz began appearing on the screen. "There were enough seemingly random killings in the Santa Cruz area that handguns and rifles started flying off the shelves. Why? Because it became obvious that some of these killers were entering homes of ordinary people and murdering them for no known reason. Coeds started disappearing from the college campus, as did girls who were out hitchhiking, a pretty popular way to get around then.

"John Frazier, for example, murdered five people for no reason other than he was trying to bring attention to his belief that the environment was being ruined by logging and other commercial interests. Makes perfect sense, right? Frazier was an extremist of the hippie lifestyle and was eventually diagnosed with paranoid schizophrenia." Brooks began showing crime scene slides that were equal to those Ressler showed in the morning. "When he was arrested and put on trial it was a circus, because Frazier wanted to appear insane for the benefit of the jury. That didn't work since evidence presented to the jury showed a combination of factors involved, including drugs. LSD was, as you'll recall, quite popular back then. Might have been a contributing factor, but the jury saw through such things as Frazier shaving off half his hair and the opposite half of his beard. He wanted to come to court looking like some sort of a certified psycho. Turned out it didn't work. Despite his claim of insanity and being driven by ecological motivations, which really didn't make a whole lot of sense, Frazier was convicted and was sent to prison." (Author's note: Frazier hung himself in his jail cell in 2009.)

Brooks switched to slides showing several crime scenes involving wide-ranging, disconnected victims such as four campers, a priest, a man working in his garden, a young girl, and a young mother and her two children. He explained what we were seeing, and then said, "In late nineteen seventy-two and early nineteen seventy-three, Herbert Mullin created an even worse period of terror in the same area." He put Mullin's picture on the screen.

"At the time of the killings, Mullin was in his middle twenties, and had been institutionalized for schizophrenia. Even though he was diagnosed as a danger to others, he was allowed to become an outpatient. His dad pleaded with the authorities to keep him in the institution, but that didn't happen and he was soon out on his own."

Brooks glanced back at the picture. "Mullin

apparently stopped taking his medication and started having psychotic episodes. Voices told him it was his mission to save the people of California from a huge earthquake that would send the state into the Pacific Ocean. Mullin's delusion was a little more complex than Frazier's. The voices told him some people he saw were communicating with him telepathically, and that this communication told him one of two things was destined to happen. He could either telepathically convince them to commit suicide to help save California, or would allow them to become human sacrifices to accomplish the same thing. And, of course, it would be his job to accomplish the sacrifices if they didn't commit suicide."

Brooks looked at us. "Makes perfect sense, doesn't it? We simply didn't have this type of thing happening in the fifties and sixties. If we did, it was so rare you never heard about it. It was always somewhere else, and we all had our own problems to deal with. There usually weren't that many victims, probably one or two, and then we'd arrest 'em. For the record, Mullin killed thirteen people."

I leaned toward Harry and whispered, "I was in Ventura when this was happening."

"Close to your town?" he asked.

"Couple hundred miles north, thank God. But my family and I went camping up there once or twice. Scary."

"Looks like a beautiful place."

"It is. Tons of redwood trees and a beautiful ocean overlook up on a cliff. Really nice place."

"Most killers are fairly selective about their weapons. Mullin wasn't." Brooks showed several more slides showing a knife, a revolver and a baseball bat. "These were what Mullin used. No pattern at all. It could have easily been many more than one killer. The authorities didn't know, and certainly nothing like it had ever happened there to provide them with much guidance. Prior experience told them that if different weapons were involved in the murder, then you *had to have* different killers. But this was something completely new. The old-school homicide detectives couldn't make sense out of it. They were used to solving their cases in a couple of days. These investigations went on for years sometimes."

Next on the screen was a photo of Mullin when he was booked by the police. "Mullin was unquestionably paranoid schizophrenic. Bob will talk about the research we've done on that, and Dr. Dietz will also explain how many men are beset with the mental disease sometime in their middle twenties. Not always, but more often than not. What we've learned, though, can be very important information in cases like these in terms of building a profile."

He added, "Don't ask me how this happened, but as crazy as Mullin obviously was, and despite his prior diagnosis, he was somehow found to be legally sane and he was convicted on ten counts of murder. Not sure what happened with the other three. Legal stuff, I guess."

It was nearing four o'clock. Brooks told us to take a little break and we'd finish up. Ressler came down in front and watched us file out.

After a quick bathroom and stretch break, we returned to the room. Brooks had assumed his spot leaning on the podium.

"So, let me wrap it up and we'll get you out of here for an early dinner. You're hungry, right?" He looked at a bunch of faces that all expressed similar thoughts: *After seeing that, I'm supposed to eat?*

"Here's what we've learned from these two cases, and one more Bob will tell you about tomorrow involving Ed Kemper. These three guys covered the spectrum of multiple murderers. We'd call Frazier a mass killer, because he killed all his victims at the same time and same place. Mullin, on the other hand, was more of a spree killer, which we think is quite similar to a serial killer on warp speed. His killings happened over a shorter period of time, about four months. And then we'll come to Kemper, who you'll see fits the description of a serial killer. That definition is still being refined, but what we're now saying is a serial killer is a person who kills three or more people over a period of time, with a *cooling off* period between the killings. The period of time can range from weeks to months, and even years. We've got a case up in Seattle right now where over forty women, mostly prostitutes, have been killed in the last two years. We simply don't know who the guy is, and we've worked hand-in-hand with the task force up there."

We wouldn't know until 2003 when Gary Ridgway, the so-called "Green River Killer," was arrested and eventually admitted to killing forty-eight women. But there were probably a lot more.

Brooks waved a hand in dismissal. "Let's get out of here and I'll see you later in the week."

CHAPTER FIFTEEN

Fifty Ways to Please Your Liver!

Harry, Denny, and I hooked up with Tim McDaniels as we were heading down toward the chow hall.

"Are you guys *really* ready to eat?" Harry asked.

"You got something else in mind?" Denny inquired.

Harry was quick to respond with, "Yeaaaah. My brain is so damn full of this crap that I need to empty it out."

"And how do you propose to do that?" I asked, as if I didn't know what the answer would be.

Harry tilted his head to the side. "I'm ready for a beer."

"This early?" Tim pointedly looked at his watch. It was barely after four o'clock.

"Hell, yes. The Boardroom opens back up at four for a reason. And I think we're it today. Plus, if you want something to eat, they've got burgers and pizza there. Some other stuff, too. Ready?"

This was a mistake of epic proportions. By six o'clock, all four of us had been dipping our beaks and talking, and had a pretty good snoot full. In short order we were joined by a bunch of other guys from the class. It appeared we were destined to drink our dinners.

While some of the talk was about what we'd seen in class, and opinions of Ressler ("He's one of the most brilliant people I've ever known"), one of the guys from Detroit commented that you simply can't get a bunch of bureau agents together without talking shop.

Listening to stories from some of the guys in big offices never failed to astound me. An agent from the Washington Field Office in D.C. was talking about an agent there who got put on "Applicants for Life" after he was caught selling Amway on duty. "He'd get in the office pretty early and grab some case files, and *bam*, he was out of there about nine every morning. Problem was, he never got any work done. So his supervisor decides they'd put a tail on him to see what in the hell he was doing. Got the surveillance squad and a plane in the air and away they go. He heads for his house and comes running out with a big signboard and stuffs it in the back seat of his bureau car. And then he hauls out some boxes, and off he goes. They follow him to about six houses all over Alexandria and Springfield, and of course he's hauling the signboard in with him wherever he stops. Finally, it's about four o'clock and he heads back toward his house. So they decide to confront him when he parks in front of his place. The signboard is professionally done by Amway showing all of their products, but worse than that he's got box after box of Amway products in the back seat. Open and shut case. Thirty days on the bricks, which is automatic for bureau car violations, and then on the Applicant Squad for the rest of the time he was in WFO. Served him right."

"Some of these guys are about one wave short of a shipwreck," an agent from the Dallas Office said. "The bureau harps about misusing bureau cars, but more guys don't pay attention than *do* pay attention. If you're in a Resident Agency, it's simply going to happen sometimes, but if you're going out to dinner, you don't throw your family in and head out to the restaurant."

"Hell, that sort of stuff happens all the time." Harry was beginning to slur his words. "We had a guy in Tampa who liked to get in these barbeque contests at county fairs. So he hitches up a tow bar to his bureau car and was apparently using it to haul this big cooker around. That's bad enough, but he's involved in something one night and can't get away. So he drives his bureau car over to his house and has another guy pick him up. What happened then was his wife gets the cooker hooked up and away she goes. In the frickin' bureau car, pulling the cooker down the freeway doing sixty-five or so and the cooker blows a tire. It starts fishtailing and she loses it. Right into a viaduct. Bureau car is wrecked. This is not good."

There were a few "oh my Gods" uttered.

"What happened?" someone asked.

"Sixty days on the beach and transferred from

Organized Crime to Applicants."

"I'm not sure which one of those two consequences is worse," someone else commented.

Another agent said, "I'd take sixty days to spending the rest of my career doing applicant work. Hoover said it's the most important work in the bureau, but Hoover never worked a damn case. That shit is boring and so repetitive I think it'd cause someone to eat their gun."

"It's all about the three B's," Tim commented. "Booze, broads, and bureau cars. Gets more damn guys in trouble than anything else in this outfit."

"We had a guy who'd take his bureau car out at about five every morning to help his son deliver papers," an agent said. "It probably worked for awhile until one of his neighbors called the SAC wondering if he was supposed to be doing it. Another thirty day vacation right there."

The stories continued and the beer flowed. The stories got even better.

An agent from L.A. talked about their last Christmas party where the Special Agent in Charge (SAC) took off a little early with one of the gals from the steno pool. "Pretty hot chick. So they're heading down the freeway and it seems she's giving him a blowjob. He's more than a little drunk and sideswipes a car, and the cops show up. 'What were you doing?' they asked. 'Uhhh, he said, my attention was diverted.' It was diverted okay, and the cops diverted him to jail, despite his protests about 'who I am.' You think a street cop gives a shit about that? Anyhow, the chick copped out to what was going on while he was driving. That story got around the cop shop in a hurry, and of course got back to our office almost as quickly. Rumors all over hell for about a week, and they start to get back to the boss. He was more than a bit of a goofball, so he calls an all agents conference for the following Monday. Everybody packs into the huge squad bay and he comes rolling out, and I'm not making this up, with a set of rose-colored sunglasses on. Don't ask me why. So he starts talking about the rumors he's heard, and everyone in the squad bay is tryin' like hell to keep from laughing. Somehow he figures out what's going on and says, 'Okay, this meeting is over. If I hear one more rumor about anything concerning this matter, I'm going to sue the

person who is spreading it.' Man, you shoulda heard
people crack up when he left."

"So, what happened to him?" someone asked.

"We were never sure, but we think he got thirty
days on the bricks, at least that's what we heard. But
worse than that, they demoted him down to ASAC
(Assistant Special Agent in Charge) and sent him to El
Paso. There again, which is worse? The sword or the
knife? That demotion cost him some serious money."

"Serves him right," someone commented. "Most of
us can do one of the B's, but it sounds like he did all
three of 'em in one fell swoop."

I got a decent laugh when I told the story about the
fugitive case and how the old farmer's wife in Iowa
looked at my credential picture and said what a bad
actor he looked like.

By this time the whole table was rocking and rolling.
The Boardroom was full, and there was a table full of
SWAT guys in for some in-service training. Most of the
SWAT group were former military guys and slightly less
evolved than some, a 'macho' group, and their table was
easily the loudest in the Boardroom. Ours was pretty
close behind. Every time a female walked in, the SWAT
table began a chorus of "There she was just walkin'
down the street." And so forth. The noise from the tables
was drowning out the music they had piped in. Pretty
normal night in the Boardroom, just as I discovered
during New Agent Training and another in-service.

It was J. Edgar Hoover who decided to put the FBI
Academy in Quantico, Virginia, about forty miles south of
D.C., and that's where it's been since about 1972. In
some ways it was a wise decision, because it didn't
enable the new agent trainees to have access to all sorts
of temptations in D.C., which happened when the
Academy was in the old post office building downtown.
How Hoover ever got the land given to the bureau by the
Marine Corps is still a subject of debate. Some think
Hoover had a file on one of the Marine Corps generals
and worked out a little trade.

Building the huge complex in Quantico undoubtedly
solved many problems. The closest town, if you could
call it that, was Quantico. It was basically all bars which
were typically patronized by drunk enlisted Marines, and
that meant fights. If you had a car to drive away from

the academy, that opened up some new doors, but it was still quite a trek to some decent watering holes in the D.C. area. So the Boardroom was the only viable option for most of us. The beer flowed freely and the price was right. There was no danger of getting arrested for drunk driving, since the dorms were only a short stagger away.

During the two weeks we were there, we'd have a 'debriefing' almost every night. It was starting to get ugly after two weeks, and some of us were thinking we'd have to get the treatment when we got home. Like joining AA with a lifetime membership.

One evening, as it started getting closer to eight o'clock, I was definitely ready to call it a night. But then we started talking about the class we were in and the profiling program as a whole. Everyone agreed it was gruesome stuff to be exposed to, but it looked like it was going to be the best in-service any of us had ever attended. No one disagreed with that.

Denny said, "They're going to train us and then expect us to go back to the field and basically do nothing other than refer cases to them back here. Right?"

"Yup, that's it," replied Dave Chamberlain from St. Louis. "I think they want us to get out there in our divisions and do some schools to make everyone in law enforcement aware of the possibilities for the program, and how it might help their cases. But we're apparently not going to be the ones doing profiles."

"Good luck with that," Denny retorted. "If I was a cop and I'm working a murder case, I don't want to give the FBI a bunch of information, which would slow me down in the first place, and then I'm supposed to sit around and wait for a profile. Sorry, I can figure this out. I was born at night, but it wasn't last night."

"Sounds like that's what they have in mind," someone else commented.

Denny took a huge gulp of his drink. "Fat chance that'll happen. The cops are gonna put a ton of pressure on us to give them a profile as soon as possible. And I don't see 'em taking 'no' for an answer. If they've gotta wait, they're gonna be pissed as hell, and what do you think are the chances of getting another call from them again?"

"Good point." Harry was tilting strongly to the

starboard side, his arm either resting on the table or keeping him from falling out of his chair. In point of fact, none of us were much better. "We're supposed to go out there and get 'em all revved up, and then when they want something, they don't want to talk to Ressler or Hazelwood. They know us, and that's who they want to talk to. Now."

It was time for me to head to bed. Full day of class tomorrow and the week wasn't close to being over. "Hey, everyone. I'm packin' it in for the night. See you guys in the morning. It'll get worked out. I hope."

CHAPTER SIXTEEN

Killing Grandma and Grandpa

"Let's finish up where Pierce left off yesterday, because if you don't know anything about this case, I think it will open your eyes even more than they are now." Bob Ressler was once again at the podium. "I've personally talked to this guy several times, and as odd as it may sound, I can honestly say I like him. I don't like what he did in killing ten people, but he is someone who you wouldn't mind shooting the bull with, but certainly under different conditions. The district attorney in Santa Cruz described him as 'the nicest serial killer I ever met.' Now, having said all of that, Edmund Kemper is someone who can give you the worst nightmares you've ever had."

Ressler punched a button on the podium, and a picture appeared on the screen depicting a plain and non-descript, seemingly harmless-appearing young man with a wispy mustache and dark, horn-rimmed glasses. Everything Ressler said from that point on was illustrated by slides, whether of people, crime scenes, or the campus of the University of California at Santa Cruz. That was the easy part. What wasn't so easy was seeing the images of body parts that were found in wooded areas, near a beach, or having floated up on shore in the ocean near Santa Cruz.

"Kemper has been quite candid with us in talking about what he did," Ressler said, "and is bright enough to understand, in large part, why he did it. To be honest about it, I'd have to say we've learned more from Kemper than any of the other multiple murderers we've talked to. Bundy *could have* done the same, but he's such a pathological liar and thinks he's so damn smart that he'll barely acknowledge having done *anything*. And that is despite being convicted of murders in Florida. If you're wondering, Bundy is awaiting execution as we speak." (Author's note: Bundy was executed in January of 1989.)

"Let me get back to Ed Kemper. We've learned a lot from him, as I said. He's very articulate and has been tested with an IQ of one hundred and thirty-five. That's quite a bit smarter than most of us. He grew up in a family where his mother was definitely the one who ran the show. Very large woman, and Kemper himself grew to six-foot-nine and three hundred pounds in his late teens and early twenties.

"His mother, Clarnelle, was verbally and physically abusive toward him. She was a woman with a lot of anger, and it also appears that same anger was passed on to Ed through continued abuse." He put up a picture of a dark-haired, pensive-looking woman with her finger against her left cheek as if in deep thought. Dark, horn-rimmed glasses dominated a slightly chubby and elongated face. The word "lesbian" almost jumped off the screen. Stereotypes notwithstanding, she was simply not an attractive person. She had an almost mean look on her face, even though she was trying to smile. It didn't appear we were looking at a woman who did a lot of that.

"When Kemper was about nine, his father had his fill of Clarnelle and filed for divorce. At the time, the Kemper family was living in Burbank, California, where Ed was born. He had an older sister and another sister who was about three years younger than him. So he was a middle kid. Ed was very close to his father, and it was difficult for him when his mother left California and moved the kids to Montana with her. As kids of divorce tend to be, Ed was unhappy about the separation from his dad, so he took his anger out on his younger sister and had temper tantrums around his mom. To this day, he believes his mother took her anger about the divorce out on him, and he admits he hated his mom. This will, by the way, be important as we proceed through the case."

Ressler kept punching buttons and putting up new slides, explaining what each meant in the grand scheme of things. Showing one of a house and basement, he explained how Kemper's mother would put him in the basement for hours, even all day. Sometimes Kemper would take one of his younger sister's dolls with him, and would mutilate the doll with a knife. He was around ten or twelve at this point, but it was a time when he had some of his most violent fantasies. Ressler said, "It's fair to assume the anger he was displaying was as a result of the constant abuse and berating by his mother. Again, this will play out as he gets older, into his early twenties.

"Kemper said he was a bit precocious in terms of having sexual fantasies. These came together with his violent ideas and behavior, and seemingly were forever linked. When he was in school, Kemper said he was a chronic daydreamer, often thinking about his sexual fantasies and imagining performing violent acts on girls in his classes." There were clearly a very perverse world and equally deviant thoughts floating around in Kemper's mind.

"Kemper told me about killing the family cat. First, he said he buried it alive. Then he decapitated it and placed the head on an altar he'd built in the woods near his house. On another occasion, when Kemper was about thirteen, he killed yet another cat, slaughtering it with a machete and put the remains in his closet, which his mother eventually found. "If you were a parent, that would make your week, wouldn't it? With this and her knowledge of the decapitations of the dolls, his mother began to keep him in the basement more often. She wanted to keep him away from his sisters, because she didn't trust him. Her instincts proved to be pretty accurate. Kemper told me, 'If anything, this fueled my violent fantasies to even higher levels.'"

At this point in Ressler's presentation, we'd seen about fifty slides which he explained thoroughly, so he decided to give us a break. We all needed one.

Milling around with coffee and donuts, several of us talked about what we were seeing.

"I've never heard of this guy," an agent from Florida said.

"I was on the police department in Ventura when these guys were literally terrorizing Santa Cruz, so I remember it," I remarked. "But we had our own issues to deal with and, frankly, I didn't pay a lot of attention to what was going on up there. Wasn't my problem."

"This guy is a sick tuna," Harry said.

"Ya think?" Denny replied before taking a sip of coffee and a bite of a donut.

"Something tells me we ain't seen nothin' yet," Dave Chamberlain commented.

"Yeah," Harry agreed. "We haven't even got to the bad stuff yet."

Ressler was at the podium, raring to go, when we started filing back into the room. Once everyone was seated, he asked, "So how's this going for everyone so far?"

"Scarin' the hell outta me," said an agent from Denver. "I had no idea these types of people even existed. I suppose I've been so immersed in my own work that it never crossed my mind."

"Well, you haven't seen anything yet." Ressler flashed a fake evil smile. "Let's get back to work." He activated the screen and started with a new slide of a young woman.

"Kemper's older sister recalled one time when she was goading him to kiss a teacher at school who he thought was pretty. She remembers him saying, 'If I did, I'd have to kill her.' In retrospect, that was a very telling comment. At about that same time, Kemper said he was fed up with things at home and decided to run away to live with his father. Somehow he succeeded in getting down to Burbank, but as soon as he got there he discovered his dad had remarried and had another son. As it turned out, his dad wasn't as happy to see him as he'd hoped. He stayed for a while, but eventually his dad sent him back to Montana.

"Here is where things get even more interesting. What he faced in Montana was a mother who didn't want him around, chiefly because she'd met a man she was planning on making her third husband. So mom decided to ship him off to live with his paternal grandparents at a ranch in California. Apparently she didn't feel she could handle the overgrown adolescent, and perhaps he would show some measure of respect toward his grandparents. Who he'd barely met, I might add.

"This plan didn't work out as well as his mother hoped, if in fact she did have any hope for her son. Kemper told me his grandmother was equally as mean as his mother, and she decided to undo the things his

mother had done by showing everyone what a terrible
parent his mother was. That didn't work out too well,
either. He became more rebellious and eventually his
grandmother shipped him back to his mother in
Montana. Kemper told me he was starting to feel like a
little pawn in a sinister chess match. He felt abandoned
by everyone. He knew no one liked him, let alone loved
him, and his view of himself got even worse when his
mother sent him back to live with his grandparents. Not
hard to understand that."

Ressler made a motion with his hand going up and
down. "You think this guy was starting to feel like a yo-
yo?" Clearly it was a rhetorical question as the answer
was obvious. "Kemper told me he felt like he was a
'walking time bomb' by the time he was fifteen and back
with his grandparents. He said he was about six-foot-five
by then, was teased by kids in school for being a 'giraffe'
or 'Jack and the Beanstalk.' He became even more
socially isolated and awkward. With no friends, a ton of
seething anger inside his head, and fantasies all over the
place, his assessment of himself was probably as
accurate as anyone could describe. He said he wished
someone knew how to defuse his rage, but instead of
that happening, everyone seemed to ensure it would
grow worse and worse. And so it all came to a head and
erupted in one day of rage and violence."

Ressler went back to the slideshow. Some showed
pictures of Kemper's grandparents, while others showed
not only the ranch, but eventually pictures of dead
bodies and the crime scenes. "Now this is where things
literally go from bad to worse, if that was possible.
Kemper told me he had fantasies of killing and mutilating
his mother and his grandmother because they were
always pushing him around and telling him what to do.
He talked about wishing everyone else in the world
would die, too, and even fantasized about killing many of
them, including himself. Things are starting to escalate
here, folks.

"One afternoon in August, Kemper and his
grandmother had an argument in the kitchen of the
ranch house. His grandmother, Maude, was sixty-six at
the time, and wasn't able to control him physically to
even the slightest degree. Kemper admitted he'd
displaced the anger for his mother to his grandmother by

this time, so it didn't take much to make him react. Some would say 'snap,' but I think the snapping process was more like a rubber band being stretched and stretched for years until it finally wore too thin and broke. He left the room in a rage and grabbed a .22 rifle that his grandfather had bought him for Christmas. He came back into the kitchen. His grandmother yelled at him for having the gun in the house, so he hit her in the head with the butt of the gun. When she fell to the floor, he shot her in the head, which killed her. And then, apparently for good measure, he shot her in the back two times. If that wasn't enough, his rage was now out of control, so he grabbed a kitchen knife and stabbed her repeatedly. All of this was completely impulsive, not even beginning to approach the planning and predatory instincts he'd display later in life."

Ressler didn't show the slightest inclination of slowing his torrent of information. "Now he realized he had a problem. A big problem. His grandfather wasn't home, and somehow he thought he had to hide the body. He dragged his grandmother's corpse into his bedroom and did his best to hide it in the closet."

He displayed photos of the blood trail and the body in the closet.

"Everything calmed down for a while according to Kemper, but about a half hour later his grandfather drove up to the house and parked. Kemper said he went into another state of frenzy. While he liked his seventy-two-year-old grandfather, whose name was also Edmund, Kemper said he had to 'finish the job.' He went to the window and pointed the gun out, and as his grandfather got out of his car, Kemper began shooting. Grandpa fell and Kemper ran out to finish him off."

More slides, these of blood near the car, which Ressler explained were from Kemper's grandfather, and a picture of the front of the garage with a body inside.

"He pulled the old man's body to the garage and tried to hide it. Now Kemper was in an even bigger mess, but some of us believe his rage calmed at that juncture. Why? Simply because he had, in his own way, avenged the rejection of both his father and his mother. He said he started thinking more clearly, but he also knew he was in serious trouble. Since he didn't know what else to do, he called his mother and told her what had happened. Clarnelle was shocked and mad, of course, and screamed at him, telling him to call the police immediately. One of his sisters later recalled Clarnelle telling her to not be surprised if Ed killed his grandparents one day. Sure enough, she had her son figured out quite well."

Ressler checked the standard, government-issue, black and white clock on the side wall. "Let's go over a few more things and then we'll take a good lunch break. For his efforts, Kemper earned a full-ride scholarship to Atascadero, which is the state mental hospital in California for violent offenders. He spent about five years there. The staff described him as a 'model prisoner' and quickly figured out he was a very bright guy. They decided to put him into a section where the staff did psychological testing and evaluations of prisoners. He eventually worked under the chief psychologist, and when he was nineteen he was the head of the lab. He learned everything there was to know about the psychological tests they gave to all newly arriving inmates. He told me he was very proud of the fact that he came up with a new scale to test and measure, calling it the 'Overt Hostility Scale.' Probably a lot of personal experience involved in that, but the staff apparently loved it and the work he did.

"Kemper said he loved being at the institution, and recalled thinking it was like he had been born again while there. He had structure, no real stress, and because of his size, few of the other inmates would tease or test him. He got in shape, lost weight, and said he never felt better in his life. He wanted to stay, since he said he felt like it was the first real home he'd had in his life. But decision time was approaching as he neared the mandatory release age of twenty-one. Despite disagreeing with the parole board, he was released, and that's where we'll pick up the rest of the story. Right after lunch."

CHAPTER SEVENTEEN

The Santa Cruz Coed Killer: Edmund Kemper

WIsh we didn't have to spend so much time on this guy Kemper," Harry whined as we were on our way to lunch.

"Pretty gruesome stuff," Denny said.

"You got that right," I agreed. Waiting in the food line, we all suspected things were going to get even more ghastly after lunch. The morning session had shown all of us just how horrifying the crimes of a serial killer could be. With more coming in the afternoon, we knew it was going to get worse. A lot worse.

"There has to be a reason Ressler's going into such detail on this guy," Denny said.

"Good point," I responded. "It's interesting, all right, but Ressler seems to be the kind of guy who always has a method to his madness."

"Madness seems like an appropriate word to describe this guy Kemper," Harry interjected. "I think you're right, Pete. This is probably heading somewhere. I'm guessing this afternoon is going to send us back to the Boardroom."

"I think you're right," Denny said.

After making our food selections from a lavish array of choices, we walked into the massive dining hall. The first time I ever walked into it was for lunch during my initial day of New Agent Training. It was truly an impressive sight, and I have never ceased to be amazed at the setting when I walk in. The walls must be thirty feet high, with huge glass windows on all three sides. Each window provides its own spectacular view of either the well-manicured courtyard, or the library and dorms. The entire academy is built out of a tan brick. On all three walls, which separate the rows of windows, are full-sized flags of every state in the United States. The lighting in the cafeteria, while not overtly decorative, is muted and indirect, giving off a soft glow and a completely different ambiance than you'd see in a normal cafeteria at a college or university campus. The tables are utilitarian, and the chairs are comfortable, though not padded. It is more of a 'get in and get out' place from that standpoint.

Several of our classmates joined us, and we spent a little time talking about the morning's presentation, but of course spent some time bitching about the bureau as well. It never ceased to amaze me the types of problems agents got themselves into in some of the larger offices like Chicago, New York, and Los Angeles, among others. Having been in Los Angeles, I could relate, but being in a small, isolated resident agency, I was well insulated from those problems. And in truth, I was glad I was. Some of the stupidity by FBI agents was simply depressing. And the biggest problem, as many saw it, was New Agent Training. The bureau had not made adaptations to modern times in training their new agents. If the public or politicians knew what was going on, there would have been a huge hue and cry. But no one did, and the sham continued.

However, to the bureau's credit the in-service training schools were exceptionally well done. This would turn out to be the best of them for me, right alongside Hostage Negotiator Training. At least in these areas, the bureau had moved training of experienced agents into modern times.

"All right, everyone here?" Ressler was scanning the classroom. Satisfied that all of his little chickens were in their coops, he activated the slide control panel on the podium and put a booking photo of Ed Kemper on the screen. "Here's Kemper after he was arrested, and here's what he did to get that way.

"When Kemper was released from Atascadero by the parole board, the real problems began almost immediately. His staff psychiatrists had recommended Kemper *not be* released to his mother, thinking that, and that alone, could trigger yet more violence. Wise advice, you'd think, but no one kept watch once he was sprung back into the real world. Having no means to support himself and no one else in his life to turn to, Kemper had to move in with his mom. He told me the verbal abuse began almost as soon as he walked in the door. She referred to him as her 'murderous son,' and blamed him for her recent divorce. It was his fault that she couldn't meet another man to marry, and on and on it went. They clearly had an unrelentingly toxic relationship at best, and certainly one that would eventuate into the catastrophic events that would develop in the coming months."

New images of a tranquil, picturesque college campus began to appear on the screen. "Kemper's mom was working as an administrative assistant at the university in Santa Cruz, living in the nearby town of Aptos. Neighbors overheard frequent arguments, and at times shouting matches. Ed was required to enroll in school as part of his parole conditions. So he enrolled in classes at a nearby community college and did well. But Kemper was fascinated by law enforcement, having watched many shows on television while he was in Atascadero. His goal was to get into the police academy, but his height and past record of murder were not the qualifications they sought for officers in the area. To compensate, he hung around in a cop bar in Santa Cruz called 'The Jury Room.' He said he enjoyed listened to their stories and took vicarious pleasure in hearing of their exploits.

"Aside from that simple amusement, Kemper told me he really didn't enjoy the newfound freedom. He felt like the world had made a quantum leap ahead while he was in Atascadero, and the train had left the station with him waiting on the platform. He was pretty close to right, because the hippie movement was in full force, campuses were erupting, violent groups were bombing college buildings and businesses, and the anti-Vietnam War movement was escalating. People didn't even look the same as they had before he went into Atascadero a mere five years before. The world had changed and he no longer fit into it, even aside from his height and ungainly appearance. He admitted he was still socially inadequate, and had a hard time approaching girls. The cops later would describe him as being a polite and attentive young man, pleasant with an easy manner, intelligent and able to articulate exceptionally well.

Kemper idolized John Wayne and could talk about every movie he'd been in. Little did the officers know it would be Kemper they would be talking about in the months to come."

Here Ressler paused. "We've found that quite a number of these multiple murderers have a fascination with law enforcement. A good example would be Kenneth Bianchi, one of the Hillside Stranglers in Los Angeles. Bianchi tried to get on LAPD and into the Sheriff's Department. When that failed, he tried getting in as a reserve officer or deputy. We'll talk about several more later on in the week and next week.

"Kemper finally landed a job with the California Department of Highways. Eventually he saved enough money to move into his own apartment in Alameda. This went back and forth because he didn't have enough money to meet the rent each month, and he sometimes ended up back at his mom's place. He bought a motorcycle and, after an accident, won a settlement for fifteen thousand dollars. Then the real problems started. He bought a used car, a yellow Ford Galaxy, which ironically looked like a police car that detectives might drive. That turned out to be handy, as well.

"So Kemper began to cruise around. He'd notice young females out hitchhiking, which was the popular mode of travel for college students and runaways in those days. When he looked them over, he started to think about things he could do to them. His violent fantasies returned, fueled in large part by his continuing poor relationship with his mother. Kemper began preparing his car for what he had in mind. He placed plastic bags, knives, a blanket, and handcuffs into the trunk. Then, all he needed was the right opportunity. For a period of time, he picked up girls and just gave them a ride where they wanted to go. These were trial runs. Practice. By his estimation, he picked up around a hundred hitchhikers, any one of whom might have been chosen to be his first victim. Finally, he started to have sexual fantasies and felt an urgent inner drive of what he called his little 'zappies.' Finally he worked up the nerve to do what he'd been planning and practicing to do for months."

Ressler showed several pictures of two young women. "His first two victims were Mary Ann Pesce and

Anita Luchessa. They were both eighteen and attending Fresno State College. He picked them up in Berkeley and took them to an isolated spot off a minor country road. He said he'd fantasized about it for so long that when the moment finally presented itself, he wasn't really sure what to do. But one thing he did know was he could get arrested for rape, so he decided to mix rape with murder, thus no witnesses or prosecution."

More slides. *How on earth does he have so many?*

"Kemper took one of the girls into the woods, but wasn't able to accomplish the rape, even after taking her clothes off. So he stabbed her to death and returned to the car and stabbed the other girl. He put her body in the trunk immediately, then went back to get the other girl. With both bodies hidden in the trunk, Kemper returned to his mother's apartment, leaving the corpses in the car, and went to sleep. The next morning, after his mother left for work, he brought both bodies into the apartment. He put both of them into the bathtub and decapitated both of the girls. He put the heads in a trash bag and hauled the mutilated corpses back to the trunk. He left one girl's body parts in a redwood grove along a mountain highway, and the other was thrown into some brush on a nearby hillside. Then he drove to another area and buried the body of Mary Ann. He'd removed the arms and legs, so the trunk of her body was all that was left." Ressler showed pictures of decomposed body parts that had been found in several places around Santa Cruz.

"Kemper kept both heads in his car for a while. As he'd drive around, he'd take one out of the bag and use it on himself to simulate oral sex. In due course of time, the heads began to decompose, so he said he threw both of them into a ravine.

"The two girls were listed as 'missing persons' for several months, until Mary Ann Pesce's head was found by some hikers, and eventually identified by dental chart comparison. After his arrest, Kemper took the investigators to a shallow grave where he had buried the remainder of her body. Anita's body was never found.

"A month later, Kemper went looking for another girl. He found Aiko Koo, a fifteen-year-old dancer, who was hitchhiking from her home in Berkeley to a dance class in San Francisco, despite promises to her parents that she'd take a bus. She never arrived for the class. Kemper took her not to San Francisco, but to an isolated spot in the mountains above Santa Cruz. He taped her mouth shut and pinched her nostrils together until she suffocated. Then he raped her lifeless body and again put it in the trunk of his car. Driving back to town, he felt stressed, so he stopped at a country bar and had a couple of beers.

"At this point, Kemper said he was 'all in.' He was the hunter, and he described it as a 'real tweak' to be out there with the power, and to have complete control over his victims. 'When I was out there, and I was killing the girls, there wasn't anything else in my mind except I was the hunter and eventually they would be mine. They were a part of me.' Kemper told me that with later victims, he would literally make two of the victims 'part of him,' by eating 'parts of them.' I'll let your imagination figure that out."

Ressler paused once more. "Let me take a quick timeout here. What you need to understand is John Frazier had been arrested for five murders, and Herbert Mullin was killing people right along with Kemper. Santa Cruz, as you might imagine, was in a total state of panic, as well they should have been. Pierce told you about those cases yesterday, so I don't need to go into details he's already covered. Suffice it to say, no one in the area felt safe since bodies were literally turning up left and right. The police and sheriff's departments were at a loss, and they had no clue if the killings were connected with the same person, or if there were several killers roaming around."

Pictures appeared of a young woman and the campus of Cabrillo Community College as Ressler continued. "This is Cindy Shall, who disappeared several weeks later while hitchhiking to a class. By then, police had issued warnings about hitchhiking, but with no law against it there was little they could do. They also told the community that, if you were going to hitchhike, do not accept a ride with anyone who didn't have a college parking sticker on their front bumper. Because Kemper's mother worked at the university, he had one. Two days after Cindy Shall went missing, dismembered arms and legs were found on a nearby cliff which overlooked the Pacific Ocean."

Still more slides.

"Then an upper torso washed ashore several days later. The coroner's office identified it as Cindy Shall's. A surfer later found her left hand, but her head and right hand remained missing. Newspapers, who *have to have* a name for killers, began calling him the 'Chopper' and the 'Butcher.' Creative huh?"

The slides went from grisly body parts to the faces of two pretty young girls. "This is Rosalind Thorpe and this is Alice Liu. Like the others, they were out hitchhiking and disappeared the same day. Police had no leads, but suspected it was all tied in with what some were calling 'The Coed Killer.'

"By almost total coincidence, Herbert Mullin was arrested about a week after the last two girls went missing. Mullin was tied to most of the shootings, but police were at a loss to connect him with the missing girls, or the disappearance of the other hitchhikers. Kidnapping and dismemberment of bodies were simply not part of his M.O. Rumors spread and grew, in large part fueled by one reporter who undertook her own investigation and formed her own theories. People believe what they read in the papers. She wrote of the deaths being satanic ritual killings, and described the decapitation and mutilation of the bodies as being 'professional.' She suggested the killer or killers were either lesbian or transvestites and continually took the police to task for their mistakes during the investigation.

"A few weeks later, a couple of hikers came across a human skull and a jawbone. The coroner said they were not from the same person. Police searched the area and found another skull that went with the first jawbone. One girl had been shot twice in the head, the other girl once. The remains were identified as Rosalind Thorpe and Alice Liu.

"As time passed, police were baffled. They had few leads, and no methods to end the killings. The colleges experienced a drop in enrollment. And then, out of the clear blue, the police got a phone call from the man who had been killing the coeds – Ed Kemper.

"Kemper had stopped the spree himself, but not before he killed his last two victims, his mother and her best friend. He told the police where to find their bodies, and admitted to being the Coed Killer. Some officers were in shock. Here was a twenty-four-year-old man who they had eaten and drank with for many months, and now he was telling them he'd committed a double murder four days before, and at least six others they knew about."

As he showed more horrific slides, Ressler explained how the police went to Clarnelle's apartment and found the two women's bodies, exactly where Kemper said they'd be. "Kemper killed his mother on Good Friday and mutilated her body. He cut out her tongue and put it in the garbage disposal, which spit it out. Failing in that, he headed to the cop bar and drank with his buddies for several hours. When he left, he called his mother's best friend and invited her over for dinner and a movie. When she arrived, he killed her, too, and removed her head. Both bodies were found stuffed in a closet.

"After killing the last two women, Kemper said he left the house, took the second woman's car, and drove aimlessly on freeways in an easterly direction for several days. He dropped off the car in Reno and rented a Chevy Impala. It was then when he decided 'the killings had to end.' He debated about whether or not to turn himself in to the police."

Ressler said Kemper was driving south on Interstate 25 in Colorado when he came to a rest stop near Pueblo. He parked and went to a phone booth to call the police in Santa Cruz. The first officer he talked to refused to listen to him, thinking it was another crackpot caller wanting to confess to some irrational crime. They'd had more than a few people do exactly that. It took Kemper about forty-five minutes and several phone calls before he talked to someone who would listen. And then the ghastly story began to unfold.

Pueblo police officers were called and raced to the rest stop, where they placed Kemper under arrest. They found several hundred rounds of ammunition and three guns in the car. Kemper told the officers he'd been taking No-Doz pills and was starting to feel 'crazy.' He talked about having an idea of stopping in a neighborhood, going from door to door and shooting people in their homes. He wanted to go out in a 'blaze of glory.' And then he decided it all had to come to an end.

Santa Cruz investigators and the District Attorney flew out to Pueblo the next day with extradition waivers and an arrest warrant. Kemper waived extradition and they began the drive back to Santa Cruz the next day. Their thinking was, if he was talking, spending hours in a car was one of the best ways to pass the time. And talk he did. He said after he killed and decapitated his mother, he put her head up on the counter and began yelling at it. Then he got out a set of darts and began peppering her skull with darts. Clearly, there was some anger coming out.

Ressler showed more pictures of Kemper's mother's body in the apartment. "He said after decapitating and mutilating his mom, he put her body on the bed and had post-mortem sex with her. He did the same to her friend, who was in her sixties.

"Investigators finally realized why the Coed Killer had been able to elude them for so long. He'd been in the bar with officers talking about the case, gleaning information and perfecting his technique. Thus, he was able to out-think and avoid them at every curve in the road. But he didn't come across as a killer to them, which is exactly what Pierce Brooks was talking about yesterday. They simply 'hide in plain sight' and are most often the last people would expect to do such heinous acts. Kemper learned how to make people feel safe around him, particularly the young girls he lured into his car and brutally killed."

Finally, the brutal parade of slides came to an end – at least, for that day. "All right, let's put a wrap on this case. I've been talking all day. Kemper did go to trial in Santa Cruz and was convicted of all eight murders. When his grandparents are factored into the equation, Kemper was guilty of killing ten people. He testified at his own trial, seemingly in an effort to show the jury he was truly insane. That didn't work out so well. He's currently serving a life term in the California state penitentiary. The death penalty had been ruled unconstitutional by a whacko California Supreme Court decision before he was convicted."

Ressler looked up at the clock, which was approaching four-thirty. "Last thing. There is a teaching point to all of this, or maybe several. Who can give me one?" Several hands went up.

"Learning how a serial killer might operate?" an agent said.

"Yup, we did that. Good. What else?"

"Learning how they do things?"

"We learned a little more about that too. Anyone else?"

With no hands raised, Ressler explained what we'd just learned. "What we're trying to accomplish in our research and with this training is *why*, rather than *what* or *how*. Think about this. Our job as psychological profilers is to look for the hidden motives. *Why* did this person do this? *Why* did they do that? Can we then take the *whys* and turn them into *who*? Our thinking is we can, and that's what we're going to spend the rest of our time working on. What Kemper was motivated by was anger. Rage. Until the end, he couldn't direct it toward his mother, so he attacked other people. Symbols of his mother. Does that make sense?"

Most of us nodded. *It makes sense, but I don't know why*, I thought. *They're telling us these people aren't crazy, but I've never seen so many crazy things in my life. Can't quite get my head wrapped around this yet.*

Ressler leaned against the side of the podium. "Another thing you may not realize you were exposed to today is the difference in types of serial killers. We've been working on these typologies, and Roy Hazelwood has sagely identified them as 'organized,' and 'disorganized.' We'll talk a lot more about those typologies, but for now I want to say we'd probably put Mullin and Frazier into the disorganized group, and Kemper would be more organized. Why? Because Kemper put a lot of planning and thought into what he did, both before and after he committed his crimes. Frazier and Mullin, on the other hand, would have been more spontaneous or impulsive in what they did. While the number of Mullin's killings was higher than Kemper's, part of that was due to the multiple killings he did a few times. Again, more on that later. Any questions?"

There were none. I looked over at Harry, then back to Denny and Dave in the back row. And then at several other guys, who nodded. Nothing had to be said. Non-verbal communication can work so well at times.

CHAPTER EIGHTEEN

A Night at the Marine Base Officers' Club

Denny Koslowski was proving to be quite the interesting character, and seemed to fit in well with not only Harry and me, but the rest of the guys. His eight-year career with the Chicago Police Department produced more than a few interesting stories. Not all of them being about the many homicide cases he'd worked.

With a taut face and receding hairline, he certainly wasn't a cop-looking guy, being about five-foot-ten and around a hundred and seventy pounds, but he was a wiry guy who obviously had familiarized himself with the weight room and didn't appear to be someone to mess with. Not to mention having grown up on the north side of Chicago in, as he referred to it, "The Polish Ghetto." Denny described it as a pretty rough place, and the turf wars sounded reminiscent of the Bloods and Crips in later years.

His best story was about a night he spent in the radio dispatch center, filling in for the dispatchers when they'd take a break. The phone rang and he answered it, and a frantic lady was on the line saying, "Officer...officer...I needs some help. I think my baby's sick." He asked what was wrong with the baby, and the woman replied, "I'm not sure, but I think the baby got the Spiral Mighty Jesus." He said it took him a few seconds to figure that out and replied, "How do you know that ma'am?" She replied, "because the baby havin' conclusions." He contacted fire/rescue and they went to her house, later to call back.

"What happened?" he asked.

"The baby had a cold." Apparently nothing as deadly as the Spiral Mighty Jesus, a dreaded and often fatal disease, I assume.

Denny recalled an occasion while out on patrol, he was looking for a kid on the south side of town, which is apparently a rough area. He went to a house where the kid was supposed to have a friend and asked a woman if her son was home.

"Which one?" she asked.

"How many you got?"

"Eight."

"Well, the one who would be about the age of this kid I'm looking for."

"Oh, that would be my..." He had no clue what the name was, so he asked her to spell it.

"L.e.m.o.n.J.e.l.l.o."

"Oh, okay." He said he was struggling to keep a straight face. "How did you come up with that?"

"How do you think?" she replied. "You not all that smart are you?"

"Nah, I'm Polish. We're not known for being very sharp people."

"I heard that."

Denny had plenty of stories, the next one usually better than the last, once he got a few beers in him and got on a roll. "So I'm out one night and arrest this guy for drunk driving. I look at his license and his first name was 'Venson.' I get all done with what we had to do on the street and haul him up to the hospital for a blood test. We're waiting for the nurse and I ask him how he got his name. And he tells me, 'My momma always liked Saint Venson, cause that be the real name of DePaul University. Saint Venson DePaul.' I'm guessing his mom wasn't one of the better spellers around."

By Friday afternoon, we'd seen an unfathomable number of dead bodies in unimaginable types of sadistic positions and places. Roy Hazelwood was completing his presentation on Auto-Erotic Death Investigation. Yet again, this was something completely new for me. People, mostly men, used a variety of means to reduce the amount of oxygen to their brain in an effort to further enhance their masturbatory orgasms. Hazelwood explained the activity had to include a release mechanism, which unfortunately didn't work on some occasions. When that didn't happen, the victim was likely to be featured in Hazelwood's slide presentation.

"Is there something wrong with plain old sex?"

Harry whispered to me.

"Apparently there is for some people," I replied. "It usually seems to work just fine for me." Harry stared at me. "Sex, I mean, not pain," I hurriedly clarified.

Hazelwood was finishing up as the hour approached four o'clock. The session had included a review of various *paraphilias*, another term I'd never heard of, used to describe a cornucopia of fetishes I'd never heard of, either. Some of these included sadistic acts, again covering things people do to each other and themselves which ostensibly increased their sexual enjoyment. The connection between extreme pain inflicted on another person and sexual pleasure was something I had a hard time understanding, but Hazelwood and other instructors explained how that was at the core of the phenomenon of serial murder.

He shut down the slideshow. "Here's the deal. When we talk to these killers, we have to put our own psychological baggage away. Most of these guys are fairly normal, and in fact a lot of them are pretty likeable and not bad to talk with. They take a realistic approach to what they've done and seem to pretty much understand the *why* of how it happened. And frankly, ladies and gentlemen, the *why* of things is what we're trying to teach you to look for. Any questions?"

There were none and Hazelwood headed for the door.

"He's a great instructor," I said to Denny as he wandered over toward Harry and me.

"So, what's the plan tonight?" Denny asked.

"Good question," I replied. "As for me, I'm not sure if my system can handle another marathon session at the Boardroom. I feel like I need to check myself into rehab."

"That's two of us. I'm not sure if I can handle another night there for awhile," Denny said. "Gotta be something better than that to do tonight."

"How about the officers' club?" Harry offered. "Might be nice to have a good steak or ribs."

"Great idea," I agreed. "Let's do it. Want to check with some of the other guys and see who might want to go along?"

The officers' club on the Quantico Marine Base was a place we'd discovered while I was in New Agent

Training. It boasted great, nicely-presented food and an exceptional ambiance with decent prices. I was hoping we wouldn't be doing much, if any, drinking, as Harry rounded up a few more guys to head over with us.

We wound up with twelve guys, which made the conversation even more lively than some nights we'd spent at the Boardroom during the week. But the atmosphere around the table was more of a decompression session about what we'd witnessed during the week than anything else. Even the usual bitching about the bureau seemed to be subdued as everyone let steam off about having seen literally hundreds of dead and mutilated bodies, albeit on slides and not in person. It still wasn't pleasant to see what humans could do to other humans.

"That guy Kemper was bad enough," someone toward the end of the table said. "But when Ressler got going on Ed Gein, I thought I was going to barf on my desk." More than a few people nodded in agreement, and we discussed what we'd seen and heard about this unusual and perverted little man.

Willis Davis was sitting directly across from me, and hadn't said much, if anything, during the session. The only black agent in the class, Willis wasn't someone who I'd had much of a chance to talk with, since he didn't often join us in the Boardroom. I'd invited him once, but he said, "I'll let you boozehounds enjoy yourselves. Just don't raise too much hell when you get back to the dorms." We were somewhat known to continue our activities after closing time, if someone had gone to the base liquor store and had a supply of appropriate adult beverages available.

When we finally got into a few bureau stories, Willis had an interesting one to report. "Did you guys hear about the shooting we had a couple of weeks ago?" All of us had, of course, heard about the famous and ill-fated "Miami Shootout" with two bank robbers, in which two of our agents had been killed and several more seriously injured. "No, not that one," Willis said. "This one probably stayed pretty close to the vest in the Miami Division."

"What happened?" asked Denny, who was sitting next to me.

"Seems like we've got a married couple, both

agents, who like to frequent a swingers' club near South Beach. So they spend the night at the club doing whatever it is they do at those places, and finally around midnight it's time to head home. They head out to their car and some guy comes running up with a gun in his hand. A robbery, right? Little did he know the female side of the pair had her nine millimeter in her purse, so she makes it look like she's trying to find her wallet, grabs the gun and shoots the guy three times right through her purse."

"Bad timing by the crook, but it sounds like a good shooting. Kill the guy?"

"Oh hell, yes. He's a frickin' bloody mess with three right in the chest. Deader than a doornail. People running all over hell in the parking lot, screaming and yelling. The male side of the pair yells at someone to call the cops, so they come rolling in. Now, of course, we have a problem, an agent-involved shooting with a bureau gun. Which is all well and good until they find out where they'd been before the guy tries to rob them. Then the shit hits the fan. Ever heard the saying 'Don't embarrass the bureau?' When the two agents gave their statement to the cops, they of course were asked where they'd been before the shooting. Naturally, they tell 'em. The SAC gets a copy of the report from the cops and faxes it straight to headquarters. No surprise with agents involved. So the bureau isn't concerned about the shooting so much as the fact they'd spent the night in a swingers' club."

"Sounds like it's their own business what they do on their own time," Harry replied.

"You'd think so," Willis said, "But the bureau apparently takes a dim view of those sorts of activities by its agents. So there's still an internal investigation underway by Professional Standards, and it's gone all the way up to the director's office."

"Any outcome yet?" I asked.

"Not yet, but the betting is on both of 'em getting fired."

"Damn," Dave said. "Just goes to show you what can happen if you're in the wrong place at the wrong time. I'm not sure if I agree with them getting fired, but the only reason they would is because they copped out to the police about where they were before the guy tried to rob them."

"Yeah," Willis replied. "It's a bitch because they're both good people, but they're sitting on pins and needles right now. Not a good way to spend any part of your career."

We managed to get out of the "O" club around eight o'clock and headed back to the academy. No sooner had we signed in at the reception desk than Harry turned and looked at me. And didn't say a word. I stared back, then turned to Denny and Dave. We knew Willis was out, but a few other guys got the clue and headed up to the Boardroom with us. It was open an hour later on Fridays and Saturdays. It'd been a stressful week. Didn't take too long to relieve at least some of the stress.

CHAPTER NINETEEN

Profiling Rapists with Roy Hazelwood.

Our second week of "Profiling Boot Camp" was, if anything, worse than the first week, if that was possible. Roy Hazelwood got us started with a session on serial sexual assault. I was surprised if not shocked to learn what he had to share.

"A rapist is not a rapist is not a rapist as we commonly believe," he said. "Rape is not a sex crime so much as a crime of three things. First is power, which is directly connected with control. Second is anger. Third would be a sadistic need. Sex is a secondary issue. There are several different types and we're going to talk about every one of them in detail."

This was a complete surprise to me. As a police officer and detective for ten years, I'd been involved in more than a few rape investigations with varying victims and suspects over the years. The thought that different psychological motives were at play had never occurred to me. It was a sex crime, plain and simple. But Hazelwood made it clear it was anything but. He'd done extensive research into serial sexual assault, and had interviewed numerous offenders in prisons. In addition to that, he'd written a book, *Sexual Assault, Methods and Motives*, citing numerous cases he was intimately familiar with including a sadistic serial offender by the name of Mike DeBardelaben who, by his own admission, raped well over one hundred women in several southern states.

Hazelwood spent a little time talking about his own background, which culminated with his appointment as an FBI agent in 1972, and his eventual assignment in 1978 to the little-known Behavioral Science Unit, then manned by nine agents. He was assigned to teach a class called "Sex Crimes" to FBI National Academy students, eventually changing the name of the class to "Interpersonal Violence" and turning it into a legitimate criminology class. He began researching sexual offenders, eventually discovering that about three quarters of all serial rapists had themselves been sexually molested as children.

As a result of his background and research into sexual assault, he made a comment unlike any I had ever heard before: "Rape is a crime of violence in which sex is the weapon." He was not trying to be cute or colloquial in any way. It was something that had never occurred to me. But how could you argue with a man who had become a legend?

Hazelwood admitted he learned almost everything he knew about the concept of criminal profiling from Howard Teten, one of the original gurus of the concept. Teten taught "Applied Criminology" classes to National Academy students for many years. He learned his craft from many of the officers attending the National Academy, and picked their brains to determine psychological reasons behind hundreds of murders they reviewed in his class sessions. Before Hazelwood put the study of rape and sexual sadism on the map, the study of sexual offenses was largely ignored, even snickered at by the FBI and law enforcement agencies around the country. His work caused law enforcement officers to focus more on the victim than the offender.

"Before we started all of this work," Hazelwood said, "law enforcement didn't seem to understand the role of the victim in the crime. We focused on the offender, but we didn't seem to understand how much information can be obtained from the victims of sexual assault crimes. It was almost like we ignored the victim, seeing her as an object only, and failing to realize she comprised one half of the crime itself."

Makes sense to me. I certainly can't argue with it.

He went on. "Psychological profiling is more of an art than a science at this point in our history. We've only been at it for ten years or so, and the extent to which we're successful depends on the experience and training of the person who is doing a profile on any given case. And here's something I want you all to understand. It's a complex process, and it's not like the TV show *Name*

That Tune. There is nothing psychic about it, and it's not 'Crystal Ball Criminology' or magic. We don't walk into any case with a pre-conceived notion, and have a laundry list to use. Each case is different from the last one we looked at. We have to examine the cases as they come to us, and no two are the same. Someday it may be a science, but right now it's an art, and that's what we're trying to impress on each of you. While you are going to be exposed to many cases we've investigated over the years, you're still not going to walk out of here at the end of a few weeks and be fully qualified to be 'profilers.' That process is going to take place over the course of the years you stay in the program, if you do. What we're trying to do here is to start making you think like the offender thinks. That's why we've gone through so many different cases with you in the past week, and we will continue to do them this week as well. We want you to understand what crime scenes may tell you. Sure, we're burying you with gore and seeming insanity. But that's what we deal with in the unit every day."

Hazelwood explained some of the cases he'd researched, and talked about work in sexual assault done by Dr. Nicholas Groth, and by Dr. Ann Burgess, a professor at Boston College. "Nick and Ann have spent years studying serial murderers, rapists, and child sex offenders. There are no two people in the country who better understand the relationship between child sexual abuse, juvenile delinquency, and the eventual effect those things may have on violent criminal behavior. I've spent a considerable amount of time with both of them, and have learned more from them than any two people I know."

He moved some papers on the podium, punched some buttons, and put a new set of transparencies on the projector.

"Now, let's spend a little time talking about the profiles we've come up with about serial sexual offenders, specifically rapists. From all the work we've compiled over the years, we break the typologies down into the power reassurance rapist, power assertive rapist, anger retaliatory rapist, anger excitation rapist, and the opportunity rapist. Each category bears distinctive elements, such as the rapist's general mode of operation, victim preference, and level of force.

They're all as important as the characteristics of the rapist himself."

To put it mildly, Hazelwood was an "old school" instructor. He didn't use the elaborate slides others had relied on; rather, he had a traditional, outdated overhead projector and transparencies. It worked well for me and I was able to take a ton of notes, which in college meant I truly got a lot out of a class. Ressler was a spectacular instructor, but Hazelwood was a superstar in my mind. I can't remember ever having an instructor I got more out of. There was no doubt my notes from his class would be a great resource in the future.

"When we look at a power-reassurance rapist," Hazelwood said, "we're talking about a person who is simply unsure of his own sexuality. He's insecure and sexually inadequate, and needs someone to reassure him he's sexually adequate. He's a guy who is going to be gentle with his victim and ask her if he is as good as her boyfriend or husband. He's going to ask the victim to rate him and may even ask her if he can see her later. Frankly, to him, it's more of a 'date' than a rape, as hard as that may be to understand. When we profile him, we're usually talking about a guy who doesn't live too far from the victim's house, and who has probably prowled in the neighborhood, peeping in windows and may have had the prospective victim under surveillance for several weeks. And, this may surprise you, he's more apt to be married or in a relationship than any of the others we'll talk about. For some reason he doesn't get what he needs out of the relationship. What we've found out about this type of guy is he's quite likely to continue his assaults until he's caught. But if the victim resists, he's much more likely to stop. It's a 'date' to him, and he relishes the fantasy of 'seducing' the victim. He is going to be more regular in his patterns. It might take a while, but we're eventually going to catch this guy."

Immediately, I could think of similar cases I'd dealt with while I was on the police department. It was almost like a light bulb turned on in my head.

He slid the transparencies around on the screen. "The other 'power' type is the power assertive rapist. Now we're talking about a horse of a completely different color. This guy has absolutely no question about his masculinity, and is a real macho man. He's more prone to be a guy who works out and wears sharp clothes to flash his feathers and look like a peacock to the women. It's all about the first impression with this guy. He may have muscles and drive a flashy car, but he's all about initial appearances. He looks attractive to women and he plays that to his advantage. His goal is to exert his power over his victims. He wants them to know who is boss, and he plays that to the hilt. He's more apt to use physical force on the victim, mainly to exert his masculinity and show her he's an alpha male. He's going to be more physically assertive with his victims, and he is absolutely going to get his way. It's hard to predict a pattern with this guy, but he's not going to stop until he's caught."

Once again, I could think back to some of these types I'd seen in the past, particularly when Hazelwood talked about the abusive behavior contradictions between the two power rapists.

"What we're dealing with is a guy who is a basic inadequate personality, and another who is anything but. The power reassurance rapist is insecure about himself, and the power assertive rapist is in the driver's seat. He's going to be more verbally aggressive with his victim, probably calling her a 'bitch' or a 'whore,' and is more liable to force her into more deviant sexual practices than regular intercourse. He's more likely to make her perform fellatio, or anally assault her, which we believe is to exert power over a woman."

"We can learn more about the rapist from what he says and what he does than anything else," Hazelwood said. "If he's verbally and physically abusive to his victim, we're more likely to be dealing with a power assertive rapist. Is there a high risk factor? What we can do then is try to determine if we can plug in the rest of the characteristics. Will he be the guy who drives a flashy car or big truck? Is he going to be a guy who has some assaults in his background, whether it's toward a woman in his life or fights in a bar? Guys like this don't become the way they are overnight. It's a completely predictable pattern."

I thought back to some of my classes in college and graduate school. If I walked away from a class with pages full of notes, I always felt like I got something good out of the class. When Hazelwood gave us a break,

I looked over at Harry and said, "I think I'm going to get carpal tunnel syndrome, but this guy is really good." Ressler was great, but Hazelwood took things to a completely different level. He was poised, relaxed in his delivery, confident and completely organized. I'd later develop my instructional style based on what I learned from watching him. Maybe the best teacher I'd ever had.

Harry responded, "You got that right. I don't think I've ever had a better instructor. This guy really gives us some information we can work with. I've been back here for a lot of in-service classes, and a lot of them were very good, but this one is definitely the best I've ever had. Hazelwood is certainly making it better."

When the break was over, Hazelwood got back into the next part of the lecture on anger rapists. "Now, we're going to see a complete contrast." Again, he put up a transparency on the screen and started talking about each point as I took notes feverishly.

"When we look at the anger-retaliatory rapist, we're talking about a guy who has a lot of repressed anger. But what we see is the anger directed toward a female other than the one he would really like to direct the anger toward. Bob Ressler talked about Ed Kemper, which is a perfect example. He spent a lifetime with a mother who was verbally and physically abusive, but typical of these people, they can't figure out a way to take it out on the person they have the anger for. I think Ted Bundy was pretty much the same. He had a girlfriend who dumped him, and he went after women who looked very much like her. For the most part, the victims he chose had long, dark hair, which was parted in a way very similar to his former girlfriend. With Bundy and Kemper, the term 'anger retaliatory' seems to be a perfect fit. Both of 'em were striking back against a woman in their lives who they couldn't control. So they found a way to control some other women and went on their murderous sprees.

"What we're dealing with here are rape suspects who are striking back. And it's usually shortly after an incident occurs with a significant woman in their lives. This might be their mother, their wife or girlfriend, or even a sister. The anger is always there below the surface. Boiling. It doesn't take much more than a single incident to set them off, and that's likely to happen on the same night." He pointed out how many of these offenders will have a long history of domestic violence or bar fights, even domestic disturbances involving their mothers. It's usually about a female, and he said we can't eliminate the wife or mother as being a significant factor.

"Any questions?" There were none. Most of us were still trying to get our notes up to date. Things were moving quickly.

"The next one I want to talk about is what we call the 'anger excitation' rapist. This is a completely different character, and the key word to this person is 'sadist.' Or perhaps more correctly 'sexual sadist.' He's the most dangerous rapist—and fortunately the most rare. He gets his kicks from seeing pain on his victim's face. We find he's outwardly charming, and incredibly cunning. Sadistic rapists are like 'the great white sharks of sexual deviance.'

"The sadist has a tremendous amount of anger, hostility, and hatred toward women," Hazelwood said. "In cases of stranger rape, he forces his victim to engage in these unspeakable, degrading acts. Which she does to save her life. Then he says, ` No decent woman would do this.' So he kills her. This is the guy we truly worry about, and he's the most likely to begin to enjoy what he does more and more. Consequently this guy is much more apt to kill his victims every time."

He described some of the characteristics of this type of individual. "They're all different and what we see done to victims is what's going to give us some clues to each individual's personality. As I said, it's not *Name That Tune* by any stretch of the imagination. It's your job to collect the information and get it back to us for evaluation. It's going to be several years before you will become reasonably competent to do these profiles. One in-service isn't going to make you the expert. You're not going to walk out of here later this week and be ready to do profiles. That's not what we want. Your job is going to be collecting the information we need and getting it to us."

He looked at the class and said, "Is everybody okay with that? We want you to understand exactly what we're going to expect out of you. No loose cannons on deck, please. No lone wolves in the forest. As soon as you find yourself involved in a case, you're going to see exactly what I mean. You don't have the experience now, but with the training we're going to give you in the coming years, that will change. For now, this is how it needs to be if this program is going to succeed."

Gottit sir. He may be a little guy, but I'm not about to tangle with him.

Hazelwood then went into the characteristics of the opportunity rapist. He said this person was not going to be someone we could profile or predict a 'pattern' for, because he didn't have one. "This guy is going to sexually assault a victim during another crime. Maybe he goes into a convenience store at two o'clock in the morning, intent on robbing the place. Then he notices the clerk is a female. Almost as an afterthought to the robbery, he decides to lock the door and take her into the back room. Here we're talking about a very impulsive person, and we can only hope there's some surveillance tape or even a witness who might have gotten a license number or a description. Or even all three."

He talked about how some of these occur during burglaries. "Let's say the victim works graveyard shift, so she comes home and sleeps during the day. This guy breaks into her house or apartment intending to steal money or property and he sees her in bed sleeping. Impulse takes over and we have a sexual assault when it otherwise would have simply been a burglary."

That made sense.

Shifting gears somewhat, Hazelwood reviewed the role of fantasy in some of the rapists' personalities. "They are all different," he said. "They might be driven by a need for power or anger, but most of them will spend a fair amount of their time in life fantasizing about what they're going to do next. The fantasy becomes a need in the person's mind, and the crimes become more and more ritualized. What they quickly discover is the fantasy they have never seems to match the reality of what happens. So they've got to work on refining the fantasy and try to improve what they want to do. Since they never can never duplicate the fantasy, they've got to continue. It's like a vicious cycle. And that's where the ritualistic nature of the crimes begins. These guys are usually pretty intelligent, but some of them are impulsive, and will go to more risk in grabbing a victim when one comes on the radar screen.

"We're going to have more luck catching the impulsive ones, because they don't consider the fact that they're leaving evidence at the crime scene. It's all about doing what they want and getting in and out. They're more apt to use a weapon of opportunity which they find at the crime scene. If we look at offenders as 'organized' or 'disorganized,' this guy is going to be the latter. He's more likely to be younger and equally likely to live in the immediate area. What we've also learned is the smarter the rapist, the more he will ritualize, and some of them are very, very smart."

When Hazelwood finally turned off the projector, a collective sigh emitted from the class, and the noise of numerous pens and pencils hitting the desks echoed around the room. It had been a long session with page after page of notes, and our collective hands and wrists were aching. At the same time, my standard was met in that having a lot of notes meant I learned something. I could see where this was going to be some extremely valuable information down the line.

CHAPTER TWENTY

The End of "Profiling Boot Camp"

There were several times during those two weeks when I wondered if Friday would ever arrive. I'd been able to call my family, but I certainly missed them and was more than anxious to be home and to sleep in the comfort of my own bed. While the accommodations at the FBI Academy were fairly adequate, the beds had always been known to be swayback-types, not firm in the places they should be, and were known to cause some back issues.

I also knew the work had piled up on my desk back in Cedar Rapids, and there was nobody who was going to do it for me. So when I got to the office the following Monday morning, I had no idea what awaited me, but I knew I was going to be buried.

We met in the classroom promptly at eight a.m. on that final day of "profiling boot camp." Several people were missing since they had early flights out of National (now Ronald Reagan) Airport. Ever energetic, Bob Ressler was at the podium, ready to greet us. "All right folks, let's get rolling and we can get you out of here. As we've told you, there will be some buses heading for National Airport at ten this morning, so everyone should be able to make their connections on time. Hopefully.

"We've thrown a lot at you in the past couple of weeks. For some of you, I'm sure it was a shock to your system, but we hope you have started to get the big picture of what we're trying to do back here. There are a few things that are important for you to understand. Psychological profiling is not some sort of mystical or psychic insight into violent crime. Hopefully we've made it clear that we can't give you a laundry list of things you can look at and then draw absolute conclusions. Since this is a new program, we want to make sure we get it right. Unlike some of the things the bureau has done over the years, this program is not going to evaporate into thin air. We're sure it's here to stay.

"Something else you need to understand is you're not going back to your field offices to become the resident expert. We realize some of your bosses won't understand that, but we've sent some very specific instructions out to your SACs. Those instructions are that when you get a case referred to you, it's your job to go out and collect the information. We don't want you doing profiles on your own right now. The time for that may come, but we want you to communicate with us and send what you've got back here where we can look at it. Yes, we've got cases piled up, but we will get to yours in due time."

I glanced back at Denny and he nodded, recalling our conversation nearly two weeks ago. As ex-cops and detectives, we knew the state and local investigators wouldn't want to be sitting around drumming their fingers on the desk, waiting for the manna to come down from above. It was going to be a tough sell, and it didn't take long for Ressler to point it out.

"Since you're now *experts*," he put a heavy emphasis on the word, "we understand you're going to be under a lot of pressure. If your agencies have a murder case, they're also under a lot of pressure to get it solved and get someone in custody. But you're not profilers so much as profiling coordinators. That means it's going to be your job to coordinate cases between the field and the unit back here. While you may think you've got the program, you're not even close yet. You're going to be coming back here at least twice a year for in-service updates. Six months from now, most of us will be sitting here in the same room going over more and more cases. The more you're exposed to, the more you're going to know."

I could see what Ressler was talking about. None of the cases we'd seen were similar to others. Clearly, in my mind, anyhow, they'd thrown a lot at us, but it was one of those things where the more you learned, the less you realized you knew. I would have been terrified to go out to work with the state or local agencies, and be expected to come up with a profile at the drop of a hat.

"Most homicide cases," Ressler continued, "are going to be solved within seventy-two hours by the local authorities. We are not going to allow ourselves to be immediately thrust into an investigation at the outset. Profiling is not meant to be a substitute for a thorough investigation. Nor a shortcut. They're much more likely to get it solved before we're even able to get away from what we're doing on our own bureau work. Yes, it's a crisis to them, but we know you can't simply drop everything you're doing and race off to help out with a profile. Particularly you guys in the Midwest and West. Where's my guy from Omaha?"

I raised my hand.

"Okay, Pete. You're out in Cedar Rapids. How far is it to the western border of the Omaha Field Division?"

"Let's see." I thought for a second. "If I had to go to Scottsbluff, Nebraska, it would be somewhere around six or seven hundred miles."

"There you go. And some of you in Texas have almost as much territory to cover. Think about it. If Pete here has to get to Scottsbluff in his bureau car and can't get out of his office for a week because of court or a Grand Jury or whatever it may be, what the heck is another option?"

A student raised his hand. "Let's say we've got a resident agency out there. Should we give them a call and set a lead to pick up what we need?"

"Pete, what do you think?" Ressler turned back to me.

"I hadn't thought about that, but it seems like it's a good idea. But you guys have trained us to look for certain things, so how well will it work having an untrained agent running around collecting all of the information? He might miss something."

"Good point." Ressler frowned at the class. "That could be a problem, but in reality what we want are reports and crime scene photos. When and if this type of scenario happens to you, and I guarantee it will, just get a hold of the resident agent and tell him to grab everything he can get his hands on. Open a case on it, or have him do it, and then have him send the stuff back to us, with an airtel explaining what's going on, generally. Make sure you've got a copy, too, because it's

Peter M. Klismet Jr.

your job, as coordinator for your division, to know something about every case you have going. So, that's generally what we want you to do. In a sense we're making this up as we go along, but we'll work out the bugs in the system as things move forward. Most of it has been well thought out, but we know we're going to have some unexpected surprises. That's a given."

He looked up at the clock. "We're still good on getting you out of here in time to make the bus. I want to make sure you understand two more things. First, you guys are going to have to do some evangelizing, so to speak. This is not going to be an easy sell to some of those old crusty detectives and sheriffs. The immediate response from them is going to be you're bringing them some more bureau hocus pocus. Or selling snake oil. We're going to send you all packets of slides. What we want you to do is get familiar with the stuff on the slides, and do a presentation at the next National Academy session. We're making copies of an HBO videotape, which I think is called *Murder: No Apparent Motive*. Get familiar with that. It's about an hour long. See if you can get on the agenda for a two-hour presentation, and simply do your best. Again, we know we're going to have to sell this program, and you're going to be our sales force. Do the best job you can, and you'll get better. If you've got a problem with the slides, or anything else we've talked about in the last two weeks, give us a call back here.

"Secondly, and you might want to think about this a bit, in about a year we're going to bring six of you back here to be assigned to the Unit. Yes, I realize that means a transfer, but you will be on the cutting edge of something that's going to get bigger and better. You need to do a good job out there and we're going to be the first ones to know if you are. We want you to tell your agencies about the National Center for the Analysis of Violent Crime and the VICAP system, and how we need as many cases in the system as we can get. You need to get the word out and work with your agencies. It'll all start coming together. It's going to take some time. We understand that back here. But we've been at this for about five years, so our patience isn't going to wear thin. It's been a real job getting all of this set up, and a real struggle at times, but we're going to get this

FBI Diary: Profiles of Evil   125

rolling and you'll like the results.

"Now, any questions?"

A few hands went up and he acknowledged the first.

"Do you know when the next in-service is going to be?"

"Good question, and I should have thought to say that. We're working with IBM right now on a date. They have an unbelievable training center up in the D.C. area, and it's just a matter of finding the right date in about six months. As soon as we know, we'll give you plenty of lead time to clear your schedules. We'd like every one of you to come back, but we also understand there are some other demands of your job. You should know in a month or two."

Ressler acknowledged another hand in the air. "Yes sir."

"Let's say we've got a major case and they want some answers right away. So we've gone out and sold the program, and they want us there yesterday. What're we supposed to do?"

"Within a month or two, that's going to happen several times around the country. That's the point where you get on the phone with us as quickly as you can. If we're talking about a series of related murders, one or more of us from back here may try to get out there as quickly as possible. Your job is going to be to get to the site and establish yourself as liaison with the agencies involved. Collect as much evidence as you can and wait for one of us. By the time we arrive, you should have things pretty well in hand, and we will work right alongside you. If I come out, or Roy, or even John Douglas, we're going to need to get our arms around the facts as quickly as possible. We've already done some on-scene profiling, and we know we're going to be doing some more, particularly with you guys out there feeding more and more cases back to us. Good question."

"What if they don't want to wait?" Denny asked, and I looked knowingly back at him. I could easily foresee law enforcement from some of the isolated places in Iowa or Nebraska wanting some answers right now. I knew Denny was thinking the same thing.

"We know that's going to be a problem, but as I said before, you're not the profilers yet. That's going to happen in the future, but we need successes, and we don't want to have you get it wrong. If that's going to happen, it needs to be done by us. Fade the heat off to us. If your SAC or ASAC is in your face, tell them to call us and we'll explain it to them, again. Right now, you're simply not ready to start profiling cases. It's a big country and there are only so many of us to cover it. That will, hopefully, change in the coming years. But at the moment, it is what it is, and until we get the funding to bring some more people like you back into the Unit, we're just going to have to do the best we can."

"Anything else?"

No hands went up.

"All right, then, let's wrap it up. You might think this is a crock of BS, but this has been the best in-service we've ever had at the academy. And I sincerely mean that. The quality of the class and your attentiveness has made it even better. All of the instructors have mentioned it to me, and I want to say I really appreciate it. You've been a great group. You've asked some important questions, and it's more than apparent that you've taken it seriously. As I said, I realize what we've thrown at you, but take a little time and let your heads clear out a bit, and we will be expecting to hear from you in the future. Good luck and we'll be seeing you in a few months."

Ressler got a well-deserved round of applause as we began to collect our materials and head for home. I was excited to be leaving, but also about being something of a pioneer on the verge of opening the door to a new frontier.

CHAPTER TWENTY ONE

Back to the Real World

Reality quickly set in once I got back to the office on Monday morning. I'd been tempted to go in on Saturday or Sunday, but I knew that meant I'd spend an entire day there, and I wanted to spend some time with my family and do a few special things with them.

Jim Whalen came in a half hour after I did, and found me sitting at my desk sorting through two week's worth of messages and other paperwork. "So how did it go?" he asked. A good question since I hadn't talked to him the whole time I'd been gone.

"Well, that's a hard question to answer." I wasn't really sure where to start. "The things we saw back there were pretty bad, but I definitely got a lot out of it. I realize I have plenty going on here, but I also think this part-time job of Profiling Coordinator is going to keep me pretty busy."

"I've been back there for in-services on new stuff a lot of times," Jim replied. "While you're back there you're immersed in one thing, so it's easy to think it's all you're going to be doing when you get back to the real world. It looks like you've got plenty on your plate right now. By the way, what's going on with the school bus case?"

"I'm not sure yet. One of the attorneys called last week, so I need to get back with them and figure out what's up. Looks like I've got a bunch of other stuff here, too, so I need to get going on that as well. A few things with short deadlines, so I suspect this will be a busy week."

"Good to have you back. By the way, I talked to the boss last week and they're sending us a new agent right out of the academy. Should be here next week. Guess who gets to train 'em?"

"That would be me, I suppose."

"Yup. All right, go ahead and catch up to the extent you can this week and maybe you can save a few things for our new agent to help you with when he gets here. Sounds like the guy we're getting has a law degree and his dad was an agent. So at least we're not getting someone completely clueless."

"That'll help."

The week flew by, and there were times I looked longingly at the three-ring binder I'd brought back with notes and handouts. I even paged through it at times, but there were some legitimate crises to deal with and I had to focus on my *real job*. There were plenty of calls back and forth between me and the Anti-Trust Division in Chicago. After all of the interviews I'd done, and Grand Jury subpoenas I'd served several months ago, they were ready to present the case to the Grand Jury in Cedar Rapids. So that was going to keep me hopping. In our first series of indictments, we charged thirteen people and companies with federal anti-trust and bid rigging violations. I had never had that many defendants or such a large case before. The next steps involved filing all of the motions and providing thousands of documents to defense attorneys. I knew I couldn't handle the demand, so the attorneys I worked with set up a temp office and a system that made documents available for copying.

I knew it would be quite a few months before we were going to face a trial, so that freed me up to do some training with our new agent and to get more and more things done and sent out of the office. Jim told me several years before that, except for big cases with indictment potential, our job was to "get them out of the office as soon as we could." A lot of things had deadlines, such as applicant cases, and others had bureau-imposed time limits. So there was a bit of pressure to keep things moving and reply back to the Office of Origin on leads they set out for us to handle.

One day the phone rang, and I picked it up on the first ring. "Hey Pete, it's Tom Moore in Omaha. How're you doing?"

"Good, Tom, what's up with you?" The last time he called me, I was off to the Psychological Profiling in-service. I immediately wondered what he had up his sleeve this time.

"Well, a couple of things, but first, did you enjoy the in-service?"

"It had its moments. Yeah, overall I'd have to say it was amazing information. A bit of an overload, though."

"I was wondering. I've read all of the paperwork from the Behavioral Science Unit, and it looks like those guys are taking this program seriously. What's your sense of that?"

"Pretty much got to agree. It's not going away, that's for sure. I just hope it doesn't become a full-time job for me, because I've already got plenty to do out here."

"We know that, Pete, and we don't want to bury you, but I've got a couple things to run by you."

"And that would be what?"

"For starters, we're having a National Academy session in Des Moines next month, and the boss would like you to do a presentation on the profiling program. Looks like there's going to be about fifty or sixty guys there. Can you be ready for that?"

"Well, I finally got the slides from Quantico, but I haven't had a chance to look at 'em. Why don't I put that up a little higher on the list—I'm guessing I can be ready in a month."

"Great, the boss will be pleased if you can. He's pretty excited about the program and to have you as the one heading it up. He seems to be a big fan of yours."

"Well, that's good," I responded, "but how quickly that can change."

"Yup. I know that, after twenty-five years in this organization."

"I'll bet."

"Got a couple more things to run by you," Tom said. "If you can be ready for the session next month, do you think you can do the same thing in Cedar Rapids a month later?"

"What's going on here?"

"They have the Iowa law enforcement yearly convention ready to go. It sounds like they're planning on having about three hundred in attendance for that, so I'm guessing that would give us a chance to really get the word out."

"Sounds good to me. If I can do one, I suppose I

can do two."

"Great, I really appreciate it, and I'll pass it on to the boss. There's one more thing."

"Okay."

"There's a hostage negotiator's in-service coming up in a couple months, and the boss told me he wants you to go."

"Damn," I said. "And just after I spent two weeks back there. We don't have a lot of hostage situations out here, Tom. In fact, I've never heard of one in the time I've been here."

"It's not so much as that. He wants you to do a few schools. I'll set 'em up and you do 'em."

"Jeez Louise. If I'm out of here too much doing profiling and hostage schools, Whalen's going to kill one of us, and I'm guessing it's going to be me."

"I've already run it by him. He's not wild about the idea, but he can't trump what the SAC wants."

I knew being in the hostage program would be fairly prestigious, but I was worried that I'd be biting off a little more than I could chew. "You know, Tom, I do have this bid rigging case with thirteen indictments, and my attorneys tell me there's no way we're not going to trial. There's a little work there."

"The boss knows that, but if you can fit it in around the trial, then he wants to do it."

"Okay with me. The way these attorneys are dragging this thing out, it's going to be about six months before we go to trial, if then."

"So I can tell him you'll do it?"

"Sure, why not?"

This stuff seemed to be coming at me pretty fast and my head was buzzing. I didn't know how I could juggle all of those balls and keep them up in the air. If I was going to get involved in something like the profiling program, I wanted to do a good job. It seemed a little overwhelming, but I guess I'd find out if I could handle it in due time. If there was enough of it.

CHAPTER TWENTY TWO

Murder: No Apparent Motive

I was a bit nervous before the first presentation in Des Moines, but surprisingly, everything went even better than I thought it would. I suspect my enthusiasm for the new program was apparent, but I also spent more than a little time poring over the material in slides and my notebook to make sure I was well-organized. I'd done a lot of teaching in colleges and police academies, and I was never one to wing it, or walk in unprepared. It seemed like the slide presentation went well, and after the break it was time for the video.

The HBO feature Bob Ressler had talked about and later sent me, *Murder: No Apparent Motive*, was a huge hit. Producers of the HBO special were allowed access to the offices of the Behavioral Science Unit, and spent a considerable amount of time talking with Ressler, John Douglas, and Roy Hazelwood. They sat in on profiling sessions with agents in the unit, and also went on-site to several locations and had some incredible footage, none of which was intended to be anything but informative. Sensationalism was not an issue. The cases the unit had been involved in were, by themselves, sensational enough. It was professionally done, and I couldn't have imagined anything more instructive in trying to get the point across of what we were ultimately hoping to accomplish with the profiling program.

Two cases featured in the HBO special were spellbinding, and I'm glad I previewed the video before I played it for the National Academy members. While watching the show, I took notes furiously and was able to match up some of the slides with what was being said on film. So I managed to look like I had more knowledge and expertise than I probably had.

The Atlanta Child Killings had gained national prominence with more than thirty young black children having been strangled over a period of several years. Roy Hazelwood had gone to Atlanta for on-scene profiling, and he had a strong feeling about the case that the local detectives didn't necessarily buy into. The biggest one was Roy believing the suspect was a black male. I recalled Roy talking about the case when we were in Quantico. He provided some other details about the profile he'd done, and talked about John Douglas also coming to Atlanta to work with him.

The case, according to Hazelwood, "was even being monitored by the President of the United States. We were making daily reports to our director, and he was giving updates directly to the White House. There was a lot of pressure on us. Rumors abounded that the Ku Klux Klan was behind the killings, essentially trying to start a race war in the South." He told us that the profiling program was in its infancy then, and they'd applied to Congress for additional funding. "We simply had to get it right. There wasn't an option. If we blew it, the entire program might die a premature death. And we wanted it to succeed."

In the video, Hazelwood talked about how he'd made a very simple conclusion that the suspect was black rather than white—the latter had been conventional thinking on the part of all of the investigators working on the case. "It was nothing more than common sense. Four of us were driving around in an unmarked police car in the area where the kidnappings took place. I was the only white person in the car, and as soon as we got to a place where people were gathered, everything on the street stopped. I asked one of the detectives what that was about and he said, 'There's a white man in the area. They're not used to seeing a white man.'" He went on to explain, as my audience watched raptly on several television sets around the room, "It didn't take a rocket scientist to figure out what that meant. Our unknown subject *had to be* a black man. No one else could move as freely around the area."

When Douglas came to Atlanta, Hazelwood said, "We worked together on the case and finally were able to come up with a profile of a younger black male who either lived in the area or not very far away. He was probably a police buff, and even may have been using that as a ruse to get the boys in a car with him. No one would have thought much about it, even if they'd seen it happen."

Douglas commented, "I was at the police station when I ran into some of the investigators. Most of the task force members still believed we should be looking for a white male. One of the guys said, 'Hey Douglas, I saw your profile, and I think it's a bunch of bullshit.' There wasn't much I could say, but I certainly was hoping he wasn't right."

Douglas and Hazelwood *weren't* wrong. The suspect, Wayne Bertrand Williams, fit virtually everything Douglas and Hazelwood had predicted in their profile. Hazelwood pointed out, "He had police badges and a car which looked like a plainclothes police car. Hairs from victims were in the car, and fibers from the car were on some of the victims. John Douglas worked with the prosecutor when the case went to trial. He suggested the prosecuting attorney violate Williams' body space when he was on the witness stand, and it worked. Williams, who had been calm and under control for the trial, suddenly burst out with an angry reply to a question. That gave the jury a bit of insight into the 'real' Wayne Williams, and he was convicted of the two murders they tried him for."

Another prominent case recounted in the video happened thousands of miles from Atlanta—in and around Anchorage, Alaska. A number of prostitutes had gone missing, and police were in a quandary to figure out what was happening, and, more importantly, who was making it happen. Alaska State Patrol sergeant Glen Flothe talked about how he'd been doing some reading, and found an article in *Psychology Today*. The article, titled "The Mindhunters," described how the Behavioral Sciences Unit back in Quantico had established the profiling program, and had some successes such as the case in Atlanta. "We were at a loss about what to do," Flothe said, "so I thought, *what the hell. I think I'll just give them a call.* And so I did. I eventually wound up on the phone with Roy Hazelwood."

Flothe explained, "I started to tell Roy all about a suspect we had developed in the case. But Roy put the brakes on me. He said, 'Don't tell me about your suspect. Tell me about the case, and let me see what I can tell you about the suspect.' We talked for a while, and then he asked me to send some reports and whatever else I might have. So I faxed a bunch of stuff back to him and he called me a couple days later. Everything Roy said fit our suspect to a 'T.' I couldn't believe it, but what I really couldn't believe was one thing Roy told me. He said he thought the guy might have a speech impediment, possibly a stutter. Our suspect was a stutterer. I still don't know how he figured that out.

"So I took the information Roy provided and drafted an affidavit for a search warrant. One of the things Roy said was their research showed that some of these guys kept souvenirs from the people they killed. He said they use them to relive what they'd done. When we searched the guy's house, every single thing Roy said would be there was there. The guy had guns, chains he used to secure the victims in the basement, and he had a bunch of jewelry and other items we later connected with some of the victims."

Perhaps one of the most sadistic serial killers of all time, Robert Hansen raped and assaulted over thirty Alaskan women. He is responsible for the brutal murder of at least seventeen women, ranging in age from sixteen to forty-one. Hansen, a prominent Anchorage citizen and skilled hunter, owned and operated a bakery in the downtown area, yet again demonstrating how most serial killers are able to hide in plain sight. He would prowl a part of town where hookers hung out and plied their trade. After raping the women in his home, he would take them at gunpoint to his airplane parked at Merrill Field. After securing them in the plane, he'd fly the victims to an area where he hunted big game. Once there, he'd tell the women they, indeed, had a chance to escape, but they would have to run and avoid him hunting them down. None escaped, and he either buried their bodies or left them in the wild for animals to feast on. After entering guilty pleas to four of the murders and a variety of other charges, Hansen was sentenced to 461 years in a federal penitentiary, which was part of the plea agreement.

CHAPTER TWENTY THREE

A Missing Paperboy in Des Moines, Iowa

It was a pretty routine day in the office. I was trying to get a few reports off to Omaha when the phone rang.

"Pete, this is Tom Moore."

"Hey Tom."

"It sounds like your presentation went very well at the National Academy."

"Really? I talked to a couple people after I was done, and a few of them seemed to be interested. I hope we can get a couple of cases referred and back to Quantico, and then I'll feel like I got something accomplished."

"Anything yet?"

"Yeah. I had some people come up to me after my session and I gave out a few cards. One has called me so far, so I'm going to get together with him in Waterloo next week. I suspect a few more got back to their own offices and pretty much forgot about what I'd talked about. A lot of booze flows at those sessions, you know," I said.

"I hear that," Tom responded. "But they haven't all forgotten about you. I've had about a half dozen calls from some chiefs and sheriffs, and they want you to do a daylong class for them. You up to that?"

"I suppose I could do a few, but I'm a little bit buried out here with my real work."

"I completely understand. Why don't you take a look at the calendar and see if you have a few days in the next couple of months we can work with?"

"Okay. Are you talking about Iowa or Nebraska?"

"Probably both. Get a few dates to me and I'll send something out to the agencies. Since it's fairly centrally located, I think Des Moines would be a logical place, and either Lincoln or Omaha would work over here. How's that sound?"

"Sounds good. Maybe I could do one in Des Moines on a Tuesday, and then head over to Omaha and do the other one on Thursday."

"Good idea. Why don't you just let me know what works for you and we'll see how we can make it work for everybody. I have a sneaking suspicion you're going to be a fairly hot commodity on the lecture circuit for a while."

"Well, I hope not too popular. I still have my real job to manage. Plenty to do out here."

Several months passed, and life returned to normal as I had previously known it. At least for a while.

Jim Whalen was cranking up his drug conspiracy investigation, expanding the focus to Dubuque, Waterloo, and Minneapolis. The latter seemed to be the source city for cocaine into Cedar Rapids. I was busy as hell trying to keep up with the demands of the school bus bid rigging case and a ton of other things I had to deal with, plus doing some occasional training with another new agent. Our headquarters office in Omaha had finally come to the realization that we were, in fact, *busy* in Cedar Rapids. They also seemed to understand that they had two hard-working agents in Jim and me, and they needed to keep us free from the annoying minutia, letting the two of us develop cases that would have some impact. Not to mention multiple indictments and convictions. I learned pretty quickly that it was all about statistics, and I took the attitude that bigger was, in fact, better where cases were concerned.

And then we started to have bank robberies. While usually not a problem in Iowa, the economy had reached a low ebb, and many people theorized some criminals were trying to solve their economic desperation by robbing banks. It'd happened in the Great Depression, and some felt that's what we were getting into again. In the previous three years I'd been in Cedar Rapids, we'd had two bank robberies in our territory. In the next eighteen months, we had twenty-four. Whalen was completely out of the picture, totally involved with his expanding drug case. I could understand that, but I was fully occupied with one huge case and several others snapping at my ankles. The United States Attorney's offices in Cedar Rapids and Des Moines, and the Anti-Trust Division in Chicago, were playing tug-of-war with me. I was probably busier than Whalen, but that didn't seem to matter. We got another new agent assigned to the office, making a total of five. But we couldn't turn a bunch of inexperienced new agents loose trying to solve a bank robbery every couple of weeks. So I had to get in the middle of those, too.

Things were starting to get more than a little stressful, and I also had Tom Moore calling me occasionally to do a profiling school somewhere. The ones I'd already done were generating some more work for me, which was exactly what I didn't need. Agencies had new cases or cold cases they wanted me to look at. My head was spinning and I was constantly going like a bat out of hell. Having weekends off was no longer an option for me. Sleeping was becoming a problem. I was waking up in the middle of the night, turning on the light, and writing down some things I needed to do. It was ridiculous. I was a grouch around my family and didn't have time to think about anything except my job. And then the phone would ring in the middle of the night and I'd have to get up and race out to an Indian settlement about forty miles away. A shooting, a rape, or a robbery had occurred, and the sheriff's department needed an agent to conduct the investigation. Since it wasn't an actual Indian reservation, the FBI was the agency in charge of investigating major crimes.

I wondered, at times, if I needed to find another job. This one was becoming like the more you did, the more they wanted you to do. I longed for the days when I was a patrol officer and every night was an event unto itself. I didn't have to carry things over from one day to the next. All I had to do was get my radio calls handled, the reports done, and look forward to what the next day would bring. How that had changed.

Just when you think things can't get worse—they do. About a year before, we'd had a kidnapping case in Des Moines which had gained national publicity. Johnny Gosch, a fourteen-year-old boy, left home in the early morning hours to deliver newspapers. Within an hour, his parents were awakened with phone calls from people on their son's route, complaining of undelivered papers. It was a quiet fall Sunday morning in September, the weather was clear, and the parents couldn't imagine what had happened. They jumped in their car and not only couldn't find their son, but found his wagon full of Sunday newspapers two blocks from their home. Other paperboys told his parents that they had seen Johnny picking up his papers that morning, and folding them before leaving the delivery station. It was not like Johnny to have suddenly decided to take off and run away from home. He was a happy kid who was doing well in school, and nothing about his home life was an apparent problem. Johnny was just gone.

No one had the slightest idea what happened to Johnny Gosch. Other paper carriers had seen a man in a car in the area at the same time, but nothing other than that piece of information was developed. Police were called and searched the area, and then expanded the search. Eventually the FBI office in Des Moines became involved because it was an apparent kidnapping, a federal violation. Hundreds, if not thousands, of hours were expended over the next several months, to no avail. It was almost like someone had come along and picked up a Christmas decoration in someone's yard, and no one had seen them do it. The police and the FBI, under constant criticism from the boy's mother, spent untold hours trying to think outside the box and solve the case. Searches were done, but nothing turned up. Stories ran in the paper for weeks. It became a national news story. The FBI director was constantly updated, but there was nothing to update. The boy was missing and he couldn't be found. Everyone assumed he was snatched off the street by a child molester and killed, but no one knew. Maybe he'd been kidnapped and he was still alive. Nobody knew that, either. Despite an unending number of theories, no one had even the slightest bit of proof what had happened to Johnny Gosch. Homosexuals in the community were rousted by police and FBI agents. Nothing was developed. And eventually the case went cold.

For many months, Johnny's mother tried to keep the case alive, constantly badgering the police, FBI, and the media, but with no success. His parents were eventually divorced, apparently as a result of the stress, but his mother persisted in her unending search for her son. Nothing worked. Johnny was gone, never to be seen again.

While I wasn't directly involved with the investigation, I followed it closely. It wasn't hard to relate to the parents' grief and to identify with them. I had a thirteen-year-old son and daughter at home. I couldn't imagine what I'd have done under the same circumstances. It became personal to me, but the investigation was in a city a hundred miles away, and I had to deal with my own problems. And so I did. There wasn't anything I could do about it.

Des Moines eventually returned to normal and we all hoped it wouldn't happen again.

CHAPTER TWENTY FOUR

A Missing Paperboy in Omaha, Nebraska

A telephone ringing at six-thirty in the morning was not usually a good thing. I was in the shower, preparing to head into the office, and so my wife answered the phone. She came into the bathroom and announced, "Pete, it's your SAC. He needs to talk to you immediately."

"Can you tell him I'm in the shower and I'll call him right back?"

She did. "He says he needs to talk to you *right now.*"

Adrenalin raced to my heart and a rapid series of thoughts hit my brain. *What in the hell did I do wrong?* I thought as I quickly toweled off. Getting an early-morning phone call was bad enough, but when it was from the Special Agent in Charge of the entire field office, that was a big clue that something was seriously wrong.

"Hey boss, what's up?"

"Pete, I need you here in Omaha as soon as you can get here."

I quickly raced through my schedule for the day, realizing I had to testify before the Grand Jury in Cedar Rapids at one o'clock. "As soon as that's over, I can head in, but it's a four-hour drive, so the earliest I could get there would be six or seven tonight. What's going on? Did I screw something up?"

"No, you're fine," he said. "It's not about you. Have you heard about the kidnapping of a paperboy we had in Bellevue the other day?"

I wracked my brain. "Just barely, but I've been pretty occupied with my own stuff here."

"A couple days ago, a thirteen-year-old paperboy

got snatched off the street in Bellevue, and we found his body in a field south of Offutt late yesterday." Bellevue was a suburb of Omaha and Offutt Air Force Base was the Strategic Air Command base which ran for several miles south of Bellevue. I'd only been on the base one or two times.

"Omigod!" I blurted. "That sounds just like the—"

He cut me off. "Yeah, I know. The Johnny Gosch case. We have no idea if it's the same guy, but you're my profiler and I need you to get in here as soon as you can."

"All right. I'll throw some clothes together before I head in to the office. My guys from Chicago won't be there until about ten this morning. We've got some work to do and then they told me I'm the first witness they're going to put on the stand at one p.m. I'll just tell 'em I'm out of there as soon as I'm done with the Grand Jury."

"Okay, thanks Pete. I'll see you later. I've got the whole damn office heading out there, so give me a call before you get here and I'll tell you where I'll be. Best guess is at the Sarpy County Sheriff's Office."

"Will do." Now my brain felt like it was on speed. I had little idea what had happened in Bellevue, and even less than no information about the crime scene. And certainly no idea how long I might expect to be in Omaha.

"Oh, by the way," he said before we hung up. "I'm going to give the Behavioral Sciences Unit a call and see if I can get one of those guys to come out. So you can work hand-in-hand with whoever they send out. If they do."

I breathed a little sigh of relief. I didn't think I was quite ready for prime time, and this case was certainly going to be that.

"Everything okay?" my wife, Mary Ann, asked as I came down to the kitchen. My twins, Kary and Loni, had just gotten up and were having breakfast before heading off to school. I filled them in on what I knew and told all three of them I didn't know how long I'd be in Omaha. Usually a trip over to headquarters city was a day or two. This time, who knew?

It was hard to focus when I got to the office. Finally, curiosity got the best of me and I called Peggy Sanders, one of our support staff in Omaha who always seemed to be in the know about office happenings.

"Peggy, it looks like I'm heading to Omaha this afternoon. Can you tell me what's happening?"

"Nobody knows for sure, Pete," she replied. "Everyone's running around here like chickens with their heads cut off right now. Two days ago this kid was out early in the morning, delivering papers. Next thing they knew his bike and papers were found lying on the sidewalk."

"Nobody saw anything?"

"Not so far as I know. I heard they found his body in a field. I guess it's south of Offutt somewhere. We don't have much information here. They've got a command post set up at the sheriff's department, so we're a little out of the loop. Everyone in the office is either down there or heading there. I did hear the little guy was stabbed and his body was cut up. Don't really know much more than that."

"Damn. All right, thanks for the info. The boss wants me there ASAP, so I'll probably see you tomorrow."

"When you leaving?"

"Can't get out of here until later. I've got Grand Jury after lunch, then I'm Omaha bound."

Depending on the amount of rain Iowa gets in late August or early September, the drive from Cedar Rapids to Omaha on Interstate 80 could be either enjoying mile after mile of fields painted in the verdant green colors of ripening corn stalks, or a seeming infinity of tall, tan stalks awaiting the sharp tines of huge John Deere harvesters to pick their bounty. Unlike what most people think, Iowa is anything but flat; it's actually made up of softly rolling hills dredged out by decades of receding glaciers thousands of years ago. The drive that day leaned toward the tan side of things, but I probably wasn't noticing much in any event. My mind simply wasn't there.

I was thrilled to hear one of the guys from Quantico may be coming, and just hoped he would get there quickly. It was clearly a case like Denny Koslowski and I had discussed several times in Quantico. It was a high-profile case, and they wanted it solved sooner rather than later. I'd been sent to a two-week school to become a profiler, but I knew I wasn't qualified to do what the guys in the unit could.

The primary thoughts I had were about Special Agent Ken Lanning's lecture on crimes against children in Quantico, specifically child molesters. I brought my binder along, with plenty of notes from Lanning's class, so I felt like that gave me a little resource material to work with. He had given us characteristics of four different *types* of child molesters, which was more than a little bit interesting to me since I had dealt with very few of them in my experience on the police force. I was hoping the police department, which was fairly small, or the sheriff's department had a detective who worked on child sex crimes, because he or she would also be someone to bounce ideas off of. And I was glad someone from the Behavioral Science Unit would be able to make it out to Omaha.

Driving through Des Moines, I couldn't help but think about the Johnny Gosch case, and how that could tie into what we had in Bellevue. It certainly seemed likely, given the relatively short distance in both time and place. Omaha is about one hundred miles from Des Moines, so anything was possible. More likely, I thought, it was going to be someone local, but who knew if he could have lived in Des Moines a year before. The facts were going to play out in their own way, and I'd find out sooner rather than later. My guess was I was facing a couple of very intense days. And I was right.

CHAPTER TWENTY FIVE

Help!

Herb Hawkins was our Special Agent in Charge, and he was truly an agent's boss. A highly decorated Marine Corps major, he'd come into the bureau as a Special Agent and, after about ten years as an agent and supervisor, the usual management track, found himself as the Assistant Special Agent in Charge in Las Vegas. While there, he'd supervised several high-profile cases, most prominently a major investigation involving a one-thousand-pound bomb placed in Harvey's Casino in Reno. That case was solved, although the bomb in the lobby exploded, doing a considerable amount of damage to the casino and hotel. The man identified as the bomber, a Hungarian immigrant, was attempting to extort three million dollars from Harvey's. Herb had also been directly involved in several other large cases in Las Vegas, so he was seemingly the right man to direct our efforts in Bellevue.

Unfortunately, Herb had an entire field office to run in two states, and plenty of other cases happening in the division, so he wouldn't be the point man on the investigation. ASAC John Evans would be working closely with the Bellevue Police Chief and Sarpy County Sheriff.

Herb was at the command post when I came rolling in the next morning after getting a good night's sleep. He seemed pleased to see me. "Pete, you ready to roll?"

"Tell me where you need me, boss, and I'm there."

"All right, first things first. I just got a call from Bob Ressler and he'll be flying into Omaha about four o'clock. Do you know him?"

"Oh, yeah. Ressler will be great. Sharp guy and he's been at it for quite a while. I'll get the info and pick him up at the airport, since I'm probably the only one here who knows him."

"Great. Why don't you get with Chuck Kempf and see what you can get together by the time Ressler lands so he can hit the ground running?" Kempf was one of the more senior agents in the office, and was not only a good investigator with an exceptional record, but well-liked by everyone including local law enforcement officers. He was a firearms and self-defense instructor, so he'd taught a lot of them those basic skills in the police academy.

"Sounds good," I said. "Any idea where he is?"

"I think he's either out at the scene or the Coroner's Office. They're doing an autopsy on the boy this morning about ten. So Chuck's probably there. See who else might be here. One of the senior guys can get you going pretty quickly."

Photos of the crime scene weren't available, but I copied off the original reports, parked myself in a quiet place in a conference room, and started reading. The facts were pretty straightforward. Thirteen-year-old Danny Joe Eberle got up early, as he always did, and headed down to a nearby convenience store to pick up his supply of seventy papers to deliver. He rolled the papers, put the entire load in the delivery bag on his bicycle, and took off on his route. But he only made three stops. When some people on the route didn't get their papers at the usual time, they were on the phone to Danny's home.

Puzzled by the number of calls, his parents headed out on the route, eventually finding Danny's bike inside the gate of a fence around a dentist's home. Folded newspapers were inside the delivery bag, but Danny Joe was nowhere to be found. There were no signs of a struggle. His parents drove around to see if they could find him but couldn't, and immediately called the Bellevue Police Department.

Police began a search for the boy right away, systematically talking to people in the area, but no one had seen anything, including Danny Joe. The search continued for the entire day with officers checking every building in the area and searching around houses. More neighbors were interviewed, but no one had seen Danny Joe with anyone. He'd simply vanished, much like Johnny Gosch did a year before, and the parallels were eerily similar.

No clues were found, despite a search by over a hundred townspeople and officers. Day became evening, and when darkness fell the search was put on hold, and began first thing the next morning. Yet again, the search teams fanned out with guidance and organization from law enforcement officers. The sheriff's department was involved, and the Bellevue police chief contacted the local FBI office in Omaha. Agents were immediately assigned to help with the search and investigation into the boy's disappearance. There were no indications of problems at home that could have made him decide to run away. To the contrary, he was conscientious about getting up, delivering his papers, and getting himself to school every morning. No problems at school. No one could understand how he could mysteriously disappear.

The search was expanded into outlying areas the next day. And, finally, a tragic break. A searcher found Danny Joe's body in some weeds just off a gravel road in an undeveloped county area. The site was about four miles southwest of where Danny Joe's bicycle was left. He was clad only in his underpants and it appeared he'd been stabbed in the front and back, numerous times. His hands and ankles were bound with rope, his mouth covered with surgical tape, and there was some evidence the boy had been tortured prior to death, a fact that would later be confirmed by the autopsy.

CHAPTER TWENTY SIX

Legendary Profiler Bob Ressler Arrives to Help

By three o'clock, I'd read every report I could find, and copied the pertinent ones. I took quite a few notes, and added my own thoughts when appropriate. I wanted to have a good handle on the facts by the time I picked up Bob Ressler at the airport.

Bob was all about business as we drove back. Eppley Field in Omaha is about thirty minutes north and east of the sheriff's department, tucked into a large, meandering turn of the Missouri River. I opted for a return route that would take us a little more time so I could bring Bob up to speed.

"So, have they been bugging you for answers yet?" he asked.

"Actually, no, thank God. My boss just told me to get up to speed as fast as I could and pretty much left me to my own devices. I landed in a quiet place and started going over reports. Some were useful and I made my own notes, plus I've got some copies for us to go over later."

"That'll help."

"Any idea what you want to do first, Bob?"

"Well, if it's not too far out of the way, I wouldn't mind driving by the scene where the boy's body was found."

"Okay, we can do that. I'm not absolutely sure where it is, but if it's on the road west of Offutt, I'm pretty sure I can find it. I'm guessing there will be some people out there, so we can see exactly where the body was left."

"That always gives me some insights, and sometimes I'm not even sure why. It eventually starts to fit together."

"Since we're doing that and it's on the way, why don't we take a quick look at the street where the boy went missing. I know I can find it."

The area was mostly post-war ranch homes, brick construction and well maintained. Since the military base was the primary engine driving the economy of Bellevue, I told Bob, "I'm guessing most of these homes are enlisted or support personnel." I pointed to a nicer house on the left. "That place is where his bike was found. Right inside that gate. A dentist lives in the house, but he didn't know anything at all."

"Did anyone see anything?"

"Nothing. Absolutely nothing. They've gone house-to-house and checked every possibility. Buildings, small fields, you name it. Nothing. It was like he just vanished into thin air. Poof and he was gone."

"Any unusual characters in the area?"

"Not sure. I suspect there's some follow-up that will be done in the next few days. I'll make a note of it and run it by the bosses when we get to the command post."

"Good idea," Bob said. "You never know. Some character in the neighborhood could have grabbed the boy and kept him in his house for a couple days. Happened before."

"That's why we've got you here."

"I just hope we can do some good."

Somehow, I managed to use wit and guile and find the country road east of the base. And, luckily, there were quite a few people tromping around on both sides of the road, searching in the area for more clues to the identity of the unknown and brutal killer.

I found a new agent I recognized searching a culvert beside the road.

"Can you point us to where the boy's body was found?" I asked him.

He turned and pointed toward the south. "Where that little group is standing. I think they're still working on the crime scene."

They were. I introduced Bob and myself, and they were quite impressed that he had come all the way out to "little old Omaha" from Quantico.

"Glad to be here." He winked at me.

Bob asked the deputies at the scene quite a few questions about the area, and when he seemed to have a sense of the demographics, he pointed to my car. "Let's head over to the command post."

Our timing was perfect. Chuck Kempf and a Sarpy County detective had just returned from the autopsy and were about to give the brass a briefing. We sat in on that in the same conference room I'd used earlier.

"The doc said it'll be a couple weeks before we get the blood work back," Chuck said, "so he couldn't tell me anything about Danny being drugged or having alcohol in his system. He didn't find any sign of sexual assault, and we used a black light on the body. Nothing there. He said he'd been stabbed a total of nine times and that he'd been hit in the face several times as well. Also, his throat was slashed."

"Any sense of what actually killed him?" the sheriff asked.

"He said the boy slowly bled out from a combination of stab wounds and the slashed throat. It took him a while to die, so he suffered, poor kid." Chuck choked up. It wasn't hard to tell he was taking the case personally. Everyone was.

"Any pictures of the scene yet?" Bob asked.

"Should have 'em tonight," Chuck said. "I'll run over to the office when we're done here and pick them up." He looked at Bob and me. "Where you guys going to be later?"

"We're heading over to the Holiday Inn on I-25 and Seventy-second Street," I replied. "I'm checked in there and I have a room reserved for Bob. We'll probably get a bite to eat and land in my room later. Want to meet us there?"

"That'll work." Chuck looked at his watch. "Should be around seven."

I gave him my room number and we took off to check in and get dinner at the hotel.

CHAPTER TWENTY SEVEN

This Stuff Isn't Magic

Bob Ressler astounded me with the insightful questions he asked Chuck Kempf and the lead detective from the sheriff's department. Both of the investigators had been immersed in the case from day one, and neither of them had slept more than a couple of hours in the previous four days. Despite that, they were both energetic and excited to run the facts past us, hoping beyond hope that we could give them some new insights into the killer.

But Bob was asking them some questions they weren't ready for. "Why do you think he tied the boy up that way?" he asked, looking at one of the crime scene pictures and flashing it to all of us.

"Well…" Chuck paused and looked at the detective. "I don't know. Maybe to secure him so he could do what he wanted to do?"

Bob nodded his head and looked over at me. "I think you've got a part of it right, Chuck. What do you think Pete?"

"Hard to say, Bob." I was at a loss to explain what I was seeing. "It's almost like he was hog-tying the boy. As soon as I saw the picture I was thinking our UNSUB (Unknown Subject) may have spent some time growing up on a farm. Bad idea?"

He nodded. "Actually, I hadn't thought of that. Not really a bad idea. I might have a meeting with myself about that later. But here's what I think it's telling us." He pointed at the ropes around the boy's wrists and ankles. "People with sadistic inclinations tend to want to completely immobilize their victims. It gives 'em a feeling of control. Power over their victim, and it lets him do exactly what he wants without any resistance."

"Don't remember covering that in profiler's boot camp," I commented.

Bob grabbed the pile of pictures the investigators had brought with them. He stacked the pile up neatly, putting it on top of the reports I'd gathered, looked at all of us, and said, "Here's what I want you to do. I think I understand *how* this happened, and I definitely know *what* happened." He put an emphasis on those two words. "We know *who* it happened to, and *where* the body of the boy was found. Right?" He looked at the three of us, our heads nodding in unison, and finally I knew where this meeting was heading.

I remembered several lectures Bob had given us. "And what you want to know is *why* all of these things happened. Right?"

Bob responded, "I'm glad to see Pete got something out of the two weeks he spent at Quantico, other than drinking with his buddies every night." That produced some smiles from all of us.

"Lucky for me." I laughed. "Those guys were pretty bad."

Bob chuckled. "Yeah, and I'm guessing they twisted your arm every night you guys went up to the Boardroom."

"Probably just a little."

"All right, here's what I want you guys to do. Every one of you has a good understanding of the case now, but here's what I want to know. Why did this guy do what he did? Did he take a big risk when he grabbed the boy off the street? What does that tell you? Did he have to use physical force on the boy or did he have a weapon with him? What does that tell us? How long did he keep the boy? What does that tell us, since there apparently wasn't any sex involved? Are we looking at a crime that was impulsive or spur-of-the-moment, or did this guy do some prior planning?" The three of us were staring at Bob like he'd just leaped off a space ship.

The Sarpy County detective replied first. "I've been a cop for over twenty years, but I've never thought about that. It's always about who, what, where, when, and how. So what you're saying is you want to put all of that aside and think about the why?"

"That's exactly what I'm saying," Bob answered. "You're starting to get it. Let's see if we can all work together and figure the *why* out for some of the things I asked you about. Just think about this for a minute. If it's not about complete control and domination of the boy, why does he tie him up the way he did, but even more importantly, why did he cover his mouth with tape?"

Chuck bristled. "He obviously didn't want the boy to say anything, to object to what he was doing. Damn. I guess I've got to start thinking about this case in a little different way then?"

"No," Bob said. "You're the case agent and he's the case detective. Both of you need to have a complete grasp of every possible fact of the investigation, at every point in the investigation. I want you to know everything, because with that information, you're indispensable to me. I just want you to add one more element to your thinking. Why did he do what he did at any given point? That's going to give us some serious clues into the motives behind this guy. See what I mean?"

The Sarpy County detective picked up the pictures. Looking at Bob and me, he asked, "So were these helpful?"

"Very helpful," Bob replied. "I'd like to pick out a few of 'em to look at later and in the morning."

"Do you think you have enough right now to do a profile on this guy?" Chuck asked, almost pleadingly. I could sense the anxiety in his voice. They wanted this case solved. Not tomorrow. Now. It was the most terrifying crime a community could experience. If an innocent boy could be snatched off the street and killed, who in the community could feel safe?

Bob reached for the pictures and selected a few. "I've got a bunch of stuff going through my head right now," he said. "It's more of a process than a lot of people think. There's no crystal ball involved or anything like mystical thinking. I have several hundred cases inside my head, and what I need to do is plug this one in there somewhere. It's almost like rolling a ball of tape across the floor and seeing what gets attached to it. It'll start to come together in the morning or sometime tomorrow. I still don't think I have all of the facts in there yet, but it'll come."

"Any initial impressions, Bob?" I asked.

"A few, but I'm not absolutely sure yet. I think this guy is going to be younger, early twenties, probably, and I don't think there's any connection with the Johnny Gosch case. I get a sense he's new to town and may have some connection to the military base."

"Interesting," Chuck said. "Do you think we're dealing with a serial killer?"

"Hard to say right now. I'd have to say this is probably his first killing. Problem is, once they get a taste of that power over a victim, they start to fantasize about what they did. Then it becomes an obsession, and eventually a compulsion to do it again because it was somehow sexually exciting to them. When they can't overcome the obsession they have, it's time to do it again."

The detective shook his head. "So it might happen again if we don't get this guy pretty soon?"

"Very possible," Bob replied.

"How soon?" The detective grabbed the pictures again, paging through them.

"Hard to say. We don't have a pattern of any sort right now. I'm hoping we can get him before he kills another kid. It could be a few days, or even several weeks. My inclination is it will be later than sooner. He is well aware we're putting a full court press on now, and until things settle down he'd be more likely to get caught. If he wants to do it, again, he doesn't want to get caught. It's the kind of a deal that when they start, it consumes them and eventually it happens again to satisfy that craving."

Chuck waved his hand to emphasize what he was going to say next. "Is this guy crazy?"

Bob shook his head. "I realize that's what most people think in a case like this, but the answer to that is almost surely not. The word *crazy* has a couple of meanings, but in the context we're talking about, it doesn't really apply. I'll almost guarantee this guy isn't insane, and that he's going to be one of the last people you'd expect to do what he's done."

"Our bosses are convinced this guy is a homosexual who wants to prey on younger victims. Any thoughts about that?" The detective from Sarpy County brought up a good point, and one that conventional wisdom would consider to be right on point.

"I doubt that," Bob said. "It's the first thing you think of, but remember there was apparently no sex act involved. We're not dealing with some guy who hangs out in gay bars or cruises wherever guys like that go. This guy is developing into a killing machine in all likelihood. If he was solely gay, he could deal with those urges without having to kill a kid."

Chuck Kempf rubbed his chin. "Our ASAC is hot on that right now. He wants some of our people out rousting the homos, because he's convinced that's what our guy is. I don't know if we can get him off that line of thinking. So you're saying he's not, right?"

"I doubt it. Somehow we've got to look beyond that. There's not a doubt in my mind that we're not going to be looking at a thirty- or forty-year-old gay guy who has made this big of a change in what he does. I'm almost positive at this point that we're going to be looking for a much younger guy who is just starting to have his previous fantasies develop into realities. *Needs* in his mind."

"That gives us something completely different to think about," the detective said. "My sheriff thinks like Chuck's boss. It's like they have their mind made up about homosexuals, and they can't see past it."

"Let me handle that," Bob replied. He looked at his wristwatch and noted the late hour. "We've been at this for a couple of hours and we all need to get a good night's sleep. Especially you guys, I suspect. Why don't we put this to bed for the night and I'll see you bright and early in the morning at the task force office?"

After the investigators left, I told Bob, "I'm really glad you're here. I don't know if I could fight through these ideas they've got. The bosses, I mean. It really helps to see we're not dealing with convention, but to change their thought processes is going to take some serious work."

"Yup, always does. Let's get a little sleep and I'll meet you in the restaurant for breakfast at about seven in the morning. Sound good?"

"See you then."

CHAPTER TWENTY EIGHT

A Hard Look at the Crime Scene

My ASAC and the Sarpy County sheriff were excited to see Bob Ressler when we rolled into the somber task force office that morning. Both men assumed he had time to deliver a profile to the officers, deputies, and agents working the case, but Bob quickly disabused them of that idea.

"Sorry, guys.," Bob sounded a little annoyed as he spoke. "There isn't any psychic thinking involved in this. It's a process and I don't feel like I've had enough time to completely digest all of the information."

"Did you meet with the primary investigators last night?" ASAC John Evans asked.

"We did, and when they left, Pete and I kicked things around. We also spent a little quality time together at breakfast this morning. There are a few more things I need to get my head wrapped around. I'm going to say we'll spend a good part of the day doing that and if I feel like I've got a handle on things, I might be ready in the morning. I want to give you some useful information and be as accurate as I can be. Just let me have a chance for all of this to sink in first."

Both bosses looked a little disappointed, but I understood exactly what Bob was saying. Our training had helped me to understand that we had to consider things such as the risk our UNSUB took in kidnapping the boy right off the street in broad daylight. Then he wanted to understand how long the boy had been with the UNSUB, why he'd selected this particular victim, and even why he dumped the body on a lonely, untraveled country road. Was he familiar with that area? If so, why? Was there anything more we could learn about the type of weapon he used, and even the rope used to restrain the victim? Why did he choose the method of essentially hog-tying the victim like he did? Was there something about any of those things that would give us some clues about his personality, and thus about him? Until Bob understood more, he didn't feel like he could do anything other than shoot from the hip, and he didn't want to do that, despite the obvious anxiety of those in charge.

"I understand they want some answers right now," Bob said as we rolled out of the sheriff's department in my bureau car. "But until I feel comfortable with what I know, they're not going to get them."

"I know what they're saying." I pulled onto the main road and headed east toward the town of Bellevue. "They're under a lot of pressure to get this solved sooner rather than later. But what I don't think they understand is you're not going to be able to pinpoint the exact guy, where he lives, and what his first name is."

"Exactly. I can give them some fairly specific things about the guy, and some general stuff, as well. But it's gonna take me a little time to process all the information, and there's obviously a lot of it."

"By the way, where do you want to go first?" I asked.

"Let's take another run past the place where the boy was snatched, and then I want to get a good handle on where the body was left in relation to other aspects of the area."

"Do you want to get the case agent down there to meet us?"

"Nah. I think we can just roll around the area for a while and try to get an idea of what direct route he might have taken and even why he dumped the body where he did rather than farther down the road, or in some other location where it wouldn't be found for months, if that."

"Good point. Some of these characters, like Bundy, tried their best to leave bodies in places where they might never be found."

"That's right, so this might give us a few more clues into what his thought processes were. One thing I can say for sure—he had to have a whole lot of anxiety when he was driving around with a kid in his car. What does that tell us?"

Looking around at the street where Danny Joe

Eberle was kidnapped seemed to give Bob some insight into the UNSUB's lack of planning in kidnapping the boy. "I've just got to think this was more of an impulsive thing than well-planned," he said as we made our second pass by the kidnapping site. "So if that's the case, what would you conclude?"

"Right out of one of your lectures at the academy," I replied. "A lack of planning and a more impulsive act tells us we're dealing with someone younger."

"Correct. My sense of this right now is we're dealing with a guy in his early twenties. What other conclusions can we arrive at?"

"Well, let's see. I'd have to go with a white male, and probably someone who isn't a very big guy. He found a victim who was young and pretty small, so he could more easily control him. The victim was a white kid, and these crimes tend to be race-on-race. Fairly easy to conclude we're looking for a white male, if not for that, just from the general demographics of the area. Virtually an all-white area here."

Bob looked over at me. "Maybe you did get something out of that training we gave you!"

"I cheated. I looked through my notes from last night."

"Good for you. There's no way you can have all of this stuff in your head right now."

"You got that right. And let me say, once again, I'm really glad you came out here. I know these guys would assume I was the *expert* since I'd gone to some training. And I'll readily admit, I don't feel like one at all."

"Yeah, but you're thinking in the right direction."

By the time we arrived at the location where the boy's body had been deposited, we'd spent more quality time coming up with some additional factors we thought would apply. "One thing I feel pretty sure about is this guy is somehow attached to that military base over there." Bob pointed toward Offutt Air Force base, which was to our east as we drove down the dirt road. "Something tells me this is a comfort zone over here, I mean a place where he's driven around when he wants to get away from it all. One of the leads I'm going to give to the sheriff is to check and see if they might have a deputy who found a car out here and talked to someone. Outside chance, but it's happened before."

It was apparent a lot of ideas were starting to come to Bob. He added, "If he's a younger guy, and I'm convinced he is, then I'd assume he's a low-ranking enlisted guy who probably hasn't been on the base very long. What happened here tells me this is his first victim. I'm not sure why I'm saying that, but just a sense I'm getting."

"So what you're saying is, wherever he might have come from, he probably isn't continuing a killing spree that started there?"

"That's right. He probably got away from there for some other reason. I'd have to say this guy left a poor family life, and by that I mean he was in a family situation that was a problem for him. His parents were likely not together and he'd lived with his mom. Usually with these characters, they grow up with an abusive parent, and the dad is absent. He probably didn't do extremely well in school, and a big part of that was because these violent fantasies wouldn't go away."

I thought about that for a few moments. "Well, that sounds familiar. That's exactly why I went in the Navy when I was seventeen."

"Same thing, probably, plus I'd say he was floundering around, and going into the military gave him some sense of direction in his life."

"Same thing with me. Helped me grow up and I was ready for life after that. But it still didn't take away the violent fantasies, right?"

"That's right. He probably has had these violent fantasies ever since he was a young kid."

"Profiling one-oh-one."

"Yup."

I parked on the road adjacent to the place where Danny Joe's body had been found. "Let me do something," Bob said. "I want to spend a little time here with my own thoughts. Some things are starting to come to me, but I want to spend a little time thinking right here. Why don't you head down the road and get a little sense of the area. Is there a south exit from the base? Anything else you might see that could help us."

"Sounds like a good idea."

I headed down the road slowly with my head on a swivel. The entire area had been searched over and over, so I wasn't going to find any obvious evidence lying out on the road, but perhaps there would be some inkling I could get about something. I didn't. I could, however, clearly see the base and the tower that was the most prominent landmark in a flat and barren part of the county. I couldn't help but think what a lonely and terrifying experience it must have been to Danny Joe, literally out in the middle of nowhere with a man who was doing things you didn't understand, and who was going to kill you. At thirteen years old. I thought of my own son. Same age as Danny Joe. It gave me the chills and an unexplainable buzzing feeling in my head.

Bob was wandering around on the road when I returned. "That helped." He buckled up and closed the door. "How about we head back to the hotel and get a bite to eat? Then I want to spend some time alone in my room going over the reports and pictures again. I think I'll be pretty close to ready later this afternoon or tonight."

CHAPTER TWENTY NINE

Here's the Type of Suspect You're Looking For

Bob pored over his notes as we drove to the sheriff's office the next morning. We had a good breakfast and it was obvious that he was ready to roll. When I parked, I said, "Looks like show time."

"Yes it is."

"Nervous?"

"Not really. I feel like I've got a good handle on it now. There might be a few things I'm not quite sure about, but if they come to me later I can add to it. Right now I've got some things that will help these guys."

Most of the investigative team was assembled in the sheriff's squad room when we walked in. Sheriff Pat Thomas introduced Bob, who took it from there.

"Let me start out by saying I appreciate all of the help I've gotten from you and the hard work everyone's done on this case," Bob said. "I want to try to give you some information I've deduced from everything that's been made available to me at this juncture. First of all, I do not believe there is any connection between this kidnapping and the Johnny Gosch case. There are a couple reasons I feel comfortable in saying that. One is that Johnny's body has never been found. In this case the body was found a couple of days after he went missing and was, in fact, probably left there the day he was kidnapped. What really differentiates these two cases is the fact that in this kidnapping, the UNSUB did what he did in a pretty random and hurried manner. Thus, I have concluded it's not the same guy."

He looked around to see if there were any questions and then continued. "The UNSUB is going to be a white male in his late teens or early twenties. There is nothing about this crime that would indicate we're dealing with an experienced and sophisticated killer. I believe this is the first person he has killed, so at this point we're not dealing with a serial killer. I believe he does something that puts him into contact with kids the age of the victim. I don't know what that may be. Perhaps coaching a youth soccer team. Something like that. He's going to be a smaller guy, by that I mean well under six feet tall and smaller in build. I say that because he chose a smaller victim he could handle if there was a confrontation."

People in the room were furiously taking notes. "Now, here's one other thing I want you to consider very closely. I strongly believe this UNSUB is a lower-ranking airman on the base. I would say you need to find out how many people have been assigned there in the past few months. That might be up to six months. I don't know how many that would be, but I'll leave it up to you to figure that out. In that group of people, you're going to find this guy.

"Let me add a few more things to that. He's not going to have any more than a high school education, and his job is going to be fairly menial and nontechnical. People he knows will consider him odd, and quiet. He has bizarre sexual fantasies, but it's not likely he will have mentioned any of that to people he works with. All of this odd sexual stuff didn't just start a few weeks ago. He's been obsessed with it for most of his life, probably even before his early teens. He's going to have a collection of pornography, and he also may have some detective magazines. We've found this with quite a few offenders in the past. So, the lead from this might be, if he has a roommate, he's probably walked in on the UNSUB reading some of this stuff. Or even caught him masturbating." Again, Bob scanned the room. "Does anyone have any questions so far?"

Everyone seemed to be busy writing and hanging on his every word. I knew they wanted that one, single clue that would lead them to the guy who committed this horrifying crime. People in the entire area were more than a little nervous, and parents were in fear to even send their kids off to school.

"We're looking for a guy who has had a recent stressful event in his life, and that was what probably pushed him over the edge from fantasy to reality," Bob said. "That could include a number of different events such as his parents getting divorced, breaking up with a girlfriend, or being fired from a job or disciplined. He's a lonely guy, so perhaps moving from one place to here put him under a lot of stress, again, something that caused him to act out in a violent manner. I think this guy has some latent homosexual tendencies, but he's not going to be someone who is active in the gay scene around town. He won't hang out in the usual haunts gay men go to, such as gay bars or other hangouts.

"I believe he's familiar with the area where the boy's body was left. Pete and I spent quite a bit of time out there, and I think it's someplace where he might go to think and just drive around. It's quiet out there and he may have just parked by himself along the road. It's possible he went back to the scene after he killed the boy, and that he'll go there again. This may sound like he wants to get caught, but the fact is, a lot of these people will return to the scene to fantasize about what they did. As hard as it may be to believe, they are highly stimulated by re-thinking the event, what they did, and how they did it. He's going to continue fantasizing about what he did, and unfortunately there is one more important thing I need to tell you."

Bob paused and looked somberly at the group of attentive officers, deputies, and agents. "If we don't figure out who it is, he's going to do it again, once the heat dies down. And that will be sooner rather than later. Right now he's living in the middle of having achieved his greatest fantasy—it finally came true. But, since it probably didn't go exactly the way he planned, he's going to refine his fantasy even more and he's going to be compelled to do it all over again."

Little did he know how true that would be.

"I don't want to put any more pressure on you than you already have," he continued, "but I do think if you use some of these leads, you're going to figure out who he is. I want to wish you the best of luck. If you have any questions, Pete and I will be around here the rest of the day. I've got to head back to Quantico tomorrow, and I think Pete needs to get back to Cedar Rapids. Good hunting."

I dropped Bob off at the airport the next morning and headed back to Cedar Rapids. It was time for life to get back to normal for me. It had been a stressful couple of days, but it had also been a great learning experience. I felt like I'd learned at the foot of the master and a man who had a body of knowledge only a few people in the world had. I didn't know if I'd ever get to that point, but I was very proud to know Bob and to now consider him a friend and confidant.

CHAPTER THIRTY

Family Life

Gradually, things began to return to normal for me, both at work and at home. My kids were starting their sophomore year at John F. Kennedy High School in Cedar Rapids and, of course, had the usual trepidation of making new friends and making adjustments at a brand-new school.

My son, Kary, had hit the puberty growth spurt over the summer, gaining several more inches up to six-foot-four, but he was still as thin as a fence post. Football was out of the question. He thought about trying out for the basketball team, but with no prior experience had few chances to even make the junior varsity. He opted for intramurals and seemed content with that, plus officiating some of the intramural games.

Because she had asthma, sports for my daughter, Loni, wasn't an issue. I wanted to make sure both of them had a better high school experience than I did, so we sat down one night and reviewed our options with their mother.

"What are the possibilities for outside activities?" Mary Ann asked.

"I don't know." I looked at the kids. "What do you guys think?"

Loni, the more outspoken of the two, seemed reluctant to speak. "I don't know, Dad. Why do we have to do anything?"

"Because I'm not going to let what happened to me happen to you. If I had played sports or gotten involved in some other activities, I doubt I would have dropped out of high school."

"But you tried to play basketball and football didn't you?" Kary asked.

"Yeah. But I just wasn't quite good enough. Frankly, I don't think that helped a lot, either."

Loni asked, "Is there something *you* want us to do?"

Mary Ann replied to that. "It's not about what your dad and I want you to do. It's more important that you pick something that you think you'll like."

"That's true," I said. "I don't want to force you guys into something you don't want to do, because then you won't be happy. And that's definitely not what I want to happen. But, we're going to figure something out."

We discussed some of the options, reviewing the handbook from the school. Finally, getting to the "T's" in the book, we hit on the theater arts program. "How about this, guys?" Since the kids had been old enough to appreciate live shows, we'd taken them to plenty of community theater and Broadway productions in California, and other shows which came through the University of Iowa in Iowa City.

Loni's reluctance came out again. "But Dad, we don't have any experience. Neither one of us has ever acted, or anything close to it."

"I realize that," I replied. "But that's exactly where you would get the experience. The kids you'd get to know in the theater program would be good students and, I assume, nice kids. I really think it's something that would work. Both of you love theater."

Kary was similarly reluctant, but he was the more passive of the two at that point in his life. "I'm not sure, Dad."

I was ready to come up with a compromise. "Okay. Let's do this. I'd like you both to think about it and talk about it. Fair enough?"

"Yes," Loni said. "If we've got to do something, this might work, but let us think about it. When do you want us to let you know?"

"How about we sit down here Friday night? No, wait, I've got a better idea. We haven't gone out to eat for a while, so let's do that. Good plan?" They all nodded their heads. No one in my family ever rejected the idea of going out to dinner. We didn't do it that often, so it was a treat when we did. That's exactly what my strategy was. I really hoped the kids would come around.

They did.

Jim Whalen, in the meantime, was spending more and more time in Dubuque, Iowa, which was one of the main distribution points for the drug network they'd identified. Plus, they had a couple of solid informants who were feeding them quality information which Jim had been compiling into an extensive affidavit in support of wiretaps on telephones in Dubuque, Cedar Rapids, and Minneapolis.

"How in the hell are you going to do all this?" I asked one day when he was in the office.

"Easy. We're going to have three phone lines to monitor, and we're going to do it all right here."

"And who's going to do the monitoring? I did a couple of these things in Los Angeles, and we had to do twenty-four hour shifts, seven days a week. These guys don't keep the same hours we do. Plus, a federal wiretap can only be monitored by federal agents. We ain't got a whole lot of them around here, you know, and I'm not interested in working twenty-four hours a day."

"Don't worry. I've got it covered." Jim smiled. "The bureau has come up with a new deal and the Department of Justice has signed off on it. With all of these drug cases we're cranking up around the country, they had to do something."

"And that would be what?"

"We're going to get some of the local officers here and in Dubuque sworn in as acting deputy United States Marshals."

"You're kidding me."

"Nope. The boss is coming out here next week. He has the authority to swear everyone in as a federal officer and we're good to go."

"Well, that's a new one on me."

"Yup. By the way, I need you to be involved. There's only one guy out here who has ever worked one of these things, and that would be you."

"Damn. It really sounds like fun Jim, but I'm more than a little buried. We've got a bunch of bank robbers in custody and the school bus case is still hanging over my head. Once we get an indictment by the Grand Jury, I'm going to be up to my you-know-what in alligators."

"I know that, but I need your experience for a few weeks if you can do it. We can figure out a way to get the young agents involved, but they're going to need some direction. Again, that would be you."

"I'll do my best," I said.

"I know that. By the way, the boss called the other day and we're both up for a QSI (Quality Step Increase). I know you got one a while back, but as soon as the indictments come out on the school bus case, you're getting another one."

"Wow. How about that?" Getting bumped up another pay grade meant some serious money, and also meant I'd get up to GS-13 two years early.

"You deserve it, Pete. You've busted your butt since the day you got here."

"Well, I suppose I've had my moments, but I sure hope I get to spend some time with my family during all of this."

"Yeah. I know exactly what you mean."

CHAPTER THIRTY ONE

Buried in Bank Robberies in Eastern Iowa

The next week we had not one, but two bank robberies in our territory. That was a first in the years I'd been in Cedar Rapids.

Jim was in Dubuque when the first call came in on a fairly quiet Tuesday afternoon. I was the only one in the office, with both of our new agents out handling some of the one-shot leads and background check cases.

The phone rang at about the time I was ready to wrap things up for the day and head home.

"Pete, its Mike Richardson in Tama." Mike was an old friend and had been the sheriff in Tama County for about ten years. Located about forty miles west of Cedar Rapids on Highway 30, Tama was best known as the location of a somewhat notorious Indian settlement. It wasn't a reservation, since it was owned by the Meskwaki tribe, but it had a complex history going back to the ancient Sac and Fox Indians and a famous Indian Chief, Keokuk, for whom a town in Iowa is named.

"Don't tell me, we've got a shooting on the settlement."

"Nope. Bad guess. Bank robbery."

"Oh damn. But there isn't a bank on the settlement, is there?"

"Nope. This one's in town. But I'm going to make this one easy for you. We've got a suspect in custody."

"No kidding. What happened?"

"You sitting down?"

"Of course. What else do FBI agents do all day?"

"Yeah, I know," he chuckled. Most local and county law enforcement officers had no clue what FBI agents did during any given day or week, so many assumed that was nothing. Mike knew better. I'd been out to the settlement many times, working closely with Mike and his deputies on a myriad of different investigations.

"So, Sheriff, before I jump in the Batmobile and race out there at about five hundred miles per hour, what've we got?"

"You're gonna love this. A young gal gets dressed up as a man and goes into the bank with a gun. Small revolver. No shots fired."

"That's always a good thing," I commented with a laugh.

"Yup, it is. Anyhow, she does the robbery and runs like hell out of the bank. One of the women tellers runs outside and sees her race a half block down the street to a parking lot. She jumps in a car, and the teller gets a description. Didn't go all the way up to the car and get a plate, but that's not too bad."

"No it isn't. Good for her."

"She comes back and by then they've got us on the phone. We put the call out and get a couple of our deputies rolling that way. The teller gives us a car description."

"Cool. So did one of 'em pull her over?"

"No, this gets even better. The parking lot she was in was icy. She tried to take off but her car high-centered on a berm of piled snow in the parking lot."

"Nice. So what happens then?"

"Well, she's stuck, so she heads over to a gas station to see if the guy can pull her out. Just so happens the tow truck driver's got a police scanner. They head back to her car and he notices the description of the car, and the gal matches what they just broadcasted. He puts two and two together and figures out what happened."

"Hopefully, he didn't try to arrest her."

"Nah, smarter than that," Mike said. "He figured she had a gun, so he gave her a story that he forgot his tow chain. He tells her to stay there and heads back to the gas station and calls us. By the time she figured out what was happening, I had a deputy there. She didn't put up any resistance, so we've got her down here now."

"Easiest bank robbery I ever solved," I said, leaning back in my chair. "I'm gonna take full credit for it, you know."

"Yeah, I know the drill. We made this one easy for

you."

"What's her story?"

"This is good, too. She said some of her girlfriends were going down to Florida for the winter, but she didn't have any money. Couldn't figure out a way to get some, so she thought she'd rob a bank."

"Definite candidate for the dean's list right there."

"No doubt about it."

"How much did she get?"

"About nine thousand bucks."

"Wow. That's actually quite a bit."

"Yeah, they had quite a bit on hand, but she still didn't get it all."

"All right, I'll be out there in about an hour. I'll set the Batmobile's speed-o-meter a little slower."

"See you when you get here. Drive safely."

"Will do."

I got on the radio to see if I could get a hold of our two new agents, and was lucky enough to catch both of them heading back into the office. We all arrived at the bank about the same time. "You guys get some statements and I'm going to head over to the sheriff's office," I told them. We had it wrapped up in a couple of hours, put the female robber in the back seat of my car and headed back to Cedar Rapids to deposit her in the county jail on a federal hold. I expressed my appreciation to Mike and told him I'd write up a nice letter on FBI letterhead and send it off to our SAC to sign and send to him and the department.

Thanks to their good work, the young woman wound up with a ten-year, full-ride scholarship to the medium security federal prison in Yankton, South Dakota. At least she was fairly close to home. But Yankton will never be confused with Florida. Particularly in the cold Midwest winters.

The second bank robbery occurred on Friday morning at about ten o'clock. It proved to be a lot more challenging.

The small farming community of Cascade, Iowa sits on prime farming land about forty miles northeast of Cedar Rapids, in Dubuque County, and about as far south and west from Dubuque as a person can travel and still be in the same county. As with most small Iowa communities, the bank was not only a revenue stream for farmers, but also something of a community meeting place. Farmers coming into town would often run into their friends, and being in no big hurry to get anywhere, would spend some time enjoying a free cup of coffee or two, and chat with the bank president. In its entire history, going back to the late 1800s, the bank had never been robbed.

That changed when two armed men appeared in the lobby that Friday morning. They both wore bandit masks, covering only their lower face, so the tellers and customers inside the bank could readily see one was a black male, and the other was white. Both men were fairly short, less than five-foot-ten inches in height, and both were slender in build. Each wore a baseball hat, one with a Pioneer Seed Corn label, and the other with an Iowa "Tiger Hawk" emblem on the front.

Upon entering the lobby, the black male shouted, "This is a robbery!" and immediately discharged what the witnesses described as a "deafening" shot from a sawed-off shotgun. Fortunately, the shot was aimed at the ceiling. He then yelled, "All y'all motha fuckas get down!" He didn't need to say it a second time. There were four customers and four employees in the bank, and none of them chose to become heroes. The white male headed directly to the bank vault, which was wide open as it always was during operating hours. A teller noticed he had what appeared to be a white pillowcase in one hand, and a pistol in the other. The black male remained in the lobby, guarding the customers and employees, and presumably assuring no one else came in the bank.

Within a matter of minutes, the white male raced out of the vault and yelled, "Okay, let's get out of here!" The black male screamed, "All right, you peoples stay on the floor for five minutes. If one of you gets up, I'm gonna be standing here to shoot your ass." The employees and customers, shocked into a state of disbelief, stayed on the floor until one finally looked up and determined both men were long gone.

Local police and the Dubuque County Sheriff's Department were immediately notified by bank employees. Officers and deputies raced to the bank and took statements from witnesses. A car description was quickly obtained and radioed to all local agencies.

Deputies in the county began checking local roads for a dark-colored Ford sedan. With that general a description, the vehicle wasn't found.

Jim Whalen happened to be at the Dubuque County Sheriff's Department when the call came in. He tried to call the office, but no one was there. I was in Iowa City, and our new agents were out getting their jobs done. Jim paged me and I called him back. I finished what I was doing and headed for Cascade, while calling both of our new agents on the radio. Eventually, I made contact with them and told them to meet me at the bank in Cascade. It took me a good hour and a half to get there, and Jim was at the scene with a sheriff's captain when I arrived. They'd rolled in a good hour before I got there, and had some useful information from witnesses.

"It's a salt and pepper team," Jim said. "One black and one white."

"Big clue there," I replied. "It's not a couple of locals." There wasn't a single black person living in Cascade, or for that matter anywhere else in Dubuque County, other than in the town of Dubuque.

"Yeah, but I think we've got something," Jim continued. He motioned toward the sheriff's captain. "Pat here checked with a few of his sources and found out a black guy and a white guy left the halfway house in Dubuque together this morning. They were both supposed to be headed for jobs they had, but neither of 'em showed up."

"That's interesting. Either one of 'em got a car?"

"We're checking it all out now."

"Great." I looked at the captain. "If we get one, can you guys put out an All-Points Bulletin? I could do it through our office in Omaha, but it'd take forever and still not get done right."

"No problem," he said. "As soon as we've got it, we'll get it out to everybody in Eastern Iowa, Wisconsin, and Illinois." Cascade was reasonably close to the borders of both states.

"That sounds great." I turned to Jim and asked, "Can you stick with us for a while on this one?"

"Sure, let's see where it goes." I knew Jim would help out to the extent possible, but if there was some paperwork to do, I was going to do it, or I'd have to get one of the youngsters to handle it. The facts were coming at us pretty fast, and I was taking notes furiously. Somewhere down the line, I suspected there was going to be a need for a search warrant. And I knew who was going to write the affidavit when that time came to pass.

CHAPTER THIRTY TWO

"Oh, Dennis...Are You in There?"

J. Edgar Hoover was reputed to be both loathsome and suspicious of resident agencies and agents, once describing them as "indispensable but necessary evils." Headquarters agents were similarly suspicious of RAs, assuming agents in outlying cities were out playing golf, working out, or simply spending all of their time goofing off. In prior years, there might have been some truth to all of that, but my experience in Cedar Rapids was quite the opposite. Jim Whalen and I were but two of the sixty agents in the entire Omaha Field Division. There were two consecutive years when Jim and I accounted for one third of all indictments and convictions for the entire field division. And with Jim's drug case and my school bus case, those numbers weren't going to change. If anything, they'd go up.

Years later, when I assessed it, I still felt Jim and I were simply two very competitive people. I made my mind up that I was going to be as good as him. I'm still not sure if I did it. He knew what he was up against, and he wasn't going to let me overtake him. It went back and forth. This bank robbery was a classic example of what could happen when hard-working resident agents worked closely together with local and state law enforcement officers. Things were going to get done. Maybe it was simple inertia. Whatever it was, Jim and I managed to get the job done, and then some.

By eight o'clock that night, we had gathered all of the information we could from witnesses at the bank and in town. Jim Whalen called a meeting at the sheriff's department. We had officers and deputies from all over the county plus all four of us agents from Cedar Rapids, so it was a pretty full house in the briefing room.

Standing in front at a podium, with sheriff's captain Pat O'Donnell at his side, Jim started the meeting. "Okay guys, here's what we've got. The bank in Cascade got robbed at about ten o'clock this morning. One of the guys cranked off a shotgun round into the roof of the bank, but no one was injured. Thank God. To make a long story short, we've developed two suspects. Dennis Ringer is a white male who is on parole for a whole variety of crimes. The second guy is Robert 'Hollywood' Henderson. He's a black male who was paroled for bank robbery a few months ago. Both of these guys were on parole to the halfway house here in Dubuque."

Jim was doing an amazing job of putting the facts in a logical format. I'd always felt fortunate to have been working with him for years, and this session told me just how lucky I'd been. He was one of the brightest guys I'd ever been around, and articulate enough that he should have run for political office. The guy could charm the scales right off a lizard.

"We think they swiped a car a couple of blocks away from the halfway house and drove it down to Cascade to commit the robbery." He held up a sheet of paper. "You've all got the description of the car and both suspects on that sheet. Everyone got one?"

Everyone seemed to have one, so he continued. "We don't know where these guys are right now. Ringer is from Council Bluffs, so that might be where he's headed. Henderson might be a bit of a loose cannon. He's from Chicago, but he grew up in East Saint Louis. He spent some time in Des Moines and got arrested down south in Burlington a few years ago." He held up another piece of paper that unfolded below his elbow. "This is his rap sheet. Why this guy is out of jail, I have no idea." Everyone nodded. "Four pages, guys. This character just doesn't get it."

"So here's the deal," Jim continued. "We don't know if these guys are still here or if they've headed for their own comfort zone, wherever that may be. If they are here, we think there's a good chance they may be holed up in a hotel or motel, but we have no idea if they are still together. If I had my guess, I'd say they split the money up and went their separate ways. They got over forty-eight thousand dollars from the robbery, but the press doesn't know that, and I don't want you to say anything if the press asks you. We never release the amount of money that was taken in a bank robbery. Everybody okay with that?"

No one had a comment, but they seemed surprised at the amount that had been taken. Many criminals think they can solve all of their financial problems by robbing a bank and landing a bounty of over a hundred thousand dollars. Little do they, know the average loss on bank robberies was closer to twenty-five hundred dollars, and usually a lot less than that.

"I've talked to the press and told them there was an 'undetermined amount' taken," Jim said. "That's our standard answer and most of 'em know it. But they'll press you for an exact amount, and we definitely don't want to tell them how much was taken in this robbery. We've had more than our share of robberies in the past year, and none of them came close to this one. If the potential bank robbers out there get a number, I'll let you guess which banks are going to be robbed in the future." A point well made. Obviously, it would be the banks in rural areas.

"Let me defer to Captain O'Donnell. He's going to give us some specific assignments to see if we can find these guys or the car."

The captain had a sheet passed out to everyone in the room. "Here's what we're going to do. I've got every hotel and motel in the area of Dubuque listed, and every one of you is part of a two-person team to check the motels and hotels to see if we can find either the suspects or the car, or both, at one of these places. We're going to have the federal agents go across the border into Wisconsin and Illinois and make the same checks. Any questions?"

The list was very clear and the responsibilities were set out for each team. It was going to take some time, but the objectives were obvious to everyone involved. By nine o'clock, all eight teams were out on the street.

Somewhere around eleven-thirty, one of the search teams was making their last assigned check at the Holiday Inn on Main Street near downtown Dubuque. "We've got the car," a deputy radioed in to the sheriff's department. That caused a flurry of activity and, of course, got the rest of the search teams headed toward the hotel. Jim and I, accompanied by Captain O'Donnell, piled into a car to head over to the hotel and direct a search for the bank robbers.

Fortunately, most of the officers, agents, and deputies were not in uniform. "Let's assume they're both in there," Jim said. "Where is the most likely place we're gonna find 'em?"

"Probably the bar," an officer answered.

"My guess too," Jim replied. "All right, here's what I want to do. Two of you head for the bar and look casual. Get a beer in the lounge. Look around. Hang out there for a while. If they're in there, don't pounce on 'em. Remember they might be armed. We don't want anyone to get shot. Got it?"

Jim looked around at the group and picked two out to check the bar. "Once you feel comfortable, if one or both of 'em aren't there, talk to a waitress and the bartender. See if these guys were in the lounge. Find out what you can. They've got tons of money to blow, so both of them are probably drunk as hell right now. The rest of you guys wait out here. Captain O'Donnell and I are going to the registration desk to see if we've got one or both of 'em checked in. Stay out of sight as best you can and we'll keep you in the loop. Any questions?" There weren't any. "Let's get this done. You guys out here might keep an eye on the car just in case they show up. And don't forget, we've got at least one sawed-off shotgun and a revolver involved. I don't know how dangerous they are, but if they've got guns with them, they're dangerous. Be careful. Please. We all need to get home tonight."

The captain and Jim were back in about ten minutes, followed shortly by the two guys who went to the bar. We all gathered in a circle. There were about twenty of us involved at this juncture. "We've got one of them checked in," Jim said. "The registration desk positively identified Dennis Ringer, but they never saw Henderson. So it looks like they split up. We've got his room number, but we don't know if he's there or not right now."

"He probably is," said one of the guys who checked the bar. "It looks like he spent about four hours in the bar, throwing money around, buying drinks for everyone and trying to pick up every woman in the place."

"How'd that work out?" O'Donnell asked.

The officer laughed. "Not well, but he's as horny as a three-peckered billy goat. He bought almost every woman in the bar at least one drink and was flashing quite a wad of money. Left the waitress a twenty-dollar tip, too. None of the women would have anything to do with him since he's such a weaselly little ugly bald guy. At least that's what the waitresses were saying, but he must think with a ton of money in his pockets, he's hotter than a dancin' bobcat."

"When did he leave the bar?" Jim asked.

"About an hour ago. The waitress said he was bagged enough that she refused to serve him anymore."

"Well, it's fair to assume he's passed out in his room by now," Jim said. "We've got his room number, so what I think we're going to do is place a pretext call to the room and see if he's there. Just pretend we called the wrong room and apologize. Let's do that first and we'll come up with a plan for how we're going to get him out of there." Jim glanced around and stopped at me. "Pete, why don't you head in there and call the room and we'll figure out what we're going to do when you get back."

By the time I got back to report that I got an answer in the room, Jim had a plan pretty well worked out. He sent one of the deputies to talk to the hotel clerk, and had him call the rooms around Ringer's, just in case. "We told him to explain to them what's going on and to have them vacate the rooms for a little while. That should be done by now."

One of the deputies was a fairly attractive young woman and Jim thought she could lure him out of the room, particularly if he was drunk and his defenses were down. We'd have several people standing outside the door, flattened out against the wall. She'd knock on the room and call out his name, sounding as seductive as possible.

"You okay with doing this, Dawn?" Jim asked, and she nodded. "Just in case, I'd like you to put your vest on. Put on a little lipstick and fluff up your hair, and he'll probably figure that his efforts in the bar finally paid off. All you've gotta do when he answers the door is bat your eyes at him and ask him if he remembers you from the bar. Before you have that said, these guys will be inside the door and on him like white on rice."

To me, Jim said, "Pete, I want you to gear up and

you're going to go in the door first."

He pointed at Mike Dudley, one of our new agents. "Mike, you go in right behind Pete."

Then he pointed at two of the other officers, both of whom were good-sized guys. "You guys good with that?" They both nodded. "All right, gear up and let's do this."

The plan worked perfectly. Dawn knocked on the door a couple of times, and then in her best seductive voice called out, "Dennis, are you in there? Oh, Dennis." She sang out the latter. "Dennis, are you in there?"

Momentarily, we heard a man's voice at the door. "Who is it?"

"I was in the bar, Dennis. You bought me a drink." He was probably looking out the peephole, and all he was seeing in his drunken stupor was a good-looking woman standing there wanting to come into the room. Surely, he thought his luck was about to change. We heard the security lock disengage and the door cracked open. No sooner did that happen than Dawn stepped back and I slammed into the door. Ringer was flattened against the wall and I reached around, grabbed him by the neck, and threw him on the floor. It all took about five seconds, if that. The others raced into the room, stepping over the two of us. I had Ringer on the floor with a chokehold around his neck. He wasn't going anywhere.

Ringer was the only one in the room, but his .38 revolver and the money were on the side of the bed he hadn't been sleeping on, along with a fifth of Jack Daniels Black, which was half empty. We booked him into the Dubuque County jail and would have a deputy haul him down to Cedar Rapids the next day for an initial appearance before the United States Magistrate.

Some plans are just meant to work out.

Ringer told us he didn't know what happened to Henderson after they'd split the money. "He said he was gonna buy a car and get the hell out of here. I dropped him off at a car lot just outside of town and I headed up here. I don't have any idea where he is now." We found the lot the next day and determined "Hollywood" Henderson had paid cash for a used Lincoln Continental, maroon in color, and took off heading south. Other than that, the car dealer didn't know anything, except that Henderson had used his true name and paid five thousand in cash, which he thought was unusual but wasn't about to turn down.

About a month later, I got a call from Ted Behne, the police chief in Burlington, Iowa. One of his officers had a few contacts in their small black community and learned there was a new guy hanging out who seemed to be flush with money, and better yet, had been seen driving a maroon Lincoln Continental.

Mike Dudley and I arrived in Burlington within a couple of hours and, working with the local officers, we found the Lincoln parked in back of a house. Burlington officers helped us talk to the residents, but they evidenced no knowledge of Henderson's whereabouts. "If he's not here, do you mind if we just check to make sure?" I asked. "We drove all the way down here and I don't feel like we'd be doing our job if we didn't check. Then we'll leave you alone and everyone can get back to their own business."

We found Henderson hiding in the attic. Dudley raked him over the coals at the police department, and I talked to the chief about harboring charges against the people in the house. We decided we had better things to do than that, and in searching the car recovered about fifteen thousand dollars of the money in the trunk.

Both of the bank robbers got twenty years in a federal prison, and we had yet more statistical accomplishments to rack up for the office.

There'd be more to come.

CHAPTER THIRTY THREE

Finally – Indictments on the Bid Rigging Case

Several weeks had passed since the kidnapping in Bellevue, and I thought it might be a good idea to get an update and then call Bob Ressler to fill him in on the latest details. I knew he'd appreciate it, and he deserved it after dropping everything and coming out to Omaha. Besides, it probably wouldn't take me more than a few minutes. So the next Monday afternoon I gave Chuck Kempf a call.

"We're not much farther along than we were when you left," Chuck said. "We've had a couple of possible suspects, but nothing panned out. We're still working on it, but we're really not getting much of anything accomplished."

"How about looking into the possibility that the guy was a newly assigned airman on the base?"

"Nothing on that yet. Still working on it. There's a lot of people out there and a lot more turnover than what you'd think, it seems."

"I can imagine. I know it's a pretty big base. Ressler sounded pretty hot on the idea that it's a new guy assigned to the base, but it's your case and you've got to do what you think is best."

"We've got a few more things going, but no luck yet." Chuck went on to tell me the ASAC had come up with what they called the "Pervert Squad," and they were out doing exactly what Ressler said wasn't going to be productive: rousting some of the homosexuals in the Omaha area. "We came up with a couple of possibilities, even an Air Force major, but while they both looked interesting for a while it just didn't work out. So we're pretty much back to square one again."

I gave Bob Ressler a call in Quantico and filled him

in on the progress, or lack of it. He was more than a little distressed with part of the squad chasing homosexuals around. "I don't know how I could have been more clear about it," he said, sounding more than a little miffed. "They're just wasting their time. The best lead is going to be on that base, dammit. I guess you can lead a horse to water..."

"I suppose they've got to keep doing *something*," I said. "Chuck's got his heart in the right place, but not all of our bosses are the sharpest nails in the box."

"Yeah, I kinda got that sense, too. Well, thanks for the info and keep me in the loop."

"You can count on it."

Little did I know how soon I would be calling him again.

By the middle of November, Jim Whalen was nearly ready to get his wiretap up and running. He had acquired a room in the basement of the federal building and had everything ready to go, short of getting the affidavit approved and the wiretap order signed by a federal judge.

A couple of days before we'd start monitoring the lines, he said, "Pete, you're the only one out here who has ever done one of these things."

"Actually, I had one of my own, and monitored on two others."

"Good. I'm going to need you to help me when we get up and running, but before we start I need you to do one thing for me."

"Tell me what and it's done."

"We're going to have one of the Assistant U.S. Attorneys give us a briefing before we start monitoring, but you and I both know they've never sat on one and had to do the actual work. So that's where I'm going to rely on you."

"Okay, you need me to go through the nuts and bolts. How it works, right?"

"Exactly."

"No problem. Tell me the date and I'm there."

"I will. I know you've got a lot going, so I don't want you to be on the lines full-time. Maybe just a couple days a week would work better. Certainly the first few days, mainly to get the guys trained and to have them understand how we've got to minimize personal calls."

"That's always an interesting problem. We had the bad guys put their girlfriends on the phones on one we did in Los Angeles. They'd let 'em talk for a while and we thought it was just girl talk, so we'd cut it off. Then we started to figure out what they were doing. The guys would let 'em talk for a couple minutes, and they'd take over. So it can be a problem."

"We'll play it by ear, but I think we'll have it figured out pretty quickly. There's never been a wiretap here in Iowa, so there's no reason for these guys to think they're being listened to. They'll probably be careful and have codes, but we can figure that out fairly soon."

A week after we had the wiretaps up and running smoothly, I was in the office when the phone rang. "Pete, it's Mark Curtis." Mark was the number two attorney on the school bus case, which I'd almost forgotten about with everything else going.

"Mark, good to hear from you. It's been a couple months, hasn't it?"

"Yeah, something like that."

"So, what's up?" My bosses had been bugging me for months about when we were going to have indictments on the bid rigging case. While I *was* the case agent, *I* wasn't the one who ultimately made the decision on when the case would go to the Grand Jury for an indictment. That had been out of my hands for months, and the Anti-Trust Division in Chicago seemed to work at a very slow pace. I had absolutely no control over that decision. I wasn't the prosecutor.

Mark said, "I just got done talking to Alonzo and our bosses in the Attorney General's office on a big conference call to D.C. They want us to present the case to the Grand Jury for indictments next week."

I doubt he heard me gulp. "Wow. It's finally here."

"Yeah, it's taken quite a bit of work, as you know." I did know that, because I'd gone over to their office for a week that summer, just to see what I could do to help. Not much. They were grinding through tons of paperwork and had several attorneys and paralegals working with the documents. "It's going to be a very document-intensive case. But at this point, we feel like we have all of the ducks lined up and we're ready to roll."

"I am too, and now I can finally get my bosses off my ass. I'll let them know what the plans are and I'll be ready. I assume I'm going to be your summary witness at Grand Jury?"

"You are. We're going to have you return some documents and explain the documents to the Grand Jury, and pretty much wrap up the case and tie a big ribbon around it."

"How about you let me know in advance what you're going to be asking me? I don't like to look like an idiot in front of the Grand Jury. I've testified a lot of times and have almost always gotten questions from members of the jury."

"Good idea. I'll work on that and get it over to you in the next few days. Certainly by the end of the week."

"That'll work. I'll talk to you later and see you next week."

I immediately drafted a memo to the file with copies to my supervisor and SAC. I knew they were sitting on pins and needles, because a big case in a small division made them look good, too.

CHAPTER THIRTY FOUR

Drugs and School Buses

By Friday of the next week, I was ready to sit down and have a glass or two of wine after I left the office. And that's exactly what I did. Mary Ann and I were planning to take the kids out to dinner so we could all catch up and connect as a family. However, they had a dress rehearsal for West Side Story, which was going to have its premiere at the high school the next day. So those plans went down the drain. Instead, we got some Chinese take-out for dinner and decided to spend the night at home watching TV. That was a fine end of the week for me. I enjoyed more than a couple of glasses of wine and got to bed a little early.

The kids had been putting in long hours at rehearsals, and often wouldn't get home until nine or ten o'clock at night. I had no clue how they were getting all of their schoolwork done, but I didn't have any indications there were problems. Loni was very self-disciplined and managed her time and work very well. Kary was simply so bright that he breezed through everything. Their days were so full that I rarely saw them.

Jim Whalen's wiretap had been approved, and was supposed to be up and running on Monday night. As luck would have it, a huge snowstorm descended on Iowa that morning, with blizzard conditions that essentially shut down the roads into Cedar Rapids. Travel was hazardous, so some of the officers and sheriff's deputies who were expected to arrive and get sworn in as deputy United States Marshals were stranded.

Iowa could quickly become a fierce place in the winter. I had discovered that in my first winter in Cedar Rapids when we had over four feet of snow, and three weekends with temperatures of thirty below zero and wind chills in the negative sixties and seventies. I'd never seen anything like it. An arctic low had descended over the Midwest, and Iowa was right in the eye of the storm. The heating bills were unfathomable, not to mention feeling like we were prisoners in our house. I wondered why I'd ever decided to leave California. When the weather changed the fourth weekend, we went out to dinner only to find everyone else in town had decided to do the same thing. Cedar Rapids had a case of mass cabin fever. We were lucky to find a restaurant.

Our SAC arrived in town the day before the snow started to fall, so he'd dodged the storm. But he was stuck at the Five Seasons Center hotel and, with a lack of people available to swear in, decided to stay in his room. Wise decision to stay off the streets, all of which were either snow packed or icy. Or both.

Jim was frustrated. "First damn federal wiretap in the history of Iowa, and we can't get it up and running." He'd called me a few times over the weekend, mainly to check on details and mechanics about how the monitoring would happen. Our technically-trained agents had rolled into town in a van on Friday, and hauled a ton of recorders and other equipment into the basement of the federal building. Jim was there for the duration, watching them set up the equipment, do all of the tests, and seemingly run wires all over the place. Setting up a wiretap on phones in several different cities was quite a bit more complicated than climbing a telephone pole with two alligator clips, putting them on a few select wires, and then donning a set of headphones, which was the way it was done in the "old days" of the FBI.

By the next morning the storm had cleared, snowplows had done their jobs, and everyone who needed to be there had arrived by noon. Our techs explained the nuts and bolts of what they had set up, showed them the mechanics of how to use the equipment, and then it was up to our supervising Assistant United States Attorney, Rich Mahoney, to explain the legalities involved in listening to calls. "When the conversation is personal, you can listen in until you feel the conversation is staying personal. Once that happens, you need to shut down the recorders. You can, however, turn the equipment back on after about thirty seconds to see if the conversation has turned to pertinent or criminal matters. If that's happened, you can continue to record." Some of the guys in the room looked around at one another and while they seemed to understand what Mahoney was saying, they didn't realize they couldn't monitor the entire conversation.

My SAC dutifully administered the oath of office to all of the officers and deputies gathered in the monitoring room, and presented each of them with a card that identified them as a Special Deputy United States Marshal. It was a formality, but was probably an important career event to some of the local officers.

Once our AUSA departed, I spent some time with the officers and deputies who would be on the lines monitoring calls.

"Rich is right," I explained. "A phone is a phone, and the people we're going to be listening to are not going to be having conversations that are criminal in nature every time the phone rings. But when they do, we need to not only listen and record the drug-related calls, but we need to take notes about what the call was generally about." I pointed out the logs they'd keep, explaining how they would need to note what the call was about, and if it was personal to indicate that. They would also need to note that they'd checked back into the call to assure that the conversation hadn't changed into a call involving drug trafficking.

"When you make your notes, indicate the times of calls in the logs, so Jim can pull the tapes and listen to them later. He's ultimately the person who will decide whether calls are pertinent or not. If you're going to err, do it on the side of caution. If we record too many personal calls, the entire wiretap might be thrown out by the court. We don't want that to happen." Each person who would be monitoring was given an opportunity to test out the system with several pretext calls we set up, so the training we needed to do was as thorough as we could possibly accomplish. Hopefully, they would all comply with the legal requirements, because the courts had set forth clear guidelines since we were dealing with a high level of personal security for people to be free and open in their communications.

Aside from that, the rest of the week was more than a little busy. My attorneys from the Anti-Trust Division in

Chicago arrived on Wednesday morning, well in advance of the storm. Lead attorney Alonzo Bradley and I spent several hours going over my testimony before the Grand Jury. I had testified a lot of times, but when we were done, I had never felt quite so prepared. These guys are really thorough, I thought.

Alonzo and Mark Curtis also spent a little time asking me some questions I might expect from jury members, but Alonzo said, "You can never anticipate what they're going to ask you. If you aren't sure what to say, just look over at me and I'll give 'em an answer." From prior experience before Grand Juries, I knew the questions could easily be as mundane as, "What is the capacity of students on the buses?" Or even, "What kind of engines do the buses use?" It was impossible to anticipate what any of them might ask. I had discovered many times that it took a simple answer to satisfy what was more about curiosity than evidence.

Thursday was more than a little frantic. The Chief of the Anti-Trust Division flew into Cedar Rapids from Chicago that morning. I hadn't met him before, so that changed. He emphasized to me that the Attorney General of the United States considered my case pretty important. I'd been in the mode of it is what it is, pretty much like with any other case I'd ever worked. I'd done my job, done the best I could, and forwarded my investigation to the next level. Now it was up to the prosecutors to decide what they were going to do. It was, without question, an important case to them.

Alonzo and Mark sat down with me and reviewed the indictment they intended to submit to the Grand Jury. I'd seen a lot of indictments, but this one was a horse of a completely different color. They'd cited an unimaginable number of specific acts and events which showed a conspiracy between the different school bus manufacturers, company owners, and employees, all of which went back a number of years, and all within the statutory limits. Every act and event was described by date and specifics. The indictment was thicker than any term paper I'd ever done in graduate school, cited with points and authorities, and asked the Grand Jury to consider the indictment of fourteen companies and people in a long-standing conspiracy. I knew we were going to indict some companies and people, but I had no clue the number would be fourteen. We'd indicted ten people in the Iowa City gambling case several years before, so this was far and away the biggest case I'd ever been involved with. It wasn't hard to assume my bosses in Omaha would be pleased with the numbers. Once again, Jim Whalen and I would lead the division in statistical accomplishments. His drug case would eventually result in the indictment of twelve people. Two agents and twenty-six indictments on two cases in an RA. And that didn't include a lot of the miscellaneous bank robbery convictions. Not bad for a statistical year.

By about nine o'clock that Friday night, I had more than a few glasses of Taylor California Vin Rose in my tummy, and had quite the feeling of warmth and contentment with life and myself. It was time to go to bed. I had a nice weekend to look forward to.

Or so I thought.

CHAPTER THIRTY FIVE

Another Missing Boy in Omaha

At about the same time I was enjoying my second glass of wine that calm Friday afternoon, two parents in the small Omaha suburb of Papillion were frantically trying to figure out where their twelve-year-old son was. He was never late getting home from school, but this day, December 2nd, was the exception.

Steve and Sue Walden had moved to the Omaha area in July, and had yet to meet or befriend anyone in the community. They had, of course, heard about the kidnapping and murder of Danny Joe Eberle several months before, and had told their son, Christopher, to be wary of talking to strangers. Chris seemed to understand this, and assured his parents he would never talk to anyone he didn't know. And certainly wouldn't get into a stranger's car.

Steve Walden was an Air Force meteorologist who was previously stationed in Hawaii. While there, the Waldens had experienced some problems with Chris that they felt had been resolved. After several instances involving missing money from both her and neighbors, Sue finally was able to confront Chris, who admitted to stealing money from her purse and from neighbors so he could play video games with friends.

The Waldens went through several sessions of counseling and felt the problem had been resolved. Returning to their former Air Force post in Omaha, they felt they had a new start, and all was going in the right direction for the family. Sue, however, worried about Chris's adjustment to a new school, as did many military families. But there didn't seem to be any immediate problems, so their lives moved forward—at least until that Friday in early December.

At seven forty-five that morning, Chris and his mother had a minor dispute about him wearing a new pair of tennis shoes to school. Sue insisted Chris wear his warm winter shoes since it had snowed the previous night. Finally, he relented and left the house after eating his normal breakfast of peanut butter and Sugar Pops cereal. Chris angrily left the house for the eight-block walk to Pawnee Elementary School. Sue didn't like to start off the morning with an argument with her son, but she at least was satisfied to know her son would be warm and dry on his walk to school that morning.

Now it was four-thirty, a half hour later than Chris should be home. Sue was less concerned than mad. Soon it would be dark. Where in the world is that boy? She considered his obsession with video games, and thought Chris might have stopped at someone's home on the way and gotten involved with playing games. She gazed out the window every few minutes because Chris had never been late coming home. Each time she looked, she was disappointed that she didn't see her son walking up the sidewalk.

Finally, she put on warm clothing and headed outside to see where he was. She recalled thinking, Just wait until I find him. I'm going to ground him for a month. She was sure he was face-to-face with a video game, killing aliens left and right, and even if he knew what time it was, he still didn't want to come home. Sue assumed Chris had finally met a new friend, and had completely lost track of the time.

She drove along the path he would have taken to the school, finding no apparent places where Chris might have stopped on the way home. Chris had been kept after school a couple of times for one reason or another, so Sue changed her line of thinking and thought perhaps this was another of those instances. When she arrived at the school, the halls were vacant. The school secretary told her there were no students in detention, in fact no students in the school at all. Sue left the school and drove back toward home, tracing the same route. Noticing some kids about Chris's age sledding on a hill, she stopped to see if Chris was there but he wasn't. She drove to the house where she knew one of Chris's friends lived. She didn't know the boy's name, but she saw him playing in the front yard.

"Have you seen Chris?" she asked.

The boy looked puzzled and said, "He wasn't in school today."

"At this point, I went from anger to panic," she later told investigators. "I got back in the car and raced home." It was only a four-block drive, and when she arrived her husband was pulling into the driveway. He looked at her and could immediately see the panic in her face.

"What's wrong?" he asked.

"Chris didn't show up for school today."

"What do you mean he wasn't in school?"

"He went to school this morning and he never showed up. I've gone down to the school and they didn't see him. He's nowhere around. I've looked all over, and I talked to one of his little friends down the street. He said he wasn't at school all day. I have no idea where he is."

"Call the police."

Sue raced into the house and did exactly what her husband had told her to do. Thinking a little more clearly, she tried to call Chris's teacher at home. But she was still in such a state of terror, she couldn't find the teacher's home phone number.

Steve had come into the house by this time. He tried to remain calm. "Maybe they made a mistake. Or maybe he skipped classes and went over to someone's house." As he said this, he knew it was out of character for his son to not make it home for dinner. By now, he'd be hungry. He later admitted the thought of his son having been kidnapped never entered his mind. All he knew was that his son wasn't home, it was dark, and it was too cold outside for Chris to be out wandering around in the neighborhood. He couldn't help but wonder, where is my son? But he tried to remain strong for his wife, who was clearly panic-stricken.

An officer from the Papillion Police Department arrived at the house about fifteen minutes later. Chris's parents explained the circumstances to the officer, who reassured them, saying, "Don't worry. We'll find your son."

CHAPTER THIRTY SIX

We Found Another Body

Omaha, Nebraska, is a town where the city quickly meets the country. The small suburb of Papillion lies to the south of Omaha, and south of that are fields and wide-open spaces. On a frigid Saturday morning, task force officers reassembled at the Sarpy County Sheriff's Department and were given a briefing by Sheriff Pat Thomas.

"We have no idea where Christopher Walden is," the ashen-faced sheriff told the gathering packed tightly into the department's squad room. "We know he left home for school about seven forty-five yesterday morning, and as far as we know, he hasn't been seen since. It doesn't look good, folks. He's not the type of kid who would just run away, so we all know we're going to be on a recovery instead of a rescue. If he somehow got trapped and had to spend the night outside in this weather, he'd be dead of exposure this morning. While that's a possibility, we suspect Chris is the second kidnapping victim after Danny Joe Eberle."

The sheriff pointed toward his detective lieutenant, explaining that his deputy had developed a grid search plan. "We will probably be getting some volunteers from the community," Thomas continued. "When and if that happens, we'll get them assigned to areas we're not covering. There's a lot of ground to cover out there, so let's get our assignments and get to work."

The phone in the monitoring room rang shortly before ten o'clock that same morning. Jim Whalen, who had been reviewing tapes from phone conversations recorded the previous day, answered it.

"Oh my God!" Jim exclaimed. "Yeah, Pete's here, just a minute." He handed me the phone.

It's amazing how many thoughts can race through your head in a matter of seconds, but my first thought was that it was my wife calling and something had happened to one of the kids.

I was wrong. It was Chuck Kempf calling from Omaha. "Pete, it looks like we've got another missing boy over here."

"You're shitting me."

"I wish I was. Twelve-year-old boy left his house for school and never got there yesterday. We've got search teams out now, and the bosses want you over here as soon as you can get here."

"I'm assuming you haven't found a body yet?"

"Nope, but we're going to keep searching until we find him."

"All right. I'm here with Jim working on the wiretaps, so let me run it by him and I'll let you know when I can get out of here. I'll call you back in a bit."

I explained what was happening to Jim, and that both the SAC and ASAC wanted me in Omaha as soon as I could get there.

Jim looked resigned. "I think we're going to be okay here, so do what you've got to do and I'll see you when you get back." He had a report to make to our federal judge in a little over a week, detailing the progress of the wiretap and providing summaries of pertinent conversations.

"Hopefully I can get back here in time to work with you on the report to the court," I said.

I headed home to pick up the clothes I'd need, making sure to grab my heavy parka since the weather in Omaha probably wasn't going to be any better than it was in Cedar Rapids.

"I'm not sure when I'll get back," I told Mary Ann.

"I understand. Just be careful driving over there. The roads probably aren't very good yet."

"Will do." And I was out the door.

My wife was right about the roads. Interstate 80 was snow-packed in spots, and worse as I drove west and through Des Moines. The drive, which usually took me about four hours, took six and I didn't roll into the sheriff's office until almost six o'clock. By then it was getting dark and search teams were returning, having found absolutely no sign of the boy's body.

Searchers were out on Sunday and Monday with the same results, but they got the break they needed late Monday afternoon. Two concrete workers had the day off because of the extreme cold temperatures, which were hovering near zero. Since they couldn't pour concrete that day, they decided to head out to their favorite place in the country and hunt rabbits. Roaming through the trees off 108th Street and feeling the cold wind whipping through the trees and tall brush, one man spooked up a rabbit. He raised his shotgun and fired.

"I got one," he yelled to his friend.

As he was walking slowly through the brush in the direction where he thought the rabbit would be, keeping alert for other critters to pop up, he suddenly stopped in his tracks. He turned and ran back toward his friend and their truck.

"We've got to get out of here!" he screamed. "There's a body out there."

"Nah, it's probably a deer," his buddy jeered.

"It ain't no fucking deer. There's a dead body out there and it looks like a young kid."

His friend looked at him. "You don't think..." He didn't need to finish the sentence. "I've got to go see."

The friend began wading through the scrubby brush and snow, going ten, twenty, and finally about forty yards before he saw the body. The young boy was clad only in underpants, and he noticed several reddish blotches in the snow. He ran back to the truck.

"It's got to be the same kid," he said as he and his pal secured their guns and jumped in the truck. They raced up the dirt road, not having a clue where they were heading.

"What're we gonna do?" said the man who first saw the body.

"Hell, I don't know, but we better get home and call the police."

Chuck Kempf and I raced out to the scene in his bureau car, since he knew the area and I didn't. It was only about five miles from the sheriff's department, and neither of us said a word on the way. A marked patrol car was parked beside the road as we rolled in, and Chuck got on the radio. "We're going to need our

Evidence Response Team (ERT) and get a hold of the state crime lab. We need them here as well."

"Did you look yet?" Chuck asked the first officer on the scene.

"Yes, I did."

"What do you think?"

"It's the missing kid. No doubt in my mind. He's frozen stiff and he only has a pair of undershorts on. I felt the body, and it's as cold as this frickin' day."

"All right," Chuck said. "We seem to have some other footprints going out there, and presumably one set is going to be our suspect. Do you have any crime scene tape in your trunk?"

"Yup." He popped the trunk and pulled out a large roll of yellow plastic tape, labeled "Crime Scene, Do Not Cross."

Chuck said, "I want to get this secured right now, before we have all sorts of people tromping out there and destroying evidence. I don't need to see the body right now. I'll take your word for it."

"Let me pull my car ahead and you can move yours back a little ways. We can run this stuff from my bumper to yours, and then we can figure out a way to put some on both sides of the field to keep everyone out."

"Sounds good."

Within an hour, there were at least forty police, sheriff, and FBI vehicles lined up on 108th Street. Officers in marked patrol units were positioned at the north and south intersections, only allowing law enforcement officers to enter the scene. Nightfall was setting upon us.

"First thing I want you to do," Chuck told the lead ERT technician, "is to get some casts made of the shoeprints out there. With the way this wind is blowing, I'm afraid they'll get covered up. We're not going to work this scene until tomorrow morning." He looked at the sheriff and the FBI bosses who were gathered around the front of the ERT van. "Is that all right with you guys?"

"If you want to get those shoeprints cast, let me get some lighting out here," the sheriff said. "I agree with what you say about tomorrow. He's dead and that's not going to change, so we might just as well accept the conditions as they are and wait until we can do it right."

Everyone around the truck agreed, and several of the ERT people began mixing up a few batches of white casting powder with water. When it was ready and looked like a white plaster for walls, they carefully started pouring casts. A sheriff's truck equipped with several portable lights drove up, and the deputy started the generator to provide power.

"I probably ought to give Bob Ressler a call," I told the brass. "Nobody's called him yet, I assume?"

Shaking heads told me what I needed to know. "Chuck, why don't you let me take your bureau car up to the office, and I'll be back in a little bit." I had my heavy parka on, but I was still cold and wouldn't mind getting out of the wind for a while and warm up a bit.

The time was creeping toward seven o'clock. I knew I wasn't going to find Ressler in the office, so I gave him a call at home.

"Looks like we've got another one," I said, and then filled in the rest of the blanks.

"Damn. Well, I can't get out of here for a couple of days. We've got a couple big crises going on, and I'm not sure when I can leave."

"If you're stuck there, can I get a hold of you in Quantico?"

"Oh, yeah. I've got a few classes to teach and then we've got several hot cases in the unit, so I'll be available. If you can't get me, I'll get back to you as soon as I can."

"That should work. Anything in particular you want me to do?"

"Yeah." Bob paused and gave a heavy sigh. "Let's do this. Since they're not going to work the scene until tomorrow, that's probably going to mean they won't be doing the autopsy until the next day."

"Probably right."

"I think it'd be best for you to just cool your jets until they've got the body at the morgue. Pick up whatever tidbits you can and keep track of things. I know you take good notes, so when you feel like you have enough to run by me, just give me a call and we'll see if anything changes. Do you think it's tied into the Eberle case?"

"Obviously no one's sure yet, but it certainly seems to have all the same earmarks."

"All right, I'll talk to you in a couple of days unless something big crops up. You know how to get me."

"You bet I do."

CHAPTER THIRTY SEVEN

Bob, I Need You Out Here, Now!

It had been a couple of days since I spoke to Bob Ressler, and I knew I had to give him an update. The news wasn't good, but he needed to know what was going on since it was such a prominent national case.

"Behavioral Science Unit, Ressler."

"Bob, it's Pete in Omaha."

"Hey Pete, how's it going out there?"

"Well, I'm not sure where to start. The body was Chris Walden's, but that isn't a big surprise. He was found about eight to ten miles away from where they found Danny Joe's body. The area is rural, not much more than some scattered scraggly trees, fields of weeds, and some rabbits running around. I suppose the occasional coyote, too. But really, it wasn't a whole lot different than where the first body was dumped beside the road."

"Was there any animal damage to the body?"

"Surprisingly, no. But there was some other weird stuff, and I'll hold that thought for a minute until I get through my notes. Chris was apparently killed right there. His clothes and school backpack were scattered within feet of his body. Just thrown around. All he had on was a pair of underpants. It looks like he died from one of two stab wounds to the back, but that's where it starts getting interesting."

"How's that?"

"The guy did some other cutting on him. On his chest and stomach. Some kind of a pattern that we can't really figure out. Everybody has a theory about what it might represent, or if there's some kind of a message there."

"It probably means something to him," Bob said.

"Were the carvings on the body done before or after death?"

"From the lack of blood, it looks like post mortem wounds."

"That's interesting. It sounds like more of a curiosity thing to me. Any signs of cannibalism?"

"Don't know that yet."

"So where does everything stand?"

"Well, the good news is we have been able to get a composite drawing done. The guy looks like he might be in his late teens. Not much more than that."

"That's a start. Hopefully they've got it out to the media."

"Oh yeah! Front page of the paper and lead story on every television station. Plenty of coverage. Hopefully, it'll turn up some leads. Never know."

"Hopefully, "Bob said. "Tell me a little more about the cutting of the boy's body."

"Like I said, everybody has a theory about the carvings. Some of them are saying it's a marijuana leaf, so there's gotta be a drug connection. Somebody came up with the theory that there's some kind of a Satanist whacko involved. Or even a cult. It's amateur hour out here, Bob. Some of these theories are crazy. But I guess they're thinking. The sheriff says it's gotta have something to do with the Hells Angels, so we need to start rounding them up."

"That's quite a step into the wild blue yonder."

"Yeah, particularly when you look at the composite. Clean cut kid. Definitely not a biker. There are a lot of guys rolling their eyes about some of these ideas they're throwing around," I said. "Chuck Kempf has the only sensible one I've heard so far. He thinks the design the guy carved in Chris' chest looks more like a Boy Scout symbol. But everyone here is in such a state, they're grasping at straws, Bob. I wouldn't be surprised if they start rousting Catholic priests next, just because in some states they've molested boys."

"What do *you* think?"

"I don't think we're dealing with some drugged out whacko Hells Angel who's a part-time Satanist. I'm sure of that. The facts just don't point in that direction. What's a Hell's Angel going to do, drive up on his hog and grab the kid? A little far-fetched. I'd probably lean more toward what Chuck says, but I don't think we really know, and you may not, either, if you can get out here to see it. Is that gonna happen?"

"I think so. My guess is I'm going to fly out of here on Friday morning. Probably roll into Omaha around noon your time."

"Sounds good."

"Hey Pete, do me a favor. Can you get a few pictures of the wounds and overnight 'em to me? Maybe some reports, too, if you can get 'em copied. It'll give me something to do on the plane. I hate flying."

"That's two of us. I should be able to get it together by tonight. If not, definitely by the morning, so it'll get there before you fly out. I'll also have as much new stuff as I can collect by the time you get here."

"Okay. Anything else you can think of right now?"

I looked at my notes. "Well, there is another thing. The body was found quite a ways off the road. Probably thirty or forty yards. The boy's clothes were spread around near the body, so it's pretty obvious he either carried him out there or made him walk. My guess is made him walk. Sound important?"

"Oh yeah, that's as important as hell. With the first boy he was probably in a state of panic, so he got rid of the body as quickly as he could. This one is much different. He learned from the first one and he wanted to keep the body out of sight."

"So no one could find it and he'd be able to go right on killing?"

"That'd be my guess. There's certainly some different stuff here, but one thing I can guarantee, like I told them last time, this guy is not gonna stop. And the next one is going to be quicker than this one."

"Weeks, not months?"

"That's my guess. I'll see you in a couple of days."

But this time, there were two potential witnesses, aside from the men who had found the body. Cheryl Baumgartner had been driving down the street where Chris was walking to school the morning he was kidnapped. After seeing the news stories on TV that night and the next day, she told her husband, "I may have seen something." She went on to explain, and later told police, how she was driving down the street and noticed a tan car parked beside the curb, and it looked like two people were struggling inside the car. "Now that I think about it, I think one of the people in the car was the young boy who is missing."

An investigator tried to get her to provide a better description of the car, but she said, "I don't really know much about cars. I'm not sure if it was a Ford or Chevy, or even something else. All I know is it wasn't a full-sized car, but it also wasn't a compact. Somewhere in between."

Another thing she remembered was that the driver's side door of the car was open. "It was so cold and windy, my first thought was, 'close the stupid door. It's cold outside.' It was just after eight-thirty and I was on my way to work, so I didn't give it much thought. I just assumed it was someone dropping his son off near the school."

Becky Trapani had been returning home from a church service when she drove past Pawnee Elementary School, where Chris Walden was headed that morning after leaving his house. "I noticed an older boy walking with a younger one, so I just thought it was an older brother walking with his younger brother. I really didn't think anything about it. I just headed home, but when I heard the story on the news, I thought I might call in to see if what I saw could provide some clues. I'm sorry, I just don't remember any more."

Two days later, Becky Trapani and Cheryl Baumgartner went through hypnosis sessions with a psychiatrist and a trained agent in San Antonio. They'd been flown down to San Antonio to see if, under hypnosis, they might be able to provide some further information about the older boy, such as a more detailed description, and even more of a description of the car parked on the roadside.

Both women tried their best, but no specific information of value came out of either session. While agents and officers were disappointed, because hypnosis had worked for other cases, they at least started to lean toward their unknown suspect as being a younger male. Exactly as Bob Ressler had told them a couple of months before.

Bob arrived in town that same Friday and was grateful for the package of information I'd provided him. We went over a few more things that had cropped up, but nothing of earth-shattering importance. Later that afternoon we headed to the sheriff's department and met with the primary investigators and brass.

"I'm one hundred percent sure we're dealing with the same guy," Bob told them. "Nothing about the kidnapping of the two boys has changed, and in my opinion he was blind to the risk he was taking. Particularly with the second boy. It was broad daylight and people were around. Possible witnesses. But he was so deep into his fantasies that the compulsion to kill had overwhelmed him, and he didn't really plan things out. He was acting more on impulse than anything else, so that confirms in my mind that we're looking for a younger man, probably not much more than twenty years old, if that.

"The victims were chosen at random, and I believe his only criteria was that they were smaller and young. There are a couple of reasons for that, but the most important was that I believe he knew he could control both boys. So if we apply a little common sense to that, he's going to be a smaller guy himself. I'd have to say he's around five-foot-seven to five-foot-ten. No more than that."

Bob went on to say the killer would be in a job or avocation that would put him in contact with boys in this same age group. "It's possible he knew both boys, but I doubt it. If you can find some connection between the boys, that may lead us right to his front door. I don't know what that might be. Maybe they played baseball or soccer together. I'd look into that possibility if you haven't yet.

"Let me just add this. I'll commit every bit of my profile to paper, but whatever you do, don't release it to the press. I don't want to terrorize the community and get you guys off on a wild goose chase. It's been a couple of months between these killings. I can guarantee you this guy is spending every hour wrapped up in his fantasies about what he's done, and what he wants to do in the future. And that *future* isn't going to be very far away. These killings become something like an addiction to these people. He's had the taste of doing two at this point, and he's going to want to feel that same high as soon as possible. Yes, it's a little like drugs, but this guy doesn't need drugs. He's on his own high with his fantasy life, and the more you get of that, the more you want. I'm going to say he'll try to do the same thing in a matter of weeks this time."

CHAPTER THIRTY EIGHT

The Killer Strikes Again

6:00 a.m., Wednesday morning

The killer was hungry and angry that morning as he finished his midnight shift and went to the mess hall on the base to get some breakfast. Sitting alone, he took his time eating, and the anger continued to well up. He could think about nothing else.

For several weeks, he'd been seething inside after hearing the sheriff call him a "coward" on the local news, and saying he should "try picking on someone his own size." He decided during his shift that night he'd show the sheriff that he wasn't a coward. He would pick on someone his own size, because he was desperately in need of some money. And little kids don't carry enough money with them.

After breakfast, he went back to his room in the barracks. Hidden in his locker was a rope, some duct tape, and the knife he'd used to kill the two boys. Putting those items into a small leather satchel, he got out of his uniform and put on some civvies, making sure to bundle up since it was cold and had snowed that night.

His own car was in for some minor repairs, so he climbed into a Chevy Citation the repair shop had loaned him for the couple of days his car would be in the shop. Despite the cold weather, the Citation started right up, and he drove toward the main gate of the base. He wasn't sure where he was going, but he'd figure it out as soon as he got there. He drove into Bellevue, then turned left onto Chandler Road, heading west. As he approached 36th Street, he removed the knife from the bag and laid it down on the seat beside him. He then turned left on 36th.

8:15 a.m.

Jennifer King was the director of the pre-school program for Aldersgate United Methodist Church, situated on the southwest corner of 36th and Green Streets. Her students weren't due to start arriving until eight-thirty that morning, so she had a little time to prepare the classroom. When she pulled the curtain back on the front window, she noticed a white car passing the front of the building slowly, but didn't think anything of it. It had snowed last night and, she thought, *anyone with a little bit of sense should be driving slowly.*

The killer noticed a middle-aged woman looking out the window. He drove to the end of the block, and then made a U-turn at the intersection of 37th Street. He drove back down Green Street, again, and thought, *I need money, and I'll bet that woman in the church has some.* He hadn't noticed the sign that would have told him Jennifer was actually standing in the window of the pre-school. He thought it was all part of the church building, and that someone involved with the church was probably flush with cash. He reached over and pulled the rope out of the bag as he drove by a second time, noticing the woman looking out the window at him.

Jennifer thought it was odd that the car came by a second time, and the youthful-looking man appeared to be staring at her. She had an instantaneous flash in her mind, thinking, *He looks a little like the drawing of the man who killed the two little boys.* The man who had literally paralyzed Bellevue and the other areas south of Omaha for nearly four months.

He made another U-turn at 36th and Green, and was then headed west once again when he pulled directly into the gravel parking lot that was in front of the window. The woman was still standing there, looking out at him through the large picture window. He had no idea who she was, and didn't care, because she surely had some money on her, and he desperately needed some. He parked and picked up the knife with his hand, holding it securely by the handle. He decided to leave the rope.

Jennifer could see the man clearly through the

windshield of the car, and now she was sure it was the same man. *Why would he be pulling in here? It isn't one of the parents who might drop their kids off early for pre-school. And there's no one else in the car with him. What is he doing here?* Her mind raced. *He probably knows this is a pre-school. If it is the same man, maybe he wants to kill one of the kids. But there aren't any here yet.*

She saw the driver's door open. The young man got out of the car, then walked quickly toward the front door of the school. She looked at the license plate and began repeating the numbers over and over in her mind. She knew it was *him*. Jennifer would later describe the encounter as "the most terrifying five minutes of my life."

He paused at the window, looked at her, and motioned with his hand for her to go over to the door. Her heart was pounding furiously. She opened it a few inches, only to hear him say, "Can you tell me where 48th Street is?" She would later recall his voice was quiet and seemed to be trembling. He immediately struck her as a little boy who had lost his mother. He seemed as scared as she was.

She tried to remain calm as her heart pounded even more rapidly, and provided him with the directions. And then he asked, "Can I use your phone?"

"There's no phone here," she lied, but she did not want him to come inside under any conditions. Consciously, she avoided looking toward the phone, which was only three feet away from the door.

With a quick motion, he pushed on the door, yelling, "Get back inside or I'll kill you!" She saw a flash of metal in his hand and was sure it was a knife. On complete impulse, she pulled the door open and bolted past the young man as he remained standing outside the door.

Her only instinct was to get away, and to do so as quickly as she could. She raced down the gravel driveway toward the road, but slipped on a patch of snow. Her knuckles and knees slammed into the pavement as she struggled to get back onto her feet and run. She could hear the cold wind whistling down the street and through the trees, burning into her flesh with its bitterness. But the sound she suddenly heard behind her made her quickly forget the wind and the pain she felt.

The engine of the car revved and the tires peeled out, throwing gravel onto the street. *He's going to run me over*, she thought as she crawled on the pavement and stumbled to her feet, running as fast as she could toward the pastor's home.

The pastor's wife, DeAnn Lindsay, was in the kitchen preparing breakfast for herself and her husband when she heard the front door crash open and Jennifer's voice screaming, "He's trying to kill me!" Suddenly in a panic herself, she ran into the living room to see Jennifer standing there repeating a series of numbers and letters over and over.

DeAnn saw blood on her hands and that her dress was wet with slush dripping off the front. "My God, Jennifer! What happened?"

"He tried to kill me...it's him..." Jennifer continued rattling off the series of numbers and letters, which DeAnn quickly figured out was for a license plate. "Get a pencil and write this number down." She kept repeating it. "He's got a knife...he tried to kill me."

The pastor, Bill Lindsay, was upstairs preparing to leave for a class he was conducting that morning when he heard the commotion. He ran down the stairs and into the kitchen, and saw his wife and Jennifer standing there. It was clear Jennifer was terrified and that *something* had happened. She was usually calm and composed, but now she was crying and nearly hysterical, her dress soaked in front, her hair a mess.

He put his arm over her shoulder and tried to calm her. "Jennifer, what's happening?"

"He attacked me. It's the man who killed those boys."

"Where is he?" the pastor asked.

"I don't know. He was in a white car. He had a knife. He came to the school."

"Are you okay?"

"I think so. Is he still out there?" She screamed, pointing toward the front of the house and the street.

"Call the sheriff," the pastor told his wife. He walked quickly toward the front window and looked outside. "There's no one out there."

8:35 a.m.

Pastor Lindsay walked carefully down the street to check the pre-school and to see if anyone was lurking around, or more importantly, was still inside the building. As he opened the door, he saw a parent inside the room with her young son. "Where's Jennifer?" she asked.

"There's been some trouble," he replied. "Would you get Jennifer's coat and things and take them up to the house?"

"What's wrong?" she asked. She could tell the pastor was nervous and that something had happened. She couldn't imagine what it was, but she hoped nothing had happened to Jennifer, who she considered to be a good friend.

"I'm not really sure, but I think someone attacked Jennifer."

"Oh my God," she breathed the words more than spoke them. "Is she all right? Can I do anything?"

"Just take the—" As he started to speak, he saw a sheriff's car pull into the driveway. "Go ahead and take those things up to the house. Jennifer and DeAnn are at the house and I'll be up there in a few minutes."

9:05 a.m.

While Jennifer King had acted on good instinct in getting out the door of the pre-school and fleeing toward the parson's house, she was wrong about one thing. The killer had *not* tried to run her down with his car. Once she raced out the door past him, he was equally as frightened as she. In a total panic, he'd leaped into his car and tried to get away as quickly as he could. He'd raced down the street, turned left on 36th Street, and barely slowed in his turn onto Chandler.

And now he was back in the safety of his room on the base. He knew he'd made a mistake, had been careless, and he knew when that happened the risk of being caught went up. But now he felt safe, and he knew no one on the base had any idea where he'd been or what he'd tried to do. He felt confident he'd gotten away from the church quickly enough that no one would ever know what happened. Surely the woman had been so afraid that she couldn't identify him or the car. Or hopefully not.

As he lay down on his bed, pulled up the covers, and went to sleep, his last thought was that he'd have to find a way to be more careful next time. And there would be a *next time*.

CHAPTER THIRTY NINE

"We've Got Him"

10:10 that same morning

By complete coincidence, or perhaps divine providence, the three lead investigators from the primary investigative agencies had decided to meet at the Bellevue Police Department that morning at nine a.m. Lieutenant Stan Jamison, the Sarpy County detective commander, Captain George Askew of the Bellevue Police Department, and Special Agent Chuck Kempf of the Omaha FBI office had been going through some of the newer reports from the past week, trying to see if there might have been some useful leads developed. Since the second boy's body had been found, the task force had been working night and day, but so far with little to no success.

All three investigators in the captain's office had been hearing police and sheriff's radio traffic that morning, mainly because a speaker was in the office. And then they heard the initial call of a possible attempted robbery at the Aldersgate church. While it sounded odd that someone would try to rob a church, their attention wasn't piqued until they later heard a description of the suspect. "Victim believes the suspect looks like the composite drawing of the guy who killed the two young boys."

The patrol deputy provided a description of the young man. "He's a white male, early twenties, about five-feet-five to five-feet-seven inches, dark hair, smaller build." The investigators looked at each other, noting the estimate of the suspect's size. The deputy went on to describe a white car and the suspect's clothing. He asked the dispatcher to run a license number, adding, "The victim believes the suspect was armed with a knife."

Kempf stood up. "Damn," he said. "The car color doesn't seem to match, but everything else does."

"Particularly the description of the guy," Jamison replied. "Plus, they got a plate, and the guy apparently had a knife."

"Stan, can you get a hold of the deputy and have him come down here?" Kempf asked.

"Sure." Jamison radioed the deputy on his hand-held portable.

"Might be a good idea to see what we've got," Kempf said. "No way to know if it's connected, but stranger things have happened."

What little did he know.

11:05 a.m.

The suspect vehicle came back registered to a car repair and sales business just north of the main gate to Offutt Air Force Base, a veritable stone's throw away from the Bellevue police building. "Let's go over there and see what we've got," Askew said. "I've known the owner of the place for years, and he certainly doesn't fit the description of the suspect."

They piled in Askew's car and were at the business within a minute of pulling out of the driveway. Facts started developing quickly.

"This kid from the base brought that car in on Monday." The owner pointed at a tan-colored Chevrolet Nova sitting on the lot. "He said the engine fan was making an odd noise, but I haven't had a chance to get to it yet. So I loaned him one of the cars we use for customers."

"Is it white?" Askew asked.

"It's white." The three investigators looked at one another simultaneously. Jamison ran the Nova's plate through his dispatch center and it came back registered to John Joubert of Portland, Maine.

"Maine?" Kempf looked puzzled.

"Yeah," Askew replied with a wave of his hand toward the base. "A lot of guys stationed here keep their cars registered in their own state."

Jamison said, "I'm going to call my office and see if he's got a Nebraska driver's license."

While he was on the phone, Askew and Kempf compared notes with the patrol deputy who had met them at the lot. "Jeez Louise, we might have something happening here," Kempf said.

"Let me call base security and have them see if they can figure out where he is right now," Askew suggested. "We have enough dealings with them that I know their guys pretty well."

"I can imagine." Kempf chuckled and looked at the business owner. "Are you sure this guy is stationed here?"

"Yeah, I'm sure. He came here in his uniform on Monday. Two-striper as I recall."

Askew hung up the phone. "I got a hold of base security and explained what we've got. One of the sergeants will meet us at the front gate."

"All right, then. Let's get out of here." Jamison looked at the shop owner. "We really appreciate your help."

They told the owner that if the guy came back, he should tell him his car wasn't done yet, but not to say anything about the police having been there.

"No problem."

11:50 a.m.

Having gathered all of the information they could, including a copy of the repair estimate for Joubert's car, the investigators drove no more than two blocks to the main gate of Offutt. A sergeant met them in a small lot just inside the gate.

"This guy is an airman and he got off shift at six this morning. Assuming he's there now, he lives in Barracks 400," the sergeant said. "You guys want to follow me or take my car?"

"We'll follow you," Askew replied.

They parked illegally outside a large, red brick barracks building. "I've got a couple of guys from OSI (Office of Security and Investigations) coming, just in case," the sergeant explained. "They should be here any minute. They've located Joubert's roommate and they're going to bring him over, just in case the room's locked."

"Good idea." Kempf looked at Jamison and Askew.

"I hate kicking doors down," he chuckled.

Two OSI agents in dark blue business suits arrived a few minutes later and Joubert's roommate led them up the stairs to the room. The sergeant knocked once, then again, even more loudly. "Open it up," he told the roommate.

Once inside, they found a dark-haired young man lying in bed, still sound asleep.

"Joubert!" the sergeant shouted. "Wake up!"

The young airman opened his eyes, rubbed them, and appeared confused, probably wondering why his room was getting inspected by a sergeant he didn't even know. "Who are you guys?" he asked.

"Get your ass out of bed and put your clothes on."

Kempf picked up some pants and a shirt from the floor and threw them on the bed. "I'm Special Agent Chuck Kempf from the FBI. This is Lieutenant Stan Jamison from Sarpy County and Captain Askew from the Bellevue Police Department. We want to talk you about an attack on a woman at Aldersgate School this morning."

Joubert looked baffled. "I don't know any Aldersgate School." He well could have been telling the truth, since he thought he was going to rob someone at a church.

One of the OSI agents pulled a card out of his wallet, and began reading Joubert his Miranda Rights. "Do you understand what I've explained to you?"

He still looked confused, saying "yes" as he finished buttoning his shirt, which he tucked into his pants.

"Same clothes," Askew said.

"I noticed that, too," Jamison said, and Kempf nodded, all three remembering the description they'd heard over the radio. "We'll get 'em later."

The OSI agent put his Miranda card back, and then asked Joubert, "Do you mind if we search your room?"

Joubert looked around for a second, and then replied, "No. Go ahead."

Kempf looked at the OSI agents. "Why don't you get both of them out of here while we check this place out."

Jamison found the black satchel stuffed under Joubert's bed and opened it, extracting a rope. "Look what I found," he sounded exuberant. "We've got this bastard!"

All three investigating officers knew the rope that had been used to tie up the boys was a completely unique color and style, and they'd spent months trying to figure out where it had come from. They'd literally looked around the world. A huge wave of relief washed over them as Jamison laid the rope down on the bed.

"There's a knife and some duct tape in there, too, but let's leave them alone," Jamison said. "Might be some good prints."

The investigators had big smiles on their faces as they slapped high fives. Kempf later said, "It was probably the best feeling I've ever had."

They decided to tow the white car to a large hangar on the base, where they'd later get a search warrant. Joubert's car, still on the lot, would be towed to the sheriff's office where it'd sit until they could get a second search warrant and conduct forensic testing on the inside of the vehicle and trunk.

CHAPTER FORTY

Interviewing the Killer

1:15 p.m.

John Joubert sat calmly in the back of Askew's car, alone with his thoughts, buckled in and cuffed behind his back. He was closely watched by one of the OSI agents while the primary investigators wrapped up their search of the room and awaited the arrival of an Air Force tow truck. When all of that work was accomplished and the evidence they'd found placed in the trunk of Askew's car, Chuck Kempf climbed in the back seat with their suspect.

The investigators had called their bosses, all of whom were anxiously awaiting their arrival at the Bellevue Police Department. The word of the arrest had spread, and a number of other task force officers had raced to the station, if for no other reason than to look at the suspect they had so diligently sought for months. Somehow, word had also spread to the media, which had sent reporters and even anchors to the station for the latest breaking news. It was easily the biggest story the Omaha area had seen in more years than anyone could count.

As they brought Joubert through the back door of the station and down a hallway, officers, agents, and deputies, not to mention staff, were transfixed on the small young man, who simply didn't fit their paradigm of what a murderous monster *should look like*. "He's so young, so harmless-looking," a woman said. Joubert was anything but what they'd expected. He didn't look like a psychotic monster, let alone a killing machine as he walked with his head down and his eyes fixed on the floor ahead of him.

Captain Askew pushed open the door to a room,

motioning for Joubert to step inside. The police chief, sheriff, and FBI ASAC had agreed to have their three lead investigators conduct the interview of Joubert.

Sitting at a table, Chuck Kempf again advised Joubert he had a right to remain silent. "Do you understand that, John?"

"Yes," Joubert said in a low voice, continuing to look at the floor.

"John, can you tell us where you were last night?"

"I was working."

"At Offutt?"

"Yes sir."

"Can you tell us why you had the loaner car?"

"Mine was in the shop for a few days, so they let me use that one."

"All right, John, let me ask you this. What were you doing at Aldersgate School this morning?"

"Do you mean the church?"

"Yes," Kempf replied. "It's a church with a pre-school attached."

Joubert sighed audibly. "All I can tell you is I needed money. I had to pay for my car and I didn't have any money."

"So what were you going to do, rob the lady?"

Joubert nodded his head.

"I need you to say something, John."

"Yes...I wanted to rob the lady."

Kempf then turned the interrogation in the direction of Joubert's background, where he was from, how long he'd been in the Air Force, when he'd arrived at Offutt and what his duties were on the base. Kempf felt it might be a good time to ease off on what was unquestionably a highly stressful situation for everyone in the room.

Jamison said, "Why don't we take a little break? John, would you like something to drink?"

Joubert nodded and Jamison left to room to find a soft drink. Kempf and Askew followed and quickly huddled to discuss their strategy.

"He's very passive with us now," Kempf said. "When we go back, let me take the cuffs off him. We can make it as relaxed in there as possible. I think he's ready to tell us everything right now."

"That's a good idea, Chuck," Jamison said. "We

don't need to turn loose the nuclear weapons right now. It may be a honey versus vinegar deal. Let's hold off on the vinegar until we need it."

Once back in the room, Jamison handed Joubert the soft drink and took the lead on the interrogation. "John, let me ask you this. Are you aware of the murders of the two boys here over the last couple of months?"

Joubert looked at Jamison and hesitated. "I've read about 'em."

Jamison then pulled out the rope, saying, "Let me show you something, John." He showed it to Joubert. "Do you recognize this rope?"

"Yes sir."

"One of the boys was tied up with this type of rope, John. We looked all over the world for it and we found this in your bag in the room."

"That rope isn't rare," Joubert said.

"Where did you get it?"

"From my Scout leader, Don Shipman. We use it all the time to practice tying knots."

For the next half hour, Joubert talked about his involvement with the Boy Scout troop. Kempf recalled thinking, *that's almost exactly what Bob Ressler said. In fact, everything Ressler said about this guy is true.*

By this time the questioning had gone on for nearly two hours. The investigators had agreed to take frequent breaks, and Askew asked Joubert if he was hungry. "A little bit."

They sent an officer to get him a Big Mac and fries.

Kempf would later describe what happened when they returned to the room to continue questioning Joubert. "The most unusual thing that ever happened to me in an interview or interrogation unfolded right before my eyes, Kempf said. "We decided to start focusing on the specifics of the boys' killings. Joubert started rocking back and forth in his chair, he looked up and down and clasped his hands in front of his face. He put his hands between his legs and said, 'Why did I kill those boys?' I was sure we were heading where we wanted to go, but this blurted-out statement shocked all three of us."

Kempf told Joubert, "Yes, John, that's why we're here. Why don't you just tell us about it?"

"I can't yet. I need to talk to Terry first."

The investigators knew he was talking about Terry

Carter, one of the boys in the Scout troop. Askew left the room, telling another officer to call Terry's parents. "See if they can bring him down here. Explain why and tell them we're going to make sure it's perfectly safe."

6:20 p.m.

Terry Carter arrived with his parents and was shown into the room after the investigators explained to his parents what was happening.

"Are you sure he'll be safe?" Mrs. Carter asked.

"Don't worry. One of us will be in the room with him," Kempf explained. "He has something to tell Terry and then we're pretty sure he'll tell us everything about the boys' killings. We're not sure what he's going to tell Terry, but we're guessing he just wants to save face and clear the air with Terry."

Askew escorted Terry Carter into the interrogation room. "Hi, John," the boy said.

Joubert looked at Askew. "Can I talk to him, alone?"

Askew shook his head. "Sorry John. I've got to stay in here as long as Terry's in here with you."

Joubert nodded. "I understand." To Terry Carter he said, "Terry, I just want you to know I'm involved in this, and I'm in a lot of trouble. But no matter what anyone says, there was never any danger to you. There's no way I would have ever hurt you."

The small blonde-haired boy simply stood and listened, showing no emotion, seemingly at a loss for what to say. "Just remember what I told you," Joubert said. He stood and put his arms out to embrace Terry. "I'm sorry," Joubert repeated as the boy left the room.

And as soon as the boy was gone, Joubert said to Askew, "Thank you. I'm ready now."

CHAPTER FORTY ONE

A Perfect Fit with the Profile

Friday, January 13th

I'm not superstitious. Never have been. Never will be. Friday the Thirteenth is just another day on the calendar to me. And I would never have thought about it until my daughter told me, "Be careful today, Dad, it's Friday the Thirteenth. Don't go under ladders and don't let a black cat run in front of you. Bad luck. You know the drill."

"Really?" I replied. "The thought never occurred to me. But I'll try to be careful. Thanks for the reminder, Loni. Now something probably *will* happen." But the way the day would play out, it would be anything but unlucky.

The weeks since I'd been to Omaha had been a handful. I was due to head back to Quantico for Hostage Negotiator's training in a couple of weeks, and was juggling my schedule around that. With thirteen companies and people under indictment in a single case, several bank robbers in jail awaiting hearings, motions, and sentencing, plus running back and forth from Cedar Rapids to Des Moines about once a week, I was glad to see this Friday on the calendar. And couldn't have cared less which day of the month it was. Well, maybe just a little bit since my thoughtful daughter had reminded me of it.

9:15 a.m.

The thought of checking in with Chuck Kempf had crossed my mind several times, but I had enough of my own problems to worry about. And I probably would have called him before I went home that Friday, except I got a phone call from someone else first.

"Pete, Bob Ressler. How're you doing?"

"Doing well, Bob. Good to hear from you. What's up?" As if I didn't know why he'd be calling.

"Just wanted to check in and see if there was anything happening with the case in Omaha."

"I haven't heard anything, but I've been up to my ears in snapping alligators since I got back."

"Whatcha got going?"

"Well, the easy answer is a lot, but we've got thirteen people and companies under indictment in a school bus bid rigging case, and the attorneys are driving me whacko."

"I hear that. They can do it. Glad I don't have to deal with 'em much, anymore."

"Bob, are you going to be around there for a while?"

"Should be. I had a class to teach at the National Academy this morning, but I'm free this afternoon as far as I know."

"All right, let me see if I can catch up with Chuck Kempf. If there's anything happening, I'll give you a call back. Otherwise, just assume there isn't and I'll check back when I hear something."

Tracking Kempf down took a little more effort than I expected it would. I tried our Omaha HQ office, Sarpy County, Bellevue P.D., and was eventually told he was probably at the Sarpy County Attorney's office. I had no idea what he'd be doing there rather than at the U.S. Attorney's office, but I finally tracked him down. And once I found him, he said "I'll have to call you back. We're filing charges on this guy now."

"Which guy?"

"Joubert."

"Joubert who?"

"John Joubert. Haven't you heard?"

"Heard what?"

"We arrested the guy who killed those boys."

You could have knocked me over with a falling aspen leaf. "You're kidding me."

"No, I'm serious. You gonna be in the office?"

"I am *now*."

"I'll give you a call back later and fill you in on all the details," Kempf said. "We should be done here in a couple of hours."

"Damn! That's great news. I'll be waiting."

I called Ressler back, immediately. "Bob, they got the guy."

"You're kidding me."

"Not unless Kempf's kidding me. I don't have any details, but I finally got a hold of Chuck and he said they were filing charges on him with the District Attorney right now. I'm not sure when they got him, or how, but Chuck is gonna call me later. How late will you be there?"

"Probably no later than six."

"That's five my time, so hopefully I'll hear from Chuck and I'll call you right away."

2:45 p.m.

Anticipating Chuck's call, I came close to sitting at my desk and doing nothing more than to look at the phone. It was Friday the Thirteenth!

But, on the old theory that a watched pot never boils, I decided to be busy and get some actual work done while I waited. Basically just killing time, but trying to be productive. I was obsessed with wondering what had happened, how they'd found him, did he finally turn himself in, did the profile help in some small way, or what? Who was he and how did they catch him?

I picked up the phone on the first ring.

"Pete, its Chuck."

"Well, I guess congratulations are due," I said. "I hadn't heard a thing until you told me. We're stuck out here in the middle of nowhere. Like mushrooms, they keep us in the dark and feed us bullshit all the time."

"I'm sorry I didn't call you, but I've been up against it the last few days. Hardly slept."

"No problem. I'm just happy to find out something good's happened. Okay, so give me the straight scoop."

Chuck rattled off everything that happened on Wednesday leading up to his arrest of Joubert in the barracks on the base. "Once we got him talking, he gave us everything. I mean the whole nine yards, and then a few more yards. A lot of things we didn't know. They're still typing his confession. We taped it all and they're doing a transcript of the whole conversation. The boss has assigned me to work on this full-time, and they transferred everything else I had to other guys on the squad. It looks like I'm in it for the long haul."

"So what's the next step?"

"Not sure, mostly lawyer stuff now, and you know how that goes. His attorney waived an initial appearance until he can review the charges. We got them pretty much done this afternoon, so I'm guessing he'll be appearing in court early next week."

"Media circus?"

"Oh man, you can't believe it. The night we got him, they were camped out at Bellevue P.D. all night, just waiting for someone to talk to."

"Who talked to them?"

"We turned the sheriff loose on 'em. Ol' Pat told 'em how the cow ate the cabbage pretty quick. He's a man of few words."

"But at least they got a story for the ten o'clock news, right?"

"Yup, they were happy. That's all they seem to want. A little talking and a face to go with it, and they just seem to make up the rest."

I could see things were concluding. "I know you've got more on your plate than you need right now, so if I can clear a few things off my calendar, I'm going to try to get into Omaha next week and copy off some of the reports. Oh, I forgot to tell you Bob Ressler called, so I'll give him a call back when we're done."

"I appreciate it. The fewer calls I have to make the better off I'll be."

"No kidding. One last thought. Have you thought about how accurate the profile was?"

"I *have* thought about that and you know what? I don't think Ressler missed anything except for the guy's size."

"Was he a big guy?"

"Not in the slightest, no pun intended. Ressler said he thought the guy might be around five-eight. Joubert's five-six. Basically a munchkin."

"And that was it?"

"That was it. Every other thing fit him like a tight shirt."

"So did it help?"

"That's a hard one to answer. When everything was

happening on Wednesday, I plugged in some of what Bob had said. I felt like we had enough on Joubert at that point to be pretty sure we had the right guy, but I think Bob's profile just added some frosting to the cake. You know what I mean?"

"Kinda confirmed that you were right about what you thought you were right about?"

"Exactly. When you talk to Bob, tell him we really appreciate what he did for us. And you, too."

"Will do. I'll probably see you in the next week or two."

CHAPTER FORTY TWO

More Victims from His Past

About three years later...

Some cases seem to never go away, and the Joubert case proved to be one of them, but in a far more gruesome way than anyone could ever have predicted. If one had thought Joubert's killings in Omaha completed his criminal history, one could not have been farther away from the truth.

Bob Ressler was conducting a class on Psychological Profiling at a session of the FBI National Academy in Quantico, Virginia, several years after being involved in the Joubert investigation. Reviewing the facts and showing slides of the victim's wounds, Ressler went on to explain the factors that had led him to arrive at the profile, which of course had been unerringly accurate. In the class was a police officer from Portland, Maine, who noted the similarity with a murder case in his jurisdiction that had occurred a number of years before. After talking with Ressler and learning Joubert had lived in Portland, the officer made contact with the investigators in Omaha.

As the investigation in Maine unfolded, John Joubert was linked to a series of similar crimes that occurred while he was living in Portland during his middle to late teen years. A nine-year-old girl, Sarah Canty, had been playing with a football in her front yard one afternoon. She stood up after picking the ball up near the sidewalk, and suddenly felt a sharp pain in her back. Simultaneously, a boy on a ten-speed bicycle went by her on the sidewalk, but she was less concerned with him than the fact that her back felt like it was on fire. Crying hysterically, Sarah ran into her house where her

parents discovered blood pouring from
a small circular wound in her back.

Police were immediately called and found a pencil lying on the grass near the sidewalk. Sarah was able to provide a description of the boy on the bike, and police searched the area for the boy with no success. No fingerprints were found on the pencil, and there were no witnesses to the stabbing.

But police would later learn Sarah was not John Joubert's first stabbing victim.

An eight-year-old boy had been attacked by an older boy matching Joubert's description about a month before Sarah was stabbed. While the boy was not stabbed, facts developed during the investigation later revealed it was Joubert who had grabbed the boy by the throat, forcing him against a wall near a bank. The boy struggled with his attacker, flailing his arms, and was able to escape, running down the street. Yet again, a report was made to police and a search of the area was conducted, but the attacker was not to be identified for years.

Almost two months after the incident involving Sarah Canty, twenty-seven-year-old Vickie Goff was walking near the campus of the University of Maine. Vickie was attending classes at the university, and was headed to a class on a cold January night. As she walked, she noticed a young man walking toward her, but had no reason to think anything was amiss. He was thin and short, probably no more than five-five or five-six. They passed on the sidewalk and she continued toward school.

She reported that several seconds later, "I heard someone running behind me on the sidewalk. I turned to see who it was, and it was the same boy who had just passed me. By then he was pacing me and I remember saying, 'Cold out tonight, isn't it?'" He said nothing, but sped up his pace, walking ahead of her, and she lost sight of him as he went around a corner. Thinking it was a little odd, but also not being concerned for her safety, she said, "I kept walking toward school. The next thing I knew I heard footsteps behind me, and before I could even turn around to see who it was, I felt a hand with a mitten on it covering my mouth. And then I felt a sharp pain in my back." As the pain spread like a wildfire had suddenly turned its wrath on her, she walked toward the school and eventually found help.

Vickie Goff was able to provide police with an excellent description of the young man who had stabbed her. Since she'd seen his face up close and personal, police were able to do a composite drawing of the young man that was circulated to all officers and businesses in the area of the college. No leads were developed and the case went cold.

A month later, a nine-year-old boy was confronted by an older boy on a hill near a nicer residential area of town. The older boy, who was in later years determined to be John Joubert, pulled what appeared to be an Exacto knife out of his coat pocket. He quickly made a slashing motion toward the smaller boy's throat, but the child was able to get away and run home. When he arrived, he was bleeding from a deep cut to his neck, but was treated at a nearby hospital and released with stitches that same night. Again, a description of the older boy was provided to all officers, but the attacker was not located that night. And, again, the case went cold.

Although all of the attacks had occurred within a two-mile radius of Joubert's house on Cottage Street in Portland, no one suspected him of the crimes. "He was so small and he looked like a little choir boy," a neighbor would tell investigators some years later. "We heard about all of this stuff happening, but the last person we'd think of suspecting was John. He was such a quiet little guy who kept to himself."

Another neighbor recalled Joubert being very involved in Boy Scouts. "I think he got all the way up to the level of Eagle Scout. From what I know, that usually means a person has accomplished something fairly meaningful at an early age, and hardly someone you'd ever think of as a person who would run around killing young boys. What little we knew."

But unknown to neighbors and teachers, lurking inside the mind of the seemingly responsible, nice young boy was a dark, unseen anger, seething inside a troubled young man who would soon go on to become a vicious and violent killer.

Six months passed and the attacks had stopped. The radiant beauty of a New England autumn was approaching that August, bringing with it the promise of unparalleled splendor the area was so well known for. A few miles from downtown Portland, an area known as Back Cove was situated in a tree-lined countryside, barely on the outskirts of town. The area was popular with joggers, having numerous trails meandering through the pleasant groves of trees and tall grasses. Even in the nighttime hours, there was rarely a time when someone couldn't be seen out on the paths, jogging along with many others.

On a cool night that same August, six witnesses would recall seeing a young boy, eleven-year-old Ricky Stetson, jogging in a "U.S.A." sweatshirt and pants. They recalled him being near Baxter Avenue, and the time was somewhere around nine o'clock. With reddish hair and freckles, Ricky wasn't hard to remember. All of the witnesses remembered seeing another young man following Ricky, riding on a ten-speed bicycle. The descriptions of the young man varied somewhat, but the witnesses were sure he was somewhere between sixteen and twenty, and had a very slight build. The young man sported a full head of thick, dark hair, was clean-shaven, and there was nothing in particular to distinguish him from anyone else out on the paths that night. And there was no reason to have any sense of alarm or concern, since bicycle riders were as frequently seen in the area as joggers.

A seventh witness recalled seeing a similarly described young man on a ten-speed bike quickly pedaling in the opposite direction on the same path where Ricky had been seen jogging. The witness recalled that the young man on the bicycle glanced back over his shoulder at least once, but the witness also reported he had not seen a small boy jogging in the area. He recalled it was around nine o'clock in the evening.

Shortly after seven o'clock the next morning, a passerby found Ricky Stetson's body beneath a pedestrian footbridge near Interstate 295. The boy was lying on his right side with his right arm extended above his head, his bloody left hand against his stomach. Blood had saturated the front of his sweatshirt, and his pants had been partially pulled down over his hips.

Portland police investigators found a three-quarter-inch stab wound in the boy's chest, and found several sharp cuts had been made to his left calf. Eventually, police identified a suspect and made an arrest, but the man would be cleared of involvement in the crime, and the Stetson case would remain on the books as unsolved.

In classes at the FBI Academy several years later, Ressler would note, "Little did the investigators in Portland know that their suspect was about fifteen hundred miles away in San Antonio, Texas. He went through boot camp there after joining the Air Force. I'm convinced he left Portland because of the Stetson murder. Shortly after boot camp, he went to Mississippi for additional training, and then was transferred to Offutt Air Force base near Omaha."

CHAPTER FORTY THREE

"Baby Billie," the Infantilist

Jim Whalen's drug investigation produced ten convictions, and spun off into yet another wiretap in which many more people in Iowa, Minnesota, and Illinois were to face charges. My school bus bid rigging case went to a jury trial in Fort Dodge, Iowa, where all fourteen companies and people were found guilty in a trial that lasted two weeks. And then the case went "viral." Anti-Trust Division attorneys were able to link violations in Iowa and Nebraska into South Dakota, Minnesota, and North Dakota. I would eventually wind up testifying before grand juries in all three states, resulting in another twenty indictments and convictions. The Anti-Trust Division sent a glowing letter to our SAC, and I received another Quality Step Increase. That was three in about five years. I was way ahead of my academy classmates.

But while all of this progress was significant, our office was going through a number of transitions. Jim Whalen decided that, after nearly fifteen years in Cedar Rapids, he would put in for a transfer. Having graduated from the University of Oklahoma law school before entering on duty with the FBI, Jim put in for an opening in the legal unit at FBI headquarters in Washington, D.C. He was gone within six months, and I'd find myself sorry to see him leave. He'd been a great Senior Resident Agent, and for the time being, I was stuck with that job.

Three new agents had been assigned to the office and were fully functioning on their own with relatively few questions or problems. One of the three, Mike Dudley, had taken over the drug task force from Whalen and stepped things up to another level. Mike was a former District Attorney in Wisconsin, and had hit the ground running as soon as I got him up to speed on the paperwork.

Bill Lauden and Kathy Keane had gotten up to speed pretty quickly and were operating quite well on their own. We had another senior agent in the office who ostensibly was assigned to work Foreign Counter Intelligence cases, but no one truly knew what he did, and most of us would find out later that he was doing virtually nothing. It mattered little to the rest of us, since we had plenty of criminal-related cases to work, including the continuing series of bank robberies. We had twenty-four in a period of eighteen months, and solved all but one of them. Bill and Kathy were certainly critical in achieving that. Mike Dudley was so involved with his drug task force cases that we rarely saw him. None of us ever questioned whether or not he was working.

With Bill and Kathy in the office, I was freed up to work anything I could develop into a big case, or focus on teaching the occasional profiling or hostage negotiations school. And then one of the weirdest cases I'd ever been involved in came into the office. The Madison resident agency of the Milwaukee Division had identified a ring of so-called "infantilists." One of these perverts had tried to kidnap a baby in Madison, and after being arrested had then provided an extensive mailing list of his compatriots around the country. Apparently, some of these people were child molesters, so the problem was fairly easy to see.

Once you think you've seen everything, you always get a big surprise. This was definitely a new one on me: people who are seemingly stuck at the infancy phase of their lives, and strive to be a "baby." It was something of a subculture in the country. There was a newsletter and even an underground market to cater to their perversions. "Mommies," essentially a different type of prostitute, were available to "baby" these individuals, and a whole variety of goods such as special diapers, "adult baby food," and many others were out there to serve their every need. Our Madison office had provided several copies of the newsletters, and I could barely believe what I was reading. "Mommies" advertised their wares and services, and members of the network would provide useful information to their fellow infantilists. I remember seeing a recipe for oatmeal mixed with brown sugar and microwaved for those who wanted to have "poopy-feeling diapers." That was gross enough, but there were more. Many more.

After fifteen years in law enforcement, not to mention my fair share of profiling in-service training sessions, I hardly considered myself naïve. But I'd never heard of this type of deviant behavior. Worse yet, we had at least one of them in Cedar Rapids, and possibly another one in an outlying part of our territory.

Bill Lauden took an immediate interest in the case, once I discussed it with him. "We've gotta work this," he said.

"It makes me sick to think about it," I replied.

"Aside from the fact these guys might be child molesters," Bill said, "this is about the funniest thing I've ever heard of."

"Well, I suppose it does sound interesting, so let's see where we can go with the lead we got from Madison."

Our Cedar Rapids "baby" was William R. Devore, according to the newsletter, and we had a confirmed address on the southwest side of town. We checked utilities and records with the police department and sheriff's office, and all had records of him living there with his parents. But while the local agencies had a record of him being involved in various offenses, most were minor crimes such as drunk driving and domestic violence on his parents. One arrest, however, was more noteworthy. Four years earlier he'd been arrested for breaking and entry of a home not far from his house. He was apparently so drunk that he was caught inside the house and nothing had been taken. However, with his prior history, he was sentenced to five years in prison. Doing the math, Devore was twenty-five years old and was on parole.

One of my favorite things to discover about a possible suspect in a crime was that he was on probation or parole. What this meant was that they had agreed to search conditions by their parole or probation officer as a condition of their release. So they could be searched at any time, as could their place of residence. However, since Devore lived with his parents, we had a new and interesting problem: since he lived with his parents, we assumed most if not all of the house would be common areas. Thus, unless we had a search warrant, our ability to search would be limited. Some very creative police work was going to be required.

"What're we gonna do?" Lauden asked me as we returned to the office.

"I'm not sure. Let me have a meeting with myself, and I'll see if I can figure something out. It's not going to be easy coming up with enough probable cause to get a search warrant." Our federal magistrate in Cedar Rapids was a bit of a stickler for detail, hardly someone who would breeze through a search warrant affidavit and give it the old rubber stamp.

CHAPTER FORTY FOUR

He's Wearing WHAT?

8:15 a.m. the next day

By the next morning I'd figured out something to try. Twenty miles down the road from Cedar Rapids was the Iowa State Prison Classification Center. Every person in Iowa who had been convicted and sentenced was required to go through a thirty-day evaluation at the Center, at which point it would be determined which facility the person would be sent to.

"Let's go down there," I told Bill the next morning. "It might be a waste of time, but I've always found checking the little things often turns into bigger things."

10:00 a.m.

The warden for the center could not have been more accommodating. He knew Devore personally because "he spent way too much time here. He was back and forth between here and Anamosa (one of the larger penitentiaries in Iowa)." He looked at us and rolled his eyes. "I don't know if I should say this, but he was an absolute pain in the ass."

"Why would that be?" I asked.

"The dumb son of a bitch was one of those jailhouse lawyers. He's not stupid, even though he's one of the biggest perverts we've ever had here. He would file one motion after another. Almost drove us crazy having to take him to court and back. Why the courts would even entertain listening to this bullshit is beyond me."

"What was he filing?" Bill asked. He had his law degree from the University of Florida, so he had plenty of background into legal affairs in the courts.

"I've got them all in the file," the warden said. "If you guys want to look, I'll let you go through the files. It's gonna take some time."

"We've got plenty of that," I said. "We're more than a little worried about this guy."

"As well you should be."

The warden provided us with a room and a stack of flies about a foot high. "Well," I said to Bill, "Let's go to work."

I was amazed at the detailed records kept by the institutions where Devore had been incarcerated. Bill and I painstakingly went through every document in the file, and the most frequent statements made that day were "Pete, look at this" or "Bill, you're not going to believe this." We took notes furiously and made an unimaginable number of copies.

Finding probable cause in all of the prison files turned out to be anything but a problem. The files showed records of Devore constantly talking to his roommates about his fetish with either being a baby, or being attracted to them in a sexual way. His court filings were more subtle, but revealing, demanding such things as being called "Baby Billy" and requiring baby food as his diet. While this was significant, even more important to us were his requests to the court to be provided with "Mother and Child" magazines every month, and to be provided with a baby crib to sleep in, rather than his bed in his cell.

It was a productive day and we thanked the warden when we left. Driving north on Interstate 380 on the way home, I made a proposal to Bill. "We've got a ton of stuff and we need to sit down and put it all together. What do you say we grab a twelve-pack of Bud and head over to my place?"

Bill was never one to turn down a beer. "Works for me. Is Mary Ann going to be okay with it?"

"Probably not, but we have some work to do and this isn't a bad way to get it done."

6:00 p.m.

Our conversations at my house drew the attention of both Kary and Loni, who were seventeen at the time.

"What is this about dad?" Kary asked.

"Hard to explain, son," I replied. "Best to say this guy we're working on is a very unusual pervert, and we need to see what he's up to. If he's into molesting children that has to be a concern to us."

Kary, who would later go on to earn a law degree from the University of Iowa, said, "But why would the FBI be involved in this?"

"We're not really sure yet," I explained. "Hopefully, we can get a search warrant and see if there are any federal violations involved."

"You want to write it?" I later asked Bill.

"Nah, you've written so many I think you're probably the right guy to do it. Why don't we be co-affiants?"

"Good idea." We'd finished the twelve-pack and it was getting late. "Let's sleep on it and I'll see you in the office tomorrow. It's gonna take a little creative writing and thinking, but I think if we put our heads together, we can get it done. What do you think?"

"I think we've got it from a legal standpoint. I'll see you in the morning."

7: 45 a.m. the following morning

Bill and I sequestered ourselves in a room in the basement of the federal building, which I'd used during the school bus case. It seemed to take forever, but by the end of the day we'd crafted an affidavit for a search warrant that I felt had a ton of probable cause. I was confident it would fly. I called our United States Magistrate and made an appointment to see him in the morning.

9:30 a.m.

John Jarvis was the U.S. Magistrate for the federal court in the Northern District of Iowa. He'd seen a number of my affidavits over the years, and I felt like I had a considerable amount of credibility with him. He knew I was a good agent, but more than that, he knew I was honest and would not provide him with anything but the truth in what I'd say in court or in an affidavit. I'd testified before him many times, and I felt like he had more than a little respect for me. But as he reviewed the affidavit, he looked up at me with some skepticism.

"This is a little bit thin, Pete," he said. "I'm not quite sure we have federal jurisdiction in this matter."

"I know, John." We'd been on a first-name basis for years, except when I was in court. Then it was "Judge" or "Your Honor." "I'm not entirely sure, yet, but my sense of things is that we have a good likelihood of interstate transportation of child pornography involved, and I think I've made that somewhat apparent in the affidavit."

"Well, I think you might be right about that. You've never been wrong in an affidavit, so I doubt you're wrong about this one."

"I don't think I am."

He signed the search warrant and we were good to go.

9:30 a.m. Friday

By the next morning, we were ready to do a search warrant at "Baby Billy's" house. I got the Sex Crimes units from the Cedar Rapids Police Department and the Linn County Sheriff's Department involved. We met that morning at the police department and I explained what we were doing and what I hoped we'd accomplish. "This guy is a pervert," I said, "and we need to find enough inside his house to assure that's the case. I don't know if he's molested kids in Cedar Rapids, but the possibility is certainly there. We just need to get him off the streets, as far as I'm concerned."

I continued to explain the circumstances. "This is not a high-risk search warrant. We've talked to the warden and this guy is very passive. We don't need the SWAT team to do a dynamic entry with flash-bang grenades or anything like that. I'm going to walk up to the door and knock. If he answers the door, fine. If his mom or dad answers the door, I'll explain what's going on to them, and I don't think there's going to be a problem. So don't worry about running in the door with your guns drawn and expect a big shootout. It's just not that type of case and we don't have anything to indicate he's got guns or is violent in any way. He apparently just wants to be a baby."

I told everyone on the search team, including Bill Lauden and Kathy Keane, that I wanted each of them to focus on a particular room in the house and search it thoroughly. "I think it's going to be more of a document case than anything else, so take your time, don't trash the place, and just look for things that are pertinent to the investigation."

10:05 a.m.

We arrived at Baby Billy's house and calmly parked our vehicles on the street. It was anything but a "lights and sirens" or "high risk" search warrant. I parked in front of the house and walked up to the front door. I had two FBI agents and four officers and deputies covering my back. Billy's mother answered the door. I explained the situation and showed her the search warrant. She acted like it was something that normally happened at the house, and didn't offer the slightest resistance or argument. Devore's father was sitting on the couch watching television. I asked his mother to sit down and told them what we were doing as other officers and agents entered through the front door.

"We have a search warrant for the house," I said. "It doesn't involve either one of you, but it does involve your son. We're going to be looking through the whole house for evidence, so I'd appreciate it if you'd just relax and cooperate with us, and we'll get this done as quickly as we can. Do you understand what we're doing?"

"Yes sir," his mother said passively. It was almost like they were used to having the police and FBI show up at the door every morning of the week. And they remained on the couch without offering any resistance or dispute about anything. Apparently, they knew their son quite well. It was the most unusual search warrant I'd ever executed. Someone in the house was usually ready to either fight or yell and scream. None of that happened at Baby Billy's house.

I made assignments for the search team, designating Kathy Keane as the person who would secure all of the pertinent items found in the house. It was a two-story house, so I told Bill Lauden to head up the stairs and search that area. And then I assigned officers and deputies to search the other rooms in the house. "Be thorough, please," I implored. "We're not looking for an elephant, we're looking for ants."

While I was sitting in the living room trying to make conversation with Baby Billy's parents, I kept hearing a laughing or chuckling noise from somewhere in the house. Not wanting to embarrass the parents, I finally walked around to some of the rooms to see what was happening. Finally, I arrived at the bottom of the stairs, and looked up. Bill Lauden was standing at the top of the steps, peering over a short wall.

"Bill, what in the hell are you doing?" I asked.

He waved his hand, motioning for me to come up the stairs. "You've gotta see this," he whispered.

I climbed the stairs quietly and looked over the short wall. Sitting in a far corner of the upstairs room was a young man, totally naked except for a diaper. He had a baby bottle in his mouth, seemed to be sucking on it, and was watching a videotape dealing with childbirth on the television set. He was completely oblivious to us. I couldn't help but muffle a laugh with my arm.

"All right you dumb shit," I told Lauden. "Get going and search the damn place."

Bill stepped into the room and said, "FBI, we've got a search warrant." Baby Billy looked back at him, continuing to suck on his bottle.

10:00 a.m. the following Monday

Bill and I met with the magistrate to return the search warrant, as was required by law. When a search warrant is issued, agents and officers are required to apprise the issuing judge of what was found as soon as it was reasonable, but absolutely within ten days.

"So, how did it go?" Judge Jarvis asked.

Bill and I both started laughing. The magistrate, like many judges, was a pretty serious guy, but seeing us both cracking up in front of him, he at least cracked a smile. "Okay, Pete, c'mon. Tell me how it went."

I could barely control myself. "John, I don't think I'll ever find anything funnier than this in my entire career. The guy was sitting in front of the TV watching a video on childbirth. It was enough to gross me out, but he was wearing diapers and sucking on a bottle. Frankly, I was surprised he wasn't choking his chicken." Lauden laughed out loud.

"You're kidding me."

"No sir." I tried to get into a more serious mood, but it was hard. "We found a ton of stuff, and I think you're gonna find you were right in authorizing the warrant."

"Okay, so tell me what you found."

I handed him a very nicely written evidence report that Kathy Keane had prepared, and he read the document. Several times he looked up at me as he reviewed Kathy's neat handwriting, then continued reading. "So how many pictures of babies did you find?"

"I'm not sure, John," I answered. "All we said was 'numerous,' but I'd guess we found over two hundred pictures of babies with their genitals showing."

"Where in the hell did he get 'em?" he asked.

"We don't know right now, but we're going to find out. Suffice it to say, this guy had tons of child porn in his room."

"Did his parents know?"

"I doubt it. They seem to be about three fish short of a full stream."

"So are we going to file on this guy here, or what?"

"Not sure. We've still got a lot of work to do."

Over the coming weeks, I assigned Bill Lauden to do whatever he could to identify as many of the babies in the pictures as possible. It was an impossible task. Bill set leads out to fifty-nine FBI offices throughout the country, but didn't receive a positive reply from any of them. No one had a clue where the pictures had come from. When the case was concluded, I sent copies of the reports and pictures to the Behavioral Science Unit in Quantico. Several days later I got a call from Special Agent Ken Lanning. Ken, who I'd known in Los Angeles, was the FBI expert in crimes against children. He'd given us an excellent presentation in our beginning profiling class several years before.

"Pete, this is really good stuff," he told me.

"Very strange case, Ken," I replied.

"I've never heard of these guys."

"It was a new one on me, too."

"I really appreciate it," Ken said. "I'm going to incorporate it into my presentations to the National Academy and see if any of the guys across the country have heard of these characters. What a bunch of perverts. I thought I'd seen everything."

"That's two of us."

Because we couldn't identify any of the babies in the pictures, the U.S. Attorney's Office in Cedar Rapids declined to prosecute Baby Billy. However, the local authorities had several statutes that seemed to apply, and they filed a number of felony charges on him. After much legal wrangling and posturing, Baby Billy Devore was allowed to enter a plea to a single felony count, but because he committed the crimes while he was on parole, it earned him another trip to state prison.

In a final and rather odd twist to the case, while Bill Lauden was reviewing membership lists, he brought several names of Iowans up to me to see if I knew any of the people. One name jumped out at me because he not only had an unusual name, he was a sheriff's deputy in the county where he lived. We debated our options and decided to turn the information over to the sheriff. I never found out, but wondered if the deputy was somehow working undercover.

CHAPTER FORTY FIVE

A Country Road and a Frozen Girl's Body

Winter mornings in the Midwest can be brutally cold and menacing, but Mother Nature seems to have a purpose for everything she does. Before the morning sun begins to peer over the horizon, its warming rays already having dimmed the light from the stars, temperatures fall to their lowest point of the day. This was such a morning, with light snow falling and the temperature hovering around zero.

Everette Dawson stepped out of his farmhouse and onto the covered porch, immediately feeling the frigid air and a biting chill hit him, as it always did, directly in the nostrils. A lifetime of living in the rolling hills of Iowa had given Dawson a nose and sinuses with a valuable and unique talent. He didn't need a thermostat to tell him it was near or below zero. The immediate surge of cold air and a quick sniff told him everything he'd need to know. He wondered at times if it was another stage of evolution for men in cold country, but he knew his nose could tell him the temperature on a cold day – within a few degrees.

It was just before six a.m. on a Friday morning when Dawson stepped off his porch and strode slowly toward his aging Ford F-150 pickup truck, parked as it always was beside his ranch-style house on the one hundred and sixty-acre farm he'd owned and cultivated since his father died more than thirty years before. A four-bay machine shed and pole barn was near the house, but Dawson chose to park his tractors and farm equipment there in the winter rather than his truck. They were the machines he used to make his living, and they needed to be protected from the bitter cold and snow to the extent possible. Rust wouldn't help them work for him. His pickup truck just got him around and into town to run errands and pick up the things he needed to keep the farm operating smoothly.

A light but constant snow was falling. Large flakes carried moisture to the ground that waited thirstily for the upcoming spring season and the rain, when crops would be planted and nurtured by Dawson and nature. He was not a man who moved quickly in the cold Iowa winters. There was no reason for it. He'd learned it wasted energy, and he was rarely in a hurry to do anything or get anywhere in the winter. And it wasn't his nature to be in a hurry, because the lot of the farmer was one of patience, mainly with the weather. Besides, there wasn't much to do in the winter, anyhow.

Dawson turned his head, gazing briefly toward the vast openness of his cornfield, which was covered by a blanket of whiteness from the storms of the past few months. The ground was a pasty white as far as the eye could see, which on some snowy mornings wasn't very far, often not even to the horizon. On this morning, soft white, low-hanging clouds obscured most of the skyline. Coupled with the falling snow, Dawson couldn't see more than two hundred yards in any direction, which told him that the welcome moisture would be falling a good part of the day. Perhaps even into the next day.

Snow and cold are constant reminders that nature has dominion in Iowa during the often foreboding winters. Because of the constant low temperatures, the snow rarely melts at all. Rather, it accumulates layer upon thin layer until spring, which signals the ages-old, time-consuming process of melting. The cycle repeats itself nearly every year, barring a minor drought – which rarely happens in this part of the country, often called the "Breadbasket of America." Even as a young man working on his dad's farm, Dawson was proud of his contribution to that effort, knowing the grain he raised, whether corn or soybeans, helped to nurture the people of his country and others. And so as nature would provide the much-needed moisture for his land, he would give back by growing crops and doing his part to feed the people of the world. For Everette Dawson, it was a fairly simple, uncomplicated life, and the only one he'd ever known. He worked hard when it was required. And that was mainly during the spring, summer, and fall, which was the time to plant, care for, and eventually harvest the crops he'd carefully tended to during those months. He led a reasonably stress-free life, aside from the fall season when the hustle-and-bustle of picking corn with his huge, deep green and yellow John Deere harvester would cause him to begin his work day before daylight broke, often continuing into the late hours of the night. Usually seven days a week, unless he decided to skip a Saturday afternoon to watch an Iowa Hawkeye football game on television. Or sometimes to attend a game in person, if he could acquire tickets for himself and his wife, Georgia. But this usually took the better part of the day, so it was wiser to simply watch the game on television. He avoided being a so-called "CBM Farmer," meaning *Corn, Beans, go to Miami*, because he had a small herd of thirty to forty hogs that he raised in a large pen at the back of the pole barn. Tending to the herd, keeping them well-fed and watered, kept him somewhat occupied during the winter months.

Thus, Everette Dawson was every bit as tied to his land as most people are to their daily jobs. In the winter, his normal routine meant getting up at five thirty a.m., checking the farm markets and weather reports on the radio station in Cedar Rapids, then heading down to West Branch around six or so to meet with his cronies from the local Co-op and surrounding farms. Between fifteen and twenty farmers would gather daily at their favorite restaurant, one of only two in town, enjoying a hearty breakfast of fried eggs, sausage and biscuits, fried potatoes, thick strips of bacon or sausage patties (or both), and heaping mounds of toast with strawberry jelly. And, of course, conversation about the weather predominated. Politics, Hawkeye basketball and football, or even the food they were eating were always secondary to the weather and market report. It was almost like cholesterol had never been invented or heard of in that part of the state. Or the memo hadn't arrived yet. Or they didn't care, because sitting around with their peers and friends in the morning was the best part of the day for many of the farmers in the cold winter months. And when they were done around nine o'clock or so, they'd all go about their various duties. For Dawson this morning, it was to be a stop at the West Branch Co-op to pick up some fifty-pound bags of food pellets for the hogs. He could pick up more, but that might mean he'd have less need to make his daily trips into town, and he enjoyed this part of his life immensely.

Dawson stared at the hood of his truck, quickly judging the depth of the snow, which he decided had probably started falling about an hour or so earlier. *About an inch*, he thought as he brushed his hand against the driver's side window and door handle, sweeping the light dusting of snow away. *Maybe a little more than that*. He opened the unlocked door and slid onto the seat. Dawson never locked his truck. There was no reason to. *Nothing* ever happened where he lived, on a lonely country road about ten miles north of Tipton in northern Cedar County. The entire county and surrounding area was all about farming, and most of the businesses the farmers dealt with were centered in Tipton. If they couldn't find what they needed in West Branch, a thriving community of about two thousand people, all they had to do was head west for Iowa City, roughly twenty miles south and west on Interstate 80. Most people who lived in West Branch had jobs in agriculture, at local businesses, and some even made the daily commute to Iowa City.

The aging farm truck slowly groaned and complained before it finally gave in and roared to a start. Winter mornings were always like that. *Gotta get a new battery one of these days.* Dawson adjusted the mirror and turned the heater up to full blast, feeling the frosty air pounding into his face and nostrils through the vents in the dashboard. He switched on the wipers, then stepped out of the truck to brush collected snow off the hood, eventually beginning to feel a slight hint of warmth from engine heat radiating upward onto metal. Looking toward the sky, he could tell, almost by instinct, that snow would be with him a good part of the day. A lifetime of living in the state gave him some insights into what to expect from the weather on such a stormy day.

Dawson walked around the truck and headed toward the pig pen. Picking up a baseball bat, he pounded on the ice which had formed overnight on top of the watering troughs. And as part of their morning routine, the hogs began collecting at the troughs to enjoy their first taste of cool, refreshing water. He grabbed a partially empty bag of hog pellets, dumping the remaining food in two dry troughs as the pigs scrambled to take their places at their dinner table. He liked to give them a bite to eat as the truck warmed, and would give them more when he returned from town.

By the time he got back to the truck, the engine and passenger compartment had warmed to a sufficient temperature that he felt ready to make his trek into West Branch. He pulled onto his rutted dirt driveway and approached the equally rutted dirt county road. The constant stream of farm trucks was hardly an issue on this frozen morning with the covering of past snows and ice providing a fairly smooth ride.

He turned right onto the road and headed south as he did most mornings, his mind occupied with listening to radio station KDSM from Des Moines. Pork bellies, corn, and soybeans were up slightly in overnight trading. Then came the commercials, touting the virtues of Pioneer corn seed and Roundup fertilizer, which provided the best protection from the blight of rootworms, always a threat to the crops. He drove aimlessly for about five miles at a slow pace, probably no more than thirty-five miles per hour. If that. He wasn't in a hurry, because the boys would be there for hours and there was always an extra table and chair to pull up to and join the crowd.

Approaching an intersection, Dawson slowed slightly, but he could see there were no vehicles coming from either direction even before he got there. As he continued south he could see a fairly large object lying in the road ahead. *Probably a deer that got hit by a car*, he thought. He slowed to avoid it with plans to continue around it. But as he got closer, he could tell it wasn't a deer. It appeared to be a person's body. *What the hell is someone doing lying out here in the road?* He brought the truck to a stop about ten feet north of where the body lay.

Dawson left the truck running and put it in park, got out, and slowly approached the body. His boot tracks were the only ones in the snow, so that told him the person hadn't been out for a morning walk, and possibly slipped and fallen on some ice or the snow. He stepped to the side of the body and could see it was a woman covered with a man's coat, which in turn was partially covered with snow. Those simple observations told him the body had been lying in the road for at least an hour, maybe even longer than that. It didn't make sense to him. Why would a dead person be lying in the middle of the county road, literally halfway to the middle of nowhere? Had she got drunk and passed out in the road? If so, how did she get there? It was too far to walk out here from West Branch, which was another five miles south. Maybe she drove out here. But where was her car? None of it made sense as his mind kicked into another gear and every possible scenario went through his brain.

Maybe she's still alive. He reached down and felt a hand that was outside the blanket. "Frozen solid," he said out loud. *No way she's alive*, he thought. "Gotta call somebody," he whispered, not wanting the person to hear what he was saying. *But how do I do that? If I leave, someone may come driving up here, not notice, and run her over*. He knew that was unlikely, but he was at a loss over what to do. *Should I pick her up and put her in the bed of the truck*? And then he noticed what appeared to be blood that was frozen to and matted on her dark brown hair. *Oh my God. Someone shot her. I've gotta get the sheriff out here.*

As he was trying to figure out what to do and how to call the sheriff's department, he heard a truck approaching from the north. Running toward the back of his truck, he waved frantically at the vehicle, quickly realizing it was one of his farmer friends, Dean Morrison, heading into town for breakfast. Dean's truck slowly pulled up beside him.

"Everette," Dean said as he lowered his window. "Your truck broke down or something? What're you doing standing out here in the middle of the road?"

"There's a dead body in front of my truck!" Everette was nearly shouting.

"What the—are you sure? Did you run someone over?"

"No, she was just lying there when I drove up. You gotta call the sheriff. Right now. Head over to that farmhouse and give 'em a call. Hurry, dammit! I think someone shot her."

"It's a woman?"

"Yeah, it's a woman. Just go over there and give 'em a call. Hurry up. I'll stay here."

"Okay. You sure it's a woman? Shot?"

"Yeah I'm sure, dammit!" Dawson's voice displayed impatience and annoyance. "I guess she's been shot. I don't know. Just get over to that damn house and call the sheriff. Now!"

Dean put his truck in reverse and gunned the engine, wildly spewing snow and dirt from the rear tires. He turned his truck around and headed toward the nearest farmhouse as Everette walked slowly back toward the front of his truck. He put his hands on the hood of his truck to warm them up, then rubbed them together, adjusted the Pioneer Seed hat on his head, and shoved both hands into his coat pockets. He didn't know what to do, but somehow he felt a need to stay outside with the body. It didn't seem right to leave her alone. *How long has she been out here?* Other thoughts continued to assault his brain. *Maybe she killed herself. That's it. Someone must have driven her out here and she killed herself. Or maybe she walked. Long walk, though. But where's the gun? Probably under her. But how do you shoot yourself in the back of the head?* He had no idea what was going on, but he knew the sheriff would be out shortly and get it all figured out.

Within several minutes, Dawson saw Morrison's truck speeding back down the road toward him. The vehicle slowed and pulled up on the shoulder. Morrison got out and walked toward Dawson. They immediately heard a siren's mournful peal across the barren land.

"They're on the way," Morrison said. "What happened?"

"I have no idea," Dawson replied. "Let's just wait here and maybe we'll find out."

"Okay. Wanna wait in my truck?"

"Nah, I think we need to stay out here with her." They stood silently and looked at the body lying in the road as the sound of the siren drew closer.

"C'mon Everette," Morrison pleaded. "It's colder than blazes out here. Let's get in my truck and stay warm. There's nothing we can do now. She's dead."

"Okay, just a minute." He went over to the young woman's body and rearranged the coat which was covering her back. "I want to make sure she's not too cold." he said.

The two farmers didn't make it to breakfast that morning.

CHAPTER FORTY SIX

Flying Solo: First Crack at a Profile in the Field

By complete coincidence, I'd done a one-day profiling school in Cedar Rapids two days before the young woman's body was found. Among those attending the class was an old friend from the Iowa Division of Criminal Investigation (DCI), Special Agent Rick Hatfield.

Early on a frigid February morning, Rick called me at the office. "Pete, I think I might need your help on a murder case."

"What happened, Rick?" I asked.

"Did you hear about the woman's body that was found north of West Branch the other day?"

I thought for a second, and then remembered reading a story in the paper the day before. "You mean the one where the body was found by a farmer out on that country road?"

"Yup. That's the one."

"So what's going on with the case?"

"We've been working on it for the last two days, and we're stuck."

"How come?"

"Well, first of all we've talked to everyone in the family, and they've all got an alibi. They say the victim went down to the convenience story to get a pack of cigarettes around ten o'clock the night before her body was found."

"Walking or driving?"

"Walking. It's only a block or so away from the house."

"Maybe somebody abducted her on the way down or back home?"

"I don't know. This just isn't the type of place where something like that would happen, but you never know.

My instincts tell me it involves someone in the family, but they all say they were home and no one went anywhere after she left. So, right now I'm looking for an unknown suspect."

"Tell me how I can help you," I said.

"You've got all of that training in profiling, so I thought you might be able to see something we might be missing," Rick responded.

"Gotcha. Where are you right now?"

"Down at the Cedar County Sheriff's Department."

"Cedar County? I thought West Branch was in Johnson County."

Rick explained the town was split almost in half, with half in one county and half in the other. "The road she was found on is in Cedar."

"I didn't know that. How long are you going to be down there?"

"How long do I need to be here?"

"It's going to take me about an hour to deal with a crisis for the U.S. Attorney in Des Moines, and then I'll head down."

"That'll be good, I'll see you in a couple of hours."

West Branch, the birthplace of President Herbert Hoover and home to his presidential library, was a good forty-five minutes south and east of Cedar Rapids. It wasn't exactly a tourist trap, but there were plenty of visitors who detoured off Interstate 80 to visit the library. That, I suspected, might have increased the possibility of a stranger killing, meaning the girl could have been picked up by a visitor to town and taken out of town to be sexually assaulted.

Sheriff Ken Whitmarsh and Rick Hatfield, along with another DCI agent from the Davenport office, were in the small conference room when I arrived. Spread out on a table were a number of photographs of the crime scene where the body had been found, autopsy photos, and reports.

Nineteen-year-old Heather Means was the victim. Rick explained, "A farmer was on the way into town and saw the body in the road. He stopped to check, and then a friend of his arrived. Since they were sure the woman was dead, he had his friend drive over to a farmhouse and call the sheriff."

Looking through the pictures, I asked, "So does it

appear she was killed there or somewhere else?"

"We have no doubt she was killed right there. There's nothing to indicate otherwise," Sheriff Whitmarsh replied.

"Looking at these pictures, it appears she got shot in the head twice. Did the coroner retrieve the slugs?"

"Yup," Rick said. "Got 'em right here. He held up a plastic evidence bag with two small bullets in it. The slugs were together in the bag, and the nose of each was flattened out. It appeared the bullets met some resistance in going through the skull, and then entered the brain with sufficient force to kill the victim.

"Looks like a .22?" I asked.

"We're pretty sure it is, but I'm going to get them to the lab tomorrow and we'll know for sure." And then Rick held up a second zip-lock baggie.

"Whatcha got there?"

"These three were found inside her body. She was shot three times in the back, as well as the two she took to the head. It appears to be the same gun, but the lab will tell us that for sure."

"Anyone in her family got a .22?" It was a pretty obvious question, but I had to ask it.

"We don't know that yet. We've got to talk to them, again."

"When do you plan on doing that?"

"We figured sometime this afternoon after we met with you."

I started looking and thinking rather than asking questions. Several immediate things came to my mind from a behavioral standpoint. "Hey guys, there are a couple little theories I'm getting in my head. First, we seem to have overkill. Do you think the shots to the head or the back were the first ones fired?"

"Don't know for sure," Rick answered. "The doc said either the two shots to the head or the three to the back would have been fatal."

In one of our profiling in-services at the FBI Academy, Roy Hazelwood had done a session on anger-related homicides. He'd shown a number of cases in which there was overkill of the victim, and the main point I got out of the session was *anger*. I recall Roy saying, "If you've got numerous stab wounds to a victim, or extreme beating to the face or head, you're probably looking for someone who knew the victim, and knew them very well. To do that much damage, you have a lot of rage coming out, and that's ordinarily going to show a close relationship between the victim and the killer." Roy went on to explain that the anger could be specific toward that victim, or general in that the killer could have been acting out of anger toward all women and may not have even known the victim.

"Is there any sign of sexual assault?" I asked.

"None, and the doc checked thoroughly," Whitmarsh said. "He was sure that didn't happen."

"So the likelihood of her being abducted by someone she didn't know and brought out here to be sexually assaulted is probably something we can eliminate?"

"I think that's fair to say," Rick answered.

"Sheriff, what do you think?" I asked.

"Makes sense to me."

I looked at several photographs of where the victim had been found. "I've probably been on this road, but I don't remember. Does it get plenty of traffic?" I looked at the sheriff to answer that.

"Well, it's certainly not the interstate or anything, that's for sure. But the farmers up in that north part of the county use it plenty. They're always needing to come into town for something, maybe the store or the co-op to get some supplies. Something like that. Or even just coming into town like a bunch of 'em do to have breakfast and chat."

Looking at the pictures again, I said, "I'd like to drive out there later, but right now I'd have to say there was a good chance the killer *wanted* the body to be found."

Rick shrugged. "Hard to say. I'm not sure where you're heading with that."

"Let me just throw out another idea," I said to the three officers. "You might think it's a little *out there*, and probably not something we'd usually think about, but I remember Bob Ressler talking about some cases like this in some of our training sessions. The point of it was, if they leave the body where they *know* it's going to be found, like with this girl that might be another behavioral clue."

Rick looked puzzled. "What do you mean by that?"

"It's pretty subtle, but think about this. After she was murdered, the killer would subconsciously want her to be found and to have a good, Christian burial. The other side of that argument is, if our killer didn't know the girl, he would care less about that. I think he'd be more apt to throw her body in his vehicle and take her out to somewhere she wouldn't be found for months. Then she'd go down as a missing person, and no one would know for the better."

"Damn," the sheriff said. "That had never occurred to me."

"Me either," Rick added.

I swallowed the last of my cup of coffee. "Here's another one, and I don't want you guys to think I'm going alien on you."

"You're already an alien." Rick laughed, as did the sheriff. Rick's partner had said little to nothing, and I assumed he was a new rookie agent who was just along to learn.

"Thanks, I love you too. But let's think about this. She was wearing a coat, but she had someone else's coat draped over her. Right?"

"Correct." Whitmarsh nodded.

"Does that tell us anything?"

"The killer wanted to cover her wounds so they wouldn't be obvious?"

Rick was reaching and I think he knew it. I didn't leap on him and say "No. That's not it." More gently I proposed another idea to them. "How about remorse? He knew her and he felt bad about killing her. So he wanted to cover up what he'd done, to insulate himself from the reality, assuming it's a 'he' we're talking about here, and I believe it is. He covered her so she wouldn't get cold. Again, it's a very subtle subconscious thing, but our subconscious mind has a lot to do with the things we choose to do. And sometimes we just can't help ourselves. How does that strike you?"

Rick looked at the sheriff, rubbed his chin, and then looked at me. "It's a theory right? But it certainly makes sense. I don't know if we can prove it one way or the other until we talked to the person who killed her."

"You're right. But my thinking is, it's another one of those behavioral clues that tells us we're not looking for a stranger. It's got to be someone who knows her well, and even had a relationship with her."

"I can't really come up with another reason, to tell you the truth," said Whitmarsh. "That pretty much narrows the number of possible suspects down a whole lot. It's either going to be someone in the family, or someone else who knew her." The sheriff looked out the office window for a second, then at Rick and me. "It's some stuff you just don't ever think about."

"Well, it's not something I could go to court and testify about," I said, "but it might give us a little insight into what was in our killer's mind. What's the family situation?"

"Five of 'em live at the house. Her mom, her stepdad, and two other kids. One's a boy about sixteen, and the other is a girl about twelve as I recall," Whitmarsh replied.

"How long have the mother and stepdad been married?"

"About two years," Rick said.

"So none of the kids are his?

"Right. I think I know where you're heading now." The sheriff looked like the light bulb just went on in his head.

"I'd have to say it was either the mom or stepdad. Unless you have some reason to suspect the brother," I added.

"Not really. Good kid as far as I know. Never been in any trouble and he's lived here all his life."

"I don't want to go statistical on you here, but most of the murders in the country are between people who know one another. So statistically, at least, the probability of it being a family member is much higher."

Rick took a long drink from his coffee cup. "Pete, we've interviewed all four of 'em. They all said none of 'em left the house after she was gone."

"Maybe someone's lying?

"Might be time to sit down and spend a little more time with her family," Whitmarsh proposed.

"Looks like it," I replied. "But before we do that, let me get a hold of someone back in Quantico. I just want to make sure I'm not flying by the seat of my pants here. We need to get this right, and we've only got one shot at it."

CHAPTER FORTY SEVEN

Incest and Murder in the Heartland

When I called the Behavioral Science Unit, Bob Ressler was my first choice to discuss the case with, but he wasn't in the office. So I asked for Roy Hazelwood.

"Pete, how're you doing?" Roy asked.

"Great, Roy. Hey, look, let me skip the preliminaries and check with you on a couple ideas. I'm down at the sheriff's department here in a little town in Iowa. They had a murder a couple of nights ago, and I just want to run a few things by you, if you've got a few minutes."

"Sure, no problem," Roy replied.

I explained the facts as we knew them, reviewing the theories I'd developed as I went through the reports and pictures.

"That sounds like good logic to me, Pete," he said. "I can't really think of anything I can add based on what you've told me so far. It does sound like someone in the family or somebody very close to her. My guess would be the stepfather, but that's more of a gut feeling."

"That's what I was thinking, too. All right, we'll take it from here. Thanks, Roy, I really appreciate it."

"Glad to help." Roy chuckled. "I'm also pleased to see you've been paying attention when you've been back here. It's good to have some guys like you out in the field who take some of the pressure off us back here."

I returned to the conference room, where the sheriff and the two DCI agents waited. "There are two guys in Quantico I really trust. I just talked to one of them, and it sounds like he agrees with what we're thinking here. You guys good with that?" All three nodded their heads, and we devised a strategy to interview the entire family, again.

"I'll have a deputy go over and ask 'em to come in,"

Ken Whitmarsh said.

"Let's talk to the kids first," Rick said. "Then let's talk to the mom and, finally, the stepdad. We can offer a polygraph. I can probably get our operator over here on Monday or so."

"Sounds good to me," I replied. "It's your case. Do you want me to sit in?"

"Yeah, I *would* like that," the sheriff said. "Maybe there's something you can pick up by the way they say it."

"That'll work," I responded. "We can evaluate what we've got after each interview, and see where we're going next."

Both of the kids were steadfast in saying they had seen their sister leave, but hadn't noticed anyone else leaving the house that night. They'd both been watching television, as had their mother and stepdad.

Carleen Roth could have been the poster girl for the words "trailer trash." She was short and dumpy with loose-fitting clothes and wore no makeup. Her hair was pulled back in a ponytail, and her teeth looked like the first row of a Willie Nelson concert. It took a while, but we finally got her to admit her husband had gone out for a cigarette after Heather left the house.

"How long was he gone?" Rick asked.

"I'm not sure," she answered. "I wasn't really payin' much attention to tell ya the truth. Maybe a half hour."

"Don't you think that's a long time to smoke a cigarette?" I asked.

"I guess. We were all just sittin' around watchin' TV and I really didn't pay much attention."

"Could it have been more than a half hour?" Rick's question was a good one, because if he had taken the car and picked up the victim to go for a drive, the time frame would work out perfectly.

"I don't know. Mighta been."

I had the feeling her IQ was somewhere around an elm tree in my front yard.

"Did he say anything when he came back inside? Or maybe act unusual?" Rick continued.

"I don't remember him saying anything at all. There wasn't anything odd about him. He don't talk much, anyhow."

We had a mini-meeting after ushering her out of the

room. Sheriff Whitmarsh was excited to see that we might finally have a useful bit of information.

"Looks like we've got something here," I said. "Assuming he took the car, he'd have had plenty of time to drive out there and back."

"Looks that way," Rick agreed. "How do you want to interview him? Good cop, bad cop?"

"Who gets to be whom?" I asked.

"I'll be the bad guy," Rick replied. "I'm good at that."

"Great, I'm not."

Delbert Roth was, if anything, even more of a bottom-feeder than his wife. No more than five-foot-five inches tall, he was probably an order of hash browns under three hundred pounds. He wore stained sweat pants of a size I couldn't imagine, and a huge Hawaiian shirt that wasn't well-laundered any more than his pants. Short, dark hair and about five-day's growth of heavy whiskers on his round face completed the look. And if all of that wasn't enough, it smelled like he hadn't showered since he last shaved.

After Rick advised him of his rights, I started out asking him to tell us about what he'd done the day of the murder. Finally, getting up to the relevant hours of the day, I asked him to recount the night.

"We just sat around watching some shows on TV all night," Roth said.

"Tell us about what happened when Heather left," I said in a neutral tone.

"What about it?"

"Did she say where she was going?"

"Yeah. Down to get some cigarettes."

"Did you follow her?"

"No, I stayed inside."

"Your wife said you went out to have a cigarette. Do you remember that?"

"Not really. Far as I know I stayed inside."

We bantered back and forth on this obvious lie and I finally looked over at Rick. "I'll be right back. I need to go to the bathroom before I punch this asshole's lights out. He's making me sick." And I walked out of the room, not sure if I was leaving as the bad cop or the good cop.

Whitmarsh and the other DCI agent were watching

through a two-way mirror, and could hear the entire conversation. I joined them and watched Rick immediately go to nuclear weapons. He paced behind Roth, asking each question louder than the previous one. I let him keep it up for about ten minutes before walking back into the room.

I sat down across the table from Roth and stared at him. "Why are you lying to us, Delbert?"

"Who says I'm lying?"

"I do and Rick does, too. But you know what? Maybe we're both wrong." I lowered my gaze to the worn tabletop and calmly said, "Delbert, let me just say something. You seem like a pretty nice guy." That was the biggest lie I'd told in a while. "Here's what I've found out over all my years in law enforcement. Some people have something like a split personality. One's good and the other one is bad. It's not unusual at all. I'm wondering if that's not what we're dealing with here. I don't think the Delbert I'm talking to would have killed Heather." Which was another lie. "But what I'm wondering is if there isn't another Delbert in there who might have. Maybe the bad Delbert. What do you think?"

He stared at me, looked at Rick and then back at me. "You're right. The good Delbert never would have done this, but the bad Delbert might have." I knew we had him on the precipice of confessing right then.

"Delbert," I said, "we're going to leave the room for a few minutes, and I want you to think about what we were just talking about."

Outside the room, everyone could see how the interrogation had taken a sudden turn.

"I've heard of good cop and bad cop," the sheriff said. "But this idea about good suspect, bad suspect is a new one on me."

"Every once in a while I come up with a good idea," I said. "This one might work."

When we got back in the room, Roth was sitting there with his face in his hands, crying. From that point on, things went quite smoothly. Roth told us he'd started a sexual relationship with Heather a year before he married her mother. It continued until about a month before the fatal night. "She started telling me about a boyfriend she had, and how she wanted to break it all off with me." Angry, he argued with her several times, but she wouldn't relent.

On the night Heather died, Roth said, "She went down to the store to get a pack of cigarettes. About five minutes later I told Carleen I was going outside for a cigarette. We don't smoke in the house, so it wasn't anything unusual. I don't think Carleen even heard me and she may not have even noticed when I got up to go. I got in my truck and drove down to the store. Heather was just coming out and stopped to light a cigarette, so I pulled into the parking lot beside her. I told her to get in and I'd give her a ride back to the house."

"Is that what you really intended to do?" Rick asked.

"Not really. I wanted to talk to her, so I just drove out the road into the country. I didn't want to stop our relationship, but she did. We argued back and forth. Finally, I was a couple miles up the road and she told me to let her out. We argued again. I told her it was too cold to walk, but she got out and started walking, anyhow. I followed her for a while, but she just kept walking. I'd honk and she'd flip me the bird. It was really pissing me off."

Roth went on to tell us he finally stopped the truck and got his .22 semiautomatic pistol out from under the seat. "I was really pissed. I got out of the truck and yelled at her and she flipped me off again. So I ran up to her and shot her in the head a couple of times. She went down right there on the road and as she was lying there, I shot her in the back. I really don't remember how many times. I figured she was dead, so I went back to my truck, trying to think of what I had just done, and what I was going to do. I'm not sure why I did this, but I grabbed my coat from the truck and went out to cover her up. I guess I must have been thinking how cold it was, and even though I knew she was dead, I didn't want her to get cold. Then I just panicked and took off like a bat out of hell and went home. That's pretty much it."

We had a few follow-up questions, one being where the gun was. "It's still in my truck." He signed a form that gave us permission to search, and we retrieved the pistol from the truck, right where he said it would be.

From there, it was a bunch of follow-up work by the investigators. Charged initially with first-degree murder,

Roth managed to avoid the possibility of a date with the gas chamber by pleading guilty to second-degree murder and received a lengthy prison sentence.

    I hoped he'd get Baby Billy as his cellmate. That would be my definition of justice!

CHAPTER FORTY EIGHT

Pete, I Need Some Help

An English writer by the name of Rebecca West once wrote, "It is always one's virtues and not one's vices that precipitate one's disaster." The FBI had a similar, but simpler quote: "No good deed goes unpunished." And of course the great philosopher and songwriter Bob Dylan once wrote a song called "The Times They Are a-Changin'." All of these started to combine into an imperfect storm as a new case loomed on the horizon.

Being an optimist by nature, I never placed much stock into any philosophy other than one I learned from my dad, which was, "If you work hard, good things will happen." That had pretty much been the guiding principal in my life, and still is.

Change is inevitable, and certainly had happened in the Cedar Rapids Resident Agency during the eleven years I was stationed there. Jim Whalen and I had both worked hard for years, breathing life into a moribund two-man office that probably would have remained at that staffing level for years to come. With a number of multi-indictment cases, we'd clearly shown there was plenty to be accomplished in Eastern Iowa. New agents were assigned, and after Jim left I continued to develop big cases, having more freedom from minor annoyances. Mike Dudley was a working machine, continuing to rack up indictments and convictions on drug task force cases.

For years, the Cedar Rapids and Davenport Resident Agencies had been overseen by a Supervisory Special Agent in Des Moines. For most of the time, that worked quite well. But as it became apparent there was more and more work directly related to the area covered by Cedar Rapids, our headquarters office in Omaha decided we needed an Eastern Iowa supervisor. I had no problem with that notion, but would later discover it was part of a disaster-in-the-making.

Surprisingly, some of the changes in our field division came about because of a series of events that occurred in Omaha. A new agent directly out of the academy had been assigned to Omaha. While he was by no means the first minority agent assigned to the division, some of the more senior agents in Omaha felt he was the most incompetent agent they'd ever seen in the field division. Over a period of about a year, everyone got their fill of him, but even worse, a few agents started a systematic process of harassment. It wasn't really racial in nature, until one culminating event took things to an entirely new level.

The two principal antagonists of the constant harassment, whose names I won't mention, decided one night to embellish a family picture the new agent kept on his desk. When he arrived at work the next morning, he was greeted with animal faces on his wife, two children and himself. Probably not one of the brighter things the two leading men had done in their bureau careers. They would later say the intent was not racial, but the implications were more than apparent.

After this final event, the targeted agent filed a racial discrimination complaint. Having a law degree, he'd kept records of the harassment, detailing each incident into a lengthy complaint. A serious complaint of this type typically prompts direct and immediate involvement of FBI headquarters. A team of inspectors was sent out to Omaha, and soon after heads began to roll. Our SAC and ASAC were reassigned, but not demoted in rank. That, of course, meant we had a new SAC and ASAC assigned to Omaha. It became apparent after a relatively short period of time that they were sent to Omaha with a clear mandate from the FBI Director: "Clean that office up."

But by that time, the principle instigator of the harassment and his target had received transfers out of Omaha. In a brilliant stroke of bureau genius, *both* of them had been assigned to the Chicago Field Division. Needless to say, the harassment continued in Chicago. The aggrieved agent would go on to file a lawsuit against the bureau, and would eventually settle out-of-court for over a million dollars.

We kept hearing rumors in Cedar Rapids that the ASAC was acting as the main henchman, and that he was going after everyone in the Omaha office, excluding support personnel. None of this had even the slightest effect on me or what I was doing. There was more than enough to do, a couple of new agents to train, and plenty of cases in the prosecution pipeline.

And then came the case that proved, as one Assistant U.S. Attorney in Des Moines described it, "that we can, in fact, convict the innocent." But the scheme I found myself involved in was anything but that.

By now I should have learned that being in the office wasn't a particularly bright move. Invariably, someone would call with something new and crazy, if not a legitimate crisis—such as having to go to Quantico for another in-service. On this occasion, it was my supervisor, Bob Conner, calling from Des Moines.

"Pete, I'm glad I caught you."

"Hey, Bob, what's up with you?"

"Well, it's more what's up for you if you can do something for us."

"Tell me what it is and I suppose we can figure it out."

"Here's the deal," he said. "We have an informant who runs a business where they buy stuff from people who are simply trying to get rid of grandma's old jewelry and such. Basically a junk dealer. A couple of yahoos came rolling into his shop the other day with a ton of jewelry, which is probably stolen. It was in a small suitcase, but there was a lot of it. He looked at it and thought it was probably worth around three hundred grand. He didn't tell 'em that, but he said there was a bunch of good stuff."

"Got that, but how do I fit into the picture?"

"Pretty easy, actually. I don't have another guy in the state who has worked undercover, and I probably don't have one who's got a line of bullshit like you do."

"I guess I'll take that as a compliment. I think."

"Well, I think you know you're one of the best guys I've got."

"Thanks. So tell me what I can do to help out."

"Our informant gave them an offer of ten thousand dollars, but they told him they need a whole lot more than that."

"Such as?"

"Closer to thirty thousand."

"Lot of money," I commented.

"You're right, it is. We think we might be able to get it for about thirty grand."

"And then as soon as the transaction goes down, handcuff time?"

"Exactly."

"What do you need me to do?'

"The informant told the guys he wouldn't give 'em more than ten grand, but he knows a guy in Omaha they might want to talk to."

"And that would be me?"

"Yep. What do you think?"

"Any background on the bad guys?"

"I've got two guys working on it. So far, nothing to go on. We'll have it by tonight, I think."

"Do we know if the jewelry's stolen?"

"He told our informant that it was part of an insurance scam in Ohio, and that it's 'sorta stolen.'"

"Which means it's stolen."

"Exactly."

"Tell me what you'd like me to do."

Bob Connor said, "The way I see things, if you can get over here, tonight, we can figure out a way to get back in touch with these guys. We know where they're staying and our informant has their number. He told 'em he'd give it to his friend in Omaha, and if he was interested he'd give them a call."

"Presumably, I'm interested...and from Omaha."

"Yup."

"It actually sounds like fun to me."

"Thought it might."

"What do you need me to do?"

"Can you get over here tonight?"

"Sure. I've got a little paperwork to finish here and I can dictate some other stuff on the way over. So, let's see. I can probably be there in about three or four hours. Gotta get this done and pick up some clothes at home, then I'm on the road. Two-hour drive and tell me where to meet you."

"Give me a call on the radio when you're getting close. I suspect a couple of us will be in the office, so I'm guessing we'll meet you here."

"Okay, see you in a couple of hours."

"Thanks, Pete. I knew I could count on you."

CHAPTER FORTY NINE

Going Undercover to Buy $300,000 in Stolen Jewelry

By the next morning, we had a plan in place, plenty of backup agents from both the Des Moines Resident Agency and Iowa Department of Criminal Investigation, and a non-bureau-looking car for me to drive to the motel. Our informant had made a call to the bad guys the previous night, and we agreed to meet at noon at the Hyatt House in Des Moines. We also got the informant to provide me with a jeweler's loupe and a couple of other tools to make me look legitimate.

"I did plenty of undercover buys when I was a cop," I told Bob. "Nobody ever shows up on time. Why don't I go rolling in around one p.m. and give 'em a line of bullshit that I had a hard time getting through the traffic in Omaha or something? They'll be waiting. If we look too anxious, it says 'cops.' They're not going anywhere. They've got some product to sell and they want to make some money."

"Good idea."

At about one-fifteen, I parked in the lot and casually walked into the hotel lounge. I sat down at the bar and ordered a draft beer. Trying to remain casual, I didn't look around, but in a couple of minutes a small, weaselly-looking guy came walking up and tapped my shoulder.

"Are you Pete?"

I turned my head to the right. "Yup, that's me."

He introduced himself with a phony name, and we later determined his true name was Thomas Reda. He was about five-foot-eight, and a maximum of a hundred and fifty pounds, if that. Somehow I pegged him as an

Italian guy from the East Coast. Dark hair slicked-back and the look of a wannabe Mafia guy, wearing a black shirt, open at the collar, and a gold necklace hanging around his neck. Being about six-foot-two and over two hundred pounds, I wasn't too concerned if a physical confrontation ensued. Unless he had a gun.

"C'mon over to our table. I've got a guy I want you to meet," he whispered. I looked over my other shoulder and slowly got off the barstool.

He introduced me to a man who was sitting at a table in a dark, far corner of the lounge. We'd later learn this guy was Michael O'Connor, and both of them were scam artists from Las Vegas. We sat and chatted for a few minutes and then Reda said, "Let's go up to my room." I finished my beer and up the elevator we went to the fourth floor.

I knew there were agents in the rooms across the hall, and I had a wire on so they could listen to our conversation. I just hoped it was working. Reda opened Room 419 and O'Connor went into Room 417. "He's got the stuff in there," Reda said. "Do you have the money?"

"Maybe I do and maybe I don't," I replied. "I haven't seen any reason to have money, yet." In fact, I didn't have the cash on me; it was secured in my undercover car. I wasn't about to get ripped off, and that was part of the plan we'd set up.

Momentarily, O'Connor came into the room with a leather briefcase. He set it down on the bed beside me and opened it up. It was literally chock-full of jewelry.

"Holy shit," I said. "You guys really have a good bit of stuff here."

"Yup, take a look." Reda sounded nervous as he said it.

I pulled out my loupe and started to examine the jewelry. Having no clue about jewelry more expensive than you could get at the local K-Mart, I spent some time acting like I knew what I was looking at as I talked to them. Many of the pieces still had price tags affixed, some showing a value of nearly two thousand dollars. Most of the necklaces and rings were in the five hundred dollar

range, some less.

O'Connor didn't say much, since Reda appeared to be acting as the point man. "Whaddya think?" he asked after I'd examined about a dozen pieces.

"I don't think anything until I look at all of this stuff." I pulled out one piece after another, closely examining each item before laying it on the bed. It took a while with me using the jeweler's loupe, and Reda paced around the room nervously. O'Connor sat comfortably on the opposite bed, saying nothing but watching closely.

By the time I'd pretty much finished going through all of the pieces in the briefcase, Reda had nearly worn a hole in the floor. He was making me a little nervous, so I said, "All right, let's see what we can work out here. I might have some interest if we can work out a decent price."

"I need fifty large," Reda replied quickly.

"In your dreams," I said. "This stuff is hot, right?"

"Well, sorta."

"Isn't that like being sorta pregnant? What the hell does sorta hot mean? I'm the one who's gonna have my neck sticking out." I didn't want to sound anxious and agree to his price. That would scream "cop" all over the room. In fact, if we couldn't agree to a number I liked, I was prepared to walk out of the room.

O'Conner finally spoke up. "Of course that shit's hot. It's worth at least three hundred K retail. Give us a number." His voice was deep and gravelly, like he'd been a life-long smoker. "If you don't want it, fine. We won't have a problem offing it somewhere."

I said, "I'll go twenty K. Final offer." It wasn't, but we were negotiating and I knew I had a little room to work upward.

"Forty," Reda shot back.

"Forget it." I got up off the bed and started to head toward the door. "I'm the one who'll be taking the risk trying to sell a bunch of hot stuff in my shop. Once you guys have it out of your hands, you're scot free and back on the road. The cops stop me, find this stuff, and I hit the bucket for a couple of years."

Back and forth we went as I stood facing both of them. It took a while, but I finally finagled the price down to thirty thousand. I knew I had that in the trunk of my undercover car.

I rubbed my chin, looked at the briefcase, acting like I had a serious decision to make. "All right, let's make it thirty. How do we want to do this?"

"You got the money with you?" O'Connor growled.

"You gotta be kidding me. It's in my car. I'll get it and be right back."

"That'll work." Reda looked pleased. "We're not going nowhere. Let's do this."

Knowing I had plenty of agents watching and listening, I took my time walking down the hall. As soon as I got on the elevator, I started telling everyone what was going on. "I'm heading down to the car to get the money. Not sure what the next step is, but hopefully you're hearing all of this. Everything is going okay. I don't feel threatened in the slightest, but who knows what's going to happen when I show up with thirty grand." I was confident they were tuned in and the word was getting where it needed to be. The guys in rooms across the hall were the ones I wanted to make sure had the clue on everything. If things went to hell, I had a code word to say, and the hotel door was coming down with a bunch of agents behind it. We do protect our own.

When I got back, Reda was alone in the room. "Where's the other guy?" I asked.

"He's in the next room. We wanna do this and get the hell out of town." And then he threw me a curve I wasn't ready for. "How interested might you be in some diamonds, or do you know anyone who would be?" That piqued my curiosity, because I knew we had a guy in Cedar Rapids who purportedly had been a fence for stolen diamonds for years.

I acted like I was thinking. "I know someone who might be, but he's not in Omaha. I've done a little business with the guy, but not much in diamonds lately."

"I've got some down in my car, well-hidden in a small sack. Do you wanna take a look?" Figuring we might have the possibility of recovering more stolen property, I agreed. In truth I couldn't tell the difference between a diamond, a cubic zirconium, and a granite boulder.

"What about all of this stuff?" I asked.

"Won't take long. We can just leave it in the room and be right back." He opened a dresser drawer. "Let's just hide it here and take a look. If you're interested or you think the guy might be, we can always give him a call. Where did you say he was?"

"I didn't, but I can get a hold of him if I think the stuff might be of interest to him." He closed the briefcase with the jewelry and put it in the drawer. I did the same with the money.

"Don't want to be walking around in a parking lot with that much money," he said, and thus began *"The Sting."* Little did I know they'd cut a hole in the wall from the adjoining room. Once we closed the door and left the room, O'Connor and another scammer I hadn't met pulled off the back of the drawer and pulled the money out with the jewelry. So now they had the whole package, including thirty thousand dollars in buy money.

As Reda and I walked to his car, O'Connor and a guy we'd later identify as Clarence Cunningham headed out of their room and went down the elevator. They eventually headed out the front door and got into a separate car parked right in front. Someone made a good decision to pull them over as soon as they pulled out of the parking lot. I didn't see any of this, since I was at Reda's car, parked as far away from the front door as possible. They had a nice little scam put together, and had probably run it several times before they got to us. Obviously, as we'd determine later, the goal was to get me as far from the room as possible, giving O'Connor and Cunningham plenty of time to get out to their car with money and merchandise, and then meet somewhere to carve up the booty.

After we'd looked at what I assumed were diamonds, we went back to the room. As we approached, agents leaped out of the rooms across the hall and pounced on both of us, screaming "FBI! FBI! Get down on the floor!"

Reda was squealing like a stuck pig, and never stopped whining or complaining as he repeatedly professed his innocence. He pointed a finger at me and claimed I was the guilty one. I was handcuffed and led out to a bureau car, and Reda was put in another one. I had no clue they had the other guys in custody.

About a month before trial in Federal Court in Des Moines, we found out the jewelry had, in fact, been stolen from a jewelry dealer's car in Las Vegas. We had the diamonds examined by the informant we'd used, and they turned out to be fake. It worked as a diversion, but I never agreed to buy them or make a referral.

Something about the entire scenario just didn't smell right from the moment I met the two scammers in the lounge. My *"If something doesn't look right, it isn't"* radar was on alert from the moment the entire meeting began, and never went to the *off* position.

Before trial, the three defendants' attorneys filed brief after brief, saying in effect the FBI had no authority to arrest the defendants for Interstate Transportation of Stolen Property, because at the time of their arrests we couldn't prove the property was, in fact, stolen. The argument was plausible, but we were fortunate to have a conservative, law and order judge assigned to the case. He denied every motion, but encouraged us to use due diligence to find out where the jewelry was stolen, and from whom. Luckily, we were eventually able to get that done.

Due in large part to an aggressive Assistant U.S. Attorney who had a set of balls, we went to trial on the case, and all three were found guilty of the charges we filed. Slam-dunk in the minds of the jury, but it was a little touch-and-go for us. You never know what's going to happen once a jury deliberates.

I learned later that the case was appealed to the United States Court of Appeals, which was the first and only time that had ever happened to me. While I wasn't needed to testify, I drove up with the AUSA who presented the government's argument to the court in St. Paul, Minnesota, and enjoyed listening to the two sides submit their divergent views of the case to the panel of judges. In a unanimous verdict, the three-judge panel upheld the convictions. The defendants' attorneys made some noise about appealing the case to the U.S. Supreme Court, but their clients apparently didn't have enough money to take things to that level.

In later years, we'd laughingly call it the "You're under arrest for possession of stolen property. Oh, by the way, we don't know if the property is stolen" caper. Thomas Reda and his merry band of thieves received their sentences to a federal institution of lower learning. It wouldn't surprise me if they went on to new and better scams, and eventually to older and worse institutions.

CHAPTER FIFTY

The Most Shocking Phone Call of My Career

"What was the most interesting case you ever worked on in the FBI?" Or perhaps, "What was the strangest case you ever had?" I'll be a little wistful here, but if I had been given one hundred dollars every time I was asked one of those questions, and invested it all, I would be pretty well off at this point in my life.

I always had a hard time answering those types of questions, because trying to determine what is or was interesting to me might not strike the average person as interesting at all. I had a bunch of cases with multiple indictments and convictions I found quite interesting. On the other hand, there were a number of murder and sexual assault cases I worked on that I found even more fascinating. It wasn't like putting a quarter in a candy machine and cases just came spitting out of my mouth.

But that all changed in 2009. I had been retired from the FBI for about nine years and was teaching criminal justice classes full-time at a large community college in Colorado. Between putting in some office hours one day and doing preparation for a class the next day, my phone rang. It seemed that I still had not learned the lesson to not spend much time in the office.

I picked the receiver up and, as I always did, said, "This is Pete Klismet."

A young-sounding female voice on the line haltingly asked, "Yes sir. Is this the same Peter Klismet who was an FBI agent?"

Immediately, I suppose I got into something of a defensive position, partly because there was no way to know what this call was going to involve. In fact, since I retired I had never had such a question. "Yes it is."

"Mr. Klismet, I'm a reporter with the Omaha World

Herald." I know she gave me her name, but I don't remember what it was. "I'm working on a story about a case involving the murder of a lady named Helen Wilson. Do you remember the case?"

I had to think for a moment, but it came back to me. "Is that the elderly woman who was killed in Beatrice, Nebraska?" Frankly, I was dumbfounded by why someone would be calling me about a case I'd done a profile on many years before. I assumed the case had been solved years ago, or was still a cold case, but I didn't know. Several times over the years, I'd wondered what happened.

"Yes sir, that's exactly the case I'm talking about."

"Sure, I generally remember the case." That was a perfectly honest answer, generally being the operative word.

"Mr. Klismet, the research I've done so far indicates you did a profile on the murderer. Do you remember that?"

"Yes I do. I did a preliminary profile and then sent everything I had back to Quantico. I don't recall, but it seems they followed up and provided a more extensive profile than the preliminary information I gave them. Is that right?"

"Yes sir, it is. What I wanted to ask you is if you would still stand by the profile?"

I probably stammered a bit, but said, "I'm sure I would. If I said it then, I would have had a good handle on the case. I don't remember what I said word-for-word all these years later, but yes, I'd certainly stand by what I said back then."

I was probably flying by the seat of my pants more than a little bit. While I generally remembered the case, I didn't have an immediate recall of the details that caused me to say what I did to the investigators and their police chief. Out of the clear blue sky, with my brain in a completely different place, this wasn't a line of questioning I was ready for in any manner of speaking. It was a bit of a pop quiz I wasn't ready for and would never give to my students.

"Are you aware of what's happened with the case since you ended your involvement in it?" she asked.

Here again, I was thinking I was the subject of a lawsuit or something worse. Maybe they were going to indict me for providing false information to investigators. I didn't have a clue. A whole lot of thoughts went through my head at Ferrari speed.

"Not really," I replied. "I know I called the police department several times after I'd been to Beatrice, but then I suppose I got involved in other things and pretty much forgot about it. Every once in a while it'd pop into my head, but not much more than a fleeting thought. So I guess the answer to your question is 'no.' I don't know what's happened, but I assume something did."

"Yes sir, something did happen. Six people were arrested for the murder and sexual assault in nineteen eighty-nine."

"Six people! No, you've gotta be kidding me." I was incredulous. There was no way six people could have been inside that woman's tiny apartment and committed this crime. Six people in the woman's apartment would have made it look like the Nebraska football team had stampeded through. The crime scene was anything but a disaster area. In fact, as I recalled, it was fairly neat. "Is this some sort of a television show to see how much you can fool someone and get their reaction? Candid Telephone or something? There is no way there were six people involved in this murder. One of my whacko friends is putting you up to this, aren't they?"

"No sir, I'm perfectly serious," she said with a matching seriousness to her tone. "Five of them pled guilty in exchange for lesser charges and shorter prison terms. One of the six maintained his innocence and took his chances with a jury. He lost and he was sentenced to life in prison in nineteen ninety."

I was still trying to wrap my brain around this mess. "This has got to be some sort of a joke. I can believe one person was convicted, and maybe he's the guy who did it, but where in the world did they come up with the other five?"

"That's part of the story we're working on. The co-defendants have now recanted their testimony and all of them said they lied on the stand. They've done a DNA match, and the person they've matched it to fits your profile perfectly."

"And that would be the guy they convicted?"

"No, and that's what the whole story is about. The DNA that was collected that night excludes the two men who were implicated in the rape and murder by their co-defendants. The man who lost the jury trial was not the person who committed the crime. They're considering releasing the other man who was supposedly involved in the case."

"And he'd be one who entered a guilty plea?"

"That's right."

"Okay, I get that, but what's happened with the guy who the DNA matched up to?"

"He died of AIDS."

"Oh my God. This has got to be the craziest thing I've ever heard about in all my years in law enforcement."

"That's what they're saying here."

"Can I have your number and call you back? I need to digest all of this."

"Yes sir." She gave me her name and number. "Let me send you a couple of links to the story which you can look at before you call me."

"That would be good. If I sound like I'm speechless, it's because I am. I've never heard of something like this, so it's gonna take me a little time to process it all. I'll call you back in a couple of days. Is that alright?"

"Yes sir. That would be fine."

CHAPTER FIFTY ONE

You Need Me WHERE?

The town of Beatrice is a small, typical Midwestern agricultural community situated on the Big Blue River in southeastern Nebraska. Beatrice is located about forty miles due south of the state capitol, Lincoln, and a virtual eternity away from modern times. But that's exactly how they like it. In the past forty years, the population of Beatrice has fluctuated between ten thousand and twelve thousand, and was closer to the latter figure in the mid-1980s.

Like many Midwestern towns, Beatrice is a quiet place, relatively crime-free, and one of those places where most people in town know one another and nothing ever happens. But fear gripped Beatrice in the summer of 1983. Someone was stalking older women, breaking into their homes, and trying to sexually assault them.

The first attack happened on June 27th. A seventy-three-year-old woman was in her apartment, knitting and watching a show on TV. She happened to look up and saw a tall, thin man standing over her. He wore a stocking cap over his face with holes cut out over his eyes so he could see. He immediately put a hand across her mouth and held a knife to her throat, then reached down to pull up her nightgown as he tried to get on top of her. She fought, kicked him in the groin, and pushed him away. He screamed in pain and fled. The struggle produced a deep cut on her thumb. She called the police who came out to take her statement. The suspect was not identified.

On August 9th, an eighty-two-year-old woman was at home when a young man suddenly appeared in her living room. She described him as having shoulder-length blonde hair, which was visible beneath a terrycloth mask he had placed over his face. He grabbed her neck with both hands and started to choke her, but she screamed, kicked, and thrashed her arms until he ran out the door.

A third attack occurred at about 12:40 a.m. two weeks later. A seventy-one-year-old woman reported she was sound asleep in her bedroom when the light went on. Suddenly awakened, she heard a man say, "If you scream I'm going to kill you." The man jumped on the bed and held a knife to her throat. She could see the man had some sort of a rag on his head. Disregarding his threat, the woman screamed and pushed the man away, receiving a cut on her throat and both of her hands in the process. She told police she managed to stand up and run out of the house, but not before he punched her in the face. She described her assailant as a young, slim, white male with long blonde hair.

Then, for some reason, the attacks stopped. Nothing happened for months, and the community returned to a state of normalcy.

Until February 5th, 1985.

That morning, Helen Wilson's sister came over to her apartment to check on her, since she hadn't gotten her usual morning phone call. She found her sister's body on the floor of her downtown apartment with an afghan wrapped around her face. She immediately called the police and an officer arrived within minutes. Other officers were at the apartment minutes later, including the Chief of Police.

No one could remember the last time a murder had occurred in Beatrice. Investigators soon learned the woman had been raped, and an autopsy revealed she had a broken breastbone, arm, and ribs. She had multiple scrapes on her face and defensive wounds on her right hand, probably caused by a steak knife taken from her kitchen. The autopsy revealed she died from suffocation, probably hastened by her pneumonia. At the time of her death, Mrs. Wilson, a widow, was sixty-eight years old.

About a week later, I was at home when the phone rang at about nine in the evening. I answered it, because at that time of night it was always for me.

"Pete, this is John Evans." John was my Assistant Special Agent in Charge.

"Hi, John," I responded, and here again immediately wondered what I'd done wrong.

"Sorry to call you at home, but we've got something happening, and I need you to get to Beatrice, Nebraska."

"Where's that?" I'd never heard of the town.

"South of Lincoln."

"Oh, okay. What's happening there?"

"They had a murder and I need you to do a profile for them."

"Tonight?"

"If you can."

"I've got to testify at the Grand Jury here tomorrow, and then I have to do the same thing in Des Moines the next day. I can't get out of that."

"All right, I need you there as soon as you can. Can you give the chief a call tonight?"

"Sure, I suppose so." I got the number and called the police department. The police chief told me about the investigation and explained they were at a standstill.

"We don't have the slightest inkling who did it," he said. He explained how the Nebraska State Police had assigned an investigator to help them, but they still didn't have a viable suspect in the case. "There are a bunch of guys we're looking at, but none of them are good enough suspects to arrest as yet."

My experience in the Midwest had shown me that smaller agencies, such as the Beatrice Police Department, are not equipped to handle much other than a smoking gun homicide. This is not meant to fault them in the slightest, because major crimes simply don't happen that often in small towns. Since that's the case, their investigators are rarely given the opportunity to attend training in homicide and other complex crimes. It's just a fact of life for small agencies, and often is driven by a lack of funding to send many officers to schools where they can learn these skills.

To Beatrice, a murder investigation certainly fit the definition of big and complex. They simply didn't have the training and experience to know where to go next. So they called the FBI in Omaha, and John Evans probably told them he'd send over his agent with a crystal ball who could pinpoint the suspect in a matter of hours. John simply wasn't sharp enough to know it wasn't *Name That Tune*, and assumed that since I was his profiler, I could have it solved in a jiffy. Like any number of higher-level FBI managers, John was anxious to feather his own bed and show people *just how good* the FBI was.

I could tell by talking to the police chief that there were plenty of leads to cover, but none of them had been at that point in the investigation. The big problem was not having enough people to work on the case. Not surprisingly, they thought an FBI profile would point them right to the suspect.

I told the chief what my dilemma was with the Grand Jury, and explained I'd head over to Beatrice right after I made my appearance at the Grand Jury in Des Moines.

"We'll be ready for you," he said. "I'll have my guys get all of the reports together."

"I assume you have crime scene photos, too?"

"Oh, yeah. We'll bring them, too."

Oh my God, I thought to myself, *what am I dealing with here?* They were expecting a savior, the Messiah, to roll into town and point the finger at the exact house where the suspect lived. They wanted an all-knowing psychic to solve the case and get back to their more basic routine of handling burglaries, thefts, vandalism, and other simple crimes. I had a strong feeling it was going to be like, "Please Mr. FBI profiler, come to town and do your magic. Solve this case for us." Knowing John Evans, he probably fomented that by boasting he had the best profiler in the FBI. I was already starting to feel the pressure. It wasn't a situation I looked forward to, and I knew there were going to be some high expectations from the time I arrived in town. It was exactly the situation Denny Koslowski and I talked about in our first weeks of training.

I still hadn't arrived at a point where I felt enough confidence to do a profile by myself, but I also knew they would assume I was *the man*. There would be expectations from the moment I arrived. It was going to be like the old cliché, "An expert is someone from more than fifty miles away who carries a briefcase." I knew I didn't have the expertise, but I hoped I would be able to provide some meaningful assistance. I was sure they needed it.

CHAPTER FIFTY TWO

The Helen Wilson Case: A Preliminary Profile

I called the police chief, Wes Scott, two days later from the U.S. Attorney's office in Des Moines. I finished testifying before the Grand Jury for the Southern District of Iowa, and spent a little time with my AUSA concerning a lengthy investigation we'd been doing into a drug case in Iowa City. We were about to charge twelve people in a sealed indictment. During the investigation I'd drafted and gotten federal wiretap authority for the home phone of our major player. The entire case had been a major fiasco with a supposed "three-headed" team of agencies in charge, meaning no one was truly in charge. Everyone had different ways to do things, and it was virtually impossible to agree on where to go next. When I agreed to work on the case, I didn't dream we would have so many problems between ourselves. We had so much conflict between the FBI, DEA, and sheriff's office that I would eventually request and be granted a transfer from Cedar Rapids to Omaha.

"Chief, it's almost three in the afternoon, and I think it's gonna take me about three hours to get there. Can you guys meet me for dinner at the hotel? Maybe we can spend some quality time reviewing what happened. It will be a good opportunity for me to get my arms around what happened."

"We'll see you here about six," he replied.

The drive was relatively easy, giving me a fair chance to clear all of the Grand Jury testimony out of my head. I hoped my mind would be ready to focus on the task ahead, even though I wasn't sure what it was going to be. As soon as I arrived, the chief and two of his officers greeted me in the lobby of the small, older motel where I planned to stay that night.

"Pete, we're really glad you're here." Chief Scott had a fairly large packet of paper in his hand and handed it to me as soon as we were inside the restaurant.

"Thanks, Chief. Let's have a bite to eat." I glanced at the reports in my hand. "I'm hungry and you guys probably are, too."

After we exchanged names and ordered our dinners, I asked the three officers to summarize what they knew at that point in the investigation. They explained what they had learned from witnesses (which was virtually nothing), the coroner's report, and the follow-up work they'd done. I could tell there were a ton of things they could have done, but hadn't. But I didn't say anything, and wouldn't until I had a chance to sit down and go through the reports.

And then one of the officers said, "We have a suspect. Let me tell you about him."

"Whoa," I said, holding up my hands. "Time out. Don't do that. The way I see my job is that I can review all of your reports and look at the pictures of the crime scene and autopsy. When I'm done with that, I'll try to give you some idea of what I think you might need to be looking for as a suspect. This is all going to be preliminary though. Before a profile is official, it has to be reviewed back in Quantico. They're the ones who will actually give you a profile. I'm mainly here to collect the information. But, based on what you have, I might be able to provide a couple nuggets of information."

"Oh," the chief said, looking surprised. "I thought you'd want to know everything about our suspect, too."

"Look at it this way," I explained. "I'm human, and we're all going to take the easy route if we can. Don't make it too easy for me. I need to do my job and that's to look at the reports and the pictures of the crime scene and autopsy information you've got for me. I'm not going to solve it for you, but what I hope is that we might be able to give you some new information and leads to work with. It's your job to solve it from there. If what we say fits the guy you were gonna tell me about, that's good. If not, we'll talk about it. Are you guys okay with that?"

While all three of them looked a little confused, I asked them to give me a couple of hours to review the reports. "Can you stick around here, or do you want me to meet you at the station in the morning? I'd guess it'll take me a couple of hours to go through all of this stuff."

Chief Scott looked at his wristwatch, and my immediate thought was he was concerned about paying his officers overtime. I didn't see that as my problem, so I stood up to head for my room. Surprisingly, he said, "We'll meet you here. Make that in the lounge."

It took me about three hours to methodically review all of the reports, the autopsy protocol, and the crime scene pictures. I busily jotted notes, and then went back through it all if I found something that didn't seem to fit with what was said earlier. I took a couple of pages of notes, and was surprised at the lack of follow-up that. Nothing had been done after the first couple of days. It was almost like they were thinking the case was going to solve itself. But I tempered that with knowing they probably lacked the training and experience to know what the next steps should be.

When I returned to the lounge, the chief and his officers were anxiously awaiting my return and appeared to be ready to hear what I had to say. I sat down with the reports and my notes, and we started going over some of the behavioral clues I felt would be of some value to them in trying to identify a viable suspect.

"Guys, there is no doubt in my mind we're dealing with a single person in this case," I said, "and there is also no doubt he's the same one who committed the other assaults on the other women. That's not only my opinion, I'd stake my reputation on it, whatever that might be worth."

"We have always thought it was only one guy, too," the chief said.

"Let me give you a couple reasons why I'm so sure of that. First, if there was a second suspect, there would have been some money taken from Mrs. Wilson's apartment. There was over fourteen-hundred-dollars in cash in her purse, and it wouldn't have been hard to find. There wasn't any ransacking, so this crime was about sexual assault and not robbery. Make sense?"

The officers scribbled notes. Chief Scott said, "Yeah, we considered that too."

"There are a couple of other things that will make even more sense in my one-suspect theory, and this is more of a 'guy thing' than anything else. If you had a partner who went into the apartment with you, are you going to have sex with an older woman while he watches? It's demeaning to him, and he'd never live down the kidding he'd get. My point here is, if it was a younger gal, then the situation would be completely different. But here we're dealing with an older lady and realistically the level of attractiveness isn't the same. I think you can see where I'm heading with this. It's fairly subtle from a behavioral standpoint, but if we just apply some common sense to the way men think, it's important."

"Hadn't thought of that," the chief commented.

"There are a few more things I want to think about, but if we can buy into the fact that the other assaults are related to this one, and I believe they are, there was only one suspect involved in those. So I'm confident you're only going to have one guy involved in this."

"But why would there have been such a gap in time?" Chief Scott interjected.

"Not sure about that," I answered. "My money would go on him leaving the city for a while. Maybe he got worried that you guys were onto him after the three earlier assaults. Time to get out of Dodge. He even might have spent some time in jail on an unrelated charge. Now here's a point where you guys might want to go through booking reports from the county jail since the last assault. It's an outside chance, but I think it might be a useful lead to cover, just to be touching all of the bases."

"Okay, if we do that, what're we looking for?" Scott asked.

"Good question. This guy is going to be a young male, early twenties. You already have some descriptive information from the earlier victims. He's tall, slender, and has long blonde hair. You can eliminate anyone over twenty-five, I'd say, and focus an age-range between twenty and twenty-five. Plus the description you have of course. That should narrow things down a lot."

The chief looked at his officers. "Write that down. It's something we need to look at." Both officers nodded.

"And one other thing. You can throw a blanket over where all four of these assaults occurred."

"Meaning this guy lives pretty close?" the chief asked.

"No question in my mind," I said. "Again, that should help to narrow it down, but I think this guy lives within walking distance of all four places. He spent quite a bit of time in Mrs. Wilson's place, which tells me he is very familiar with the area."

"Why is that?" one of the officers asked.

"It's a fairly subtle psychological thing, because if you think about it, it would make sense he was comfortable in the apartment for a couple of reasons. One would be that he knew what the best escape routes would be on the streets and alleys if he heard a siren, or saw a police car. It'd just be out the door, down the stairs, and he's lost in the night."

"You said a couple of reasons," one of the officers replied.

"You're right, I did. I'd suspect he's either been in the apartment before, maybe to do some repair work like plumbing or something simple. I'm not sure about that, but it's possible and it's another lead that can be checked out."

"Put that down too," Chief Scott said.

"Another thing to consider is that this probably isn't his first attempt at rape."

"So, he might have a record?"

"Yes, most likely he will."

We spent another half hour kicking around some other possibilities before I said, "It's getting late, and I pretty much turn into a zombie or a werewolf after ten o'clock. Why don't I meet you guys down at the station in the morning? I'll think about it a little more tonight, but I tend to be a whole lot sharper in the morning. I'll just have a bite to eat here in the morning and meet you there around nine?"

"That should work," the chief said, and we all got up and went our separate ways. I still had all of the reports, and figured I'd look at them in the morning when my brain was fully operational. That often happened after one or two cups of coffee. There would be no Pabst Blue Ribbon beer involved.

CHAPTER FIFTY THREE

And the Years Went By...

The next morning they carved out a space for me to work at the police station. I started typing out some of my thoughts to give them, which was something of a preliminary profile. Once again I explained that nothing was official until I'd sent everything back to Quantico. Then one of the agents in the Behavioral Science Unit would review the facts and provide them with a report. Those were the rules, and those of us in the field had agreed to abide by them from day one. But, as had been the case on some other investigations I'd worked on over the years, the local officers didn't want to wait a couple of months for some answers. They were desperate for something, but I was fearful of giving them more than I was qualified to do. It was a very slippery slope and a difficult position to be into. I certainly wanted to avoid getting into hot water with the Behavioral Science Unit in Quantico.

I had opened the case with an official FBI file number, packaged everything up, and sent it on its way to Quantico. I included my initial assessment of the facts in typed form, knowing it would help the agent who was assigned the case at the BSU. I added as much explanation and rationale to my opinions as I could and provided a copy of that to the chief. When I left that afternoon, I felt like I'd given them my best effort, and provided some new and viable leads to consider. My job wasn't to roll into town on golden wheels in a chariot and solve the case for them with magic or psychic powers. They seemed very appreciative of my help when I left. It was a long drive back to Cedar Rapids, and I felt brain-dead by the time I pulled into my driveway about six hours later.

Over the next couple of months, I periodically checked in with Chief Wes Scott in Beatrice and received the same responses. They hadn't developed a solid suspect, or a suspect at all. It was tempting to ask him if they'd followed up on any of the suggestions I'd made, but that wasn't appropriate. It was their case, and it wasn't my job to check up on them. My part in the investigation was fairly limited, I had done it to the best of my ability, and now they had to take the ball and run with it.

About three months after I'd sent everything in to Quantico, the official profile came to me in bureau mail. I reviewed it, saw it as a good reason to call the chief again, and told him I'd fax a copy directly to him. In reality, there was very little added to my assessment of the crime. Their assessment was that the crime was committed by one man acting alone, and they added several other things:

He will be a white male, in his late teens or early 20s. He was and probably still is described as a nice, quiet, and shy boy.

He is thin and of average- to below-average height.

The suspect lives close to Mrs. Wilson's apartment because all of the similar attacks occurred within a four-block area. In addition, he will probably live with his mother or another older female relative.

He is very dependent on this mother figure in his life, has been dominated by her through his life. He resents this domination, and has had significant conflict with either this woman or another significant woman in his life.

The suspect likely has a poor self-image and low self-esteem. He wouldn't be comfortable in a relationship with a woman his own age.

In school, he would have been seen as a loner or, at the very least, odd. He would not have been involved in activities and probably would have been of slightly below-average intelligence.

He would care little about personal hygiene. He is not someone women would be attracted to.

His car, if he owns one, would have been drab and old and probably unkempt inside, and poorly maintained.

It's also possible he knew Mrs. Wilson, and may have performed errands or work for her in the past. The likelihood that he had been in her apartment previously cannot be discounted.

There is even a possibility that the suspect lived in the apartment building at one time.

The suspect has, in all probability, been interviewed early in the investigation.

He may have approached the police under the guise of a concerned citizen, or may have provided information to take the focus away from himself.

The suspect was motivated by rape and probably did not mean to kill Mrs. Wilson.

It is probable the suspect will have a past record of sexual assault.

As a result, he may have felt remorseful and may have visited her grave in an effort to make peace with himself and minimize the stress he felt.

Within the next several months and years, I completely lost contact with the officers in Beatrice, probably assuming they'd call me if a suspect was identified and charged with the murder. A phone call from Beatrice never came, and I went on to other duties. But in large part, I had plenty of things to work on, and the Wilson case eventually faded from my memory. I received a transfer into Omaha, working gang and drug cases, and eventually received my Office of Preference transfer to the Denver Division's Grand Junction Resident Agency. That wasn't my first choice, but the Denver office wanted someone who understood the inner workings of a resident agency, and I'd done that for over ten years in Cedar Rapids. If I turned the transfer down, it would have been three more years before I'd be up for another one. And I wanted to get back to Colorado where I'd grown up. I'd been away for twenty-seven years. It was time to go home.

A case in Grand Junction garnered me the 1999 Law Enforcement Officer of the Year award. I was flown to San Francisco to accept the award from a multi-national organization with nearly two thousand people in attendance at the yearly convention. It seemed to me that if you were going to go out, you might as well do it when you were on top. It worked out quite well for John Elway and some other athletes. I didn't see how I could be more on top than I was that year.

After several meetings with myself, I put in my

retirement papers. My bosses were surprised, because I could have stayed in the bureau four more years if I chose to do so. My last day in the FBI was December 31, 1999. I was ready, after nearly thirty years in law enforcement. There had to be something else out there for me.

And then the something else appeared. A teaching position at a small community college in northwest Colorado opened up. Teaching had been something I had wanted to do since I was in college, and here was the chance, only months after I retired. Three years teaching at that college led to a job teaching at a much bigger school on the other side of the state. I couldn't have drawn up the plan any better than it turned out.

CHAPTER FIFTY FOUR

Picking Low-Hanging Fruit

The investigation into Helen Wilson's murder has been called "the greatest miscarriage of justice in modern Nebraska history." Some have even said in United States history. After scouring every story I could find about the case on the Internet, researching for nearly two years, reading an incredible number of newspaper articles, making phone calls, and generally thinking about how something like this could happen, I would have to join in that belief. Piece by piece, a horror story of incompetence at several levels, a need to convict *someone*, a lack of integrity, and a complete absence of ethics formed into a whirlwind of gross injustice. It simply has to be among the worst cases in the annals of law enforcement in the United States. And indeed may be the worst.

The question that drove and mystified me for several years was: How on earth could five people plead guilty to something they hadn't done? What was in their personalities that would allow them to do it? And not only to enter guilty pleas, but to exacerbate the problem by lying to a jury to convict a sixth man who had absolutely nothing to do with the murder.

In the final analysis, it comes down to questionable investigation by law enforcement, browbeating by a hard-charging prosecutor, and deception by a psychologist masquerading as a deputy. Presumably, they were well-intended, but how they could perpetrate a disaster of this magnitude is unfathomable. This wasn't the Thomas Reda case in which we laughed about convicting the innocent—none of whom *were* innocent. This was a case in which truly innocent people were convicted, and that goes against everything I've believed in during my many years of involvement with law enforcement.

The second investigation of the Helen Wilson case began nearly four years after the murder when a sheriff's deputy re-interviewed a young woman who was seventeen years old at the time of the crime. She told the deputy she knew a woman named Ada JoAnn Taylor, and had "partied with her several times." She went on to say that Ada Taylor had admitted to the murder of Mrs. Wilson while she and Taylor stood near Helen Wilson's apartment building at seven thirty on the same morning Mrs. Wilson's body was found. This somewhat fragmentary statement eventually led to a firestorm of activity, resulting in charges against Ada Taylor and five other defendants.

On its face, the statement of Ada Taylor simply can't be true, because there was a murder *and* a rape committed. How could Ada Taylor do both? There is a certain amount of common sense to be applied in any investigation, and that was lacking from the outset. But then it got worse. Much worse.

Ada JoAnn Taylor was born to a father in prison and a mother who was suicidal. She was placed in foster care at eleven, was married at fourteen, and was lodged in a psychiatric hospital at the age of seventeen. During her post-conviction evaluation, a psychiatrist described Ada as being "overweight, mildly disheveled with Borderline Personality Disorder." In the research I did on this case, I've discussed the latter aspect (Borderline Personality Disorder) with people who have a background in psychology, with all of the required degrees. While no one can say with certainty, there was agreement that a person of this type could easily be manipulated in interviews and certainly influenced by figures of authority. Or at another level, to make a statement which was completely untrue to embellish her own poor self-esteem. Or to satisfy the person he or she might be interviewed by. How admitting to a murder could accomplish this is anyone's guess.

However it happened, Ada Taylor's initial interview was the springboard to identify five other individuals, all of whom were ostensibly involved in the murder of Helen Wilson. Statements of another woman, and Thomas Winslow (who would eventually be charged as well) were taken. Both statements seemed to enhance what investigators already thought they had. They presented their specious findings to the district attorney and arrest warrants were authorized. Within a matter of days, Joseph White and Ada Taylor were in custody. The dominoes then started to fall.

White was interrogated at the time of his arrest in Alabama. He denied knowing Helen Wilson, denied ever having been in her apartment, and denied knowing anything about the murder. Investigators asked him to provide hair and body fluid samples, saying, "You know the samples can put you at the scene."

White was apparently not concerned about that, since he knew he hadn't been there. He replied, "Yep, and it can also positively prove I wasn't there." Samples were collected before White was returned to Nebraska to face initial charges.

Following her arrest in North Carolina, Ada Taylor appeared confused, as had White when he was taken into custody. Both were oblivious to how they could be arrested for a crime they didn't commit. White, however, steadfastly maintained his innocence. Ada Taylor, on the other hand, told the arresting officers she must have been at Wilson's apartment that night "because the other officers told me I was there." Completely exhausted while holding her head in her hands and crying, Taylor told Nebraska cops over and over she couldn't remember. She went on to tell them she believed her personality disorder made it impossible for her to know, particularly since someone had told her she was in the apartment.

Like circling sharks in a feeding frenzy, two investigators helped Taylor come up with a story. She told them on the night Wilson died, she and White went to the widow's one-story house early in the evening to do yard work. One of the investigators told Taylor that White wouldn't be doing yard work in February. Not to mention that Helen Wilson would not be responsible for yard work at an apartment building. Or even that the building didn't have a yard. These would seem to be important facts, but apparently common sense had long-since gone by the wayside at this juncture.

The videotaping was discontinued for twenty minutes as the officers talked to her off camera. When they returned to the interview, the one-story house became a three-story brick building, and a summer evening of doing yard work became a bitterly cold winter night. In fact, the night Helen Wilson was killed, temperatures plummeted to seven degrees below zero. From recalling almost nothing to telling a story of rape and murder, Taylor was clearly led down the primrose path, and then said White and another boy had stabbed the woman. Wilson's death was caused by suffocation. All of this is called developing a theory, and then forming a set of facts to conform to the theory. It is not something that is encouraged in police work. But it obviously was happening to a person with a very weak and susceptible personality.

The officers worked Taylor over verbally, trying to get her to admit the "other boy" inside the apartment was Thomas Winslow, later to become a defendant in the case as well. Surprisingly, Taylor didn't fall into this trap, but the ones she did fall into gave investigating officers even more fuel for their ill-conceived theories. Someone was going down, and the more the merrier it seemed at this juncture.

When he was arrested, Thomas Winslow did little to contribute to his own innocence. He told investigators that he was in Helen Wilson's apartment on the night she was killed. While he later recanted that statement, Winslow effectively put the rope around his neck. Ada Taylor had told officers that Winslow's future wife, Beth Johnson, was in the apartment that night with what was now becoming a veritable flock of uninvited guests. The logical conclusion seemed to be that if Beth Johnson was there, Thomas Winslow *must have been*. And better yet, he'd admitted it, for reasons only he might know since it was obviously untrue. Trying to recant was like trying to un-ring the bell. It simply wasn't going to happen.

Winslow did say a portion of his story was true, and that part was placing White and Taylor in Helen Wilson's apartment on the night she was raped and killed. He also said his girlfriend, Beth Johnson, was there. Overlooked was the fact that, if he said he wasn't there, how could he know who was? Including his own girlfriend.

Was Winslow mistaken? Did he lie? Either way, he was wrong. Johnson had an alibi for that night, and it could not be broken. While this was obviously a lie by

Winslow, everything else he said was *deemed* to be true. If the theory doesn't fit the facts, throw out the facts, except those that might seem to relate to the facts.

At this point in the investigation, despite a number of inconsistencies, investigators were up to three potential defendants. Whether or not all of those people could have ever fit comfortably in Helen Wilson's small apartment while a brutal crime was occurring seemed irrelevant. The case was clearly *coming together* for the investigative team, and the prosecutor was apprised of developments at every stage. The level of excitement was palpable. Not only had the case been "solved," but three people *involved* in the murder had been arrested.

Early into my law enforcement career, I learned that the statement "Case Closed by Arrest" could not be anything further from the truth. An investigation was an effort to seek the truth, and an arrest was simply a part of the process. The truth of a matter would ultimately be determined in several ways. First would be an assessment of the facts by a competent prosecutor. Second would be a determination to lodge charges based on that evaluation of provable facts. Third would be a preliminary hearing to determine if probable cause existed to believe the defendant(s) were the likely person(s) who committed the crime. Finally would be the trial, whether in front of a jury or a judge. Unless, of course, the parties involved in the case chose to enter pleas of guilty. Most criminal cases in the country are resolved by guilty pleas. This would prove to be instructive in how six people were found guilty of crimes they didn't commit.

Meanwhile, the zealous investigative team wasn't even close to being done. A woman by the name of Debra Shelden was Helen Wilson's grandniece, but had not met her until she was in her twenties. Debra was a mentally challenged person who had gone through special education classes offered in the Beatrice School District. She had grown up in foster care for most of her childhood. Following the initial arrests, the primary investigator showed up at Debra's trailer-home in Lincoln to take a statement from her. The essence of the statement was that Ada Taylor had confessed to the killing of her great-aunt in a letter, but she no longer had that letter in her possession. Several weeks later, the investigator interviewed Debra's husband, Cliff, who was about to start a nine-year prison sentence for his role in the robbery of a motel in Lincoln. Cliff Shelden implicated Ada Taylor, Joseph White, and Thomas Winslow in the murder. And, seemingly as an afterthought, he threw his own wife and a young construction worker by the name of James Dean under the bus. Why that happened, no one knows, since the statement was later determined to be absolutely false on its face. Perhaps Cliff Shelden wanted to have some familiar faces with him in prison.

Nonetheless, Debra Shelden was promptly arrested. She didn't help her case by admitting she went to her great-aunt's apartment that fateful night with Winslow, White, and Taylor. She recalled hearing Helen Wilson scream and also recalled her aunt being injured during the attack. She remembered her head was bleeding. In short, Debra gave investigators what amounted to a full-blown confession. This was, by far, the best statement they had gotten. How the statement was obtained and the methods involved in influencing a mentally challenged person to confess to something she didn't do are still up for debate. One might assume Debra Shelden was *force-fed* information, and promptly regurgitated it back to the investigators. And one might be correct.

James Dean was promptly arrested. He admitted he knew the other suspects, but said he had no involvement in Helen Wilson's murder. But then he began to question himself two weeks later when he learned he had failed a polygraph examination. Following that, the prosecutor, the sheriff, and Dean's public defender agreed to have a Beatrice psychologist evaluate Dean. In the report, the psychologist said Dean understood the results of the polygraph "revealed something at the subconscious level," namely that "he was present in the apartment, but could not reconcile his being present with the conscious belief that he was not there." (I've read that a hundred times, and I'm still not quite sure what it says.)

The psychologist went on to conclude that James Dean likely witnessed Helen Wilson's death, but had *repressed* the memory. He recommended therapy for Dean, which Dean agreed to, but said he wanted to talk to someone else. The psychologist, as it turned out, happened to be a part-time deputy for the sheriff's department in Gage County.

If all of this hasn't reached the level of bewilderment beyond the comprehension of the ordinary person, another interesting twist of fate was entered into the equation. Some have labeled the investigation at this point as being an "incestuous relationship." A psychologist had worked with Beatrice police shortly after Helen Wilson's death. His evaluation of the murder led him to believe the killing was committed by a single person acting alone, and that this person had considerable anger toward older women. I wasn't aware of this profile, but anecdotal information shortly after the death would clearly state that the police, the psychologist, and a seemingly competent profiler from the FBI agreed there would be only one suspect involved in the case. But why pay attention to that! The investigation was on a roll like a snowball heading down a steep mountain slope.

The picture became yet more involved when Ada Taylor first got back to Beatrice after her arrest in North Carolina. The same psychologist the police used four years before was the first person she asked to see. Perhaps not coincidentally, he had been her therapist when she was living in Nebraska. He later said, "I wanted to see her, too. I wanted to see if she knew what was going on, both for her sake and the state's (the prosecution)." His statement would seem to add credence to the probability that he had some serious questions about her involvement, and the involvement of all of the other people. But *justice* continued to march forward.

The psychologist also met with Debra Shelden after her arrest to evaluate her competency. By this time, Shelden had entered a guilty plea in the case, but said she was having trouble remembering details from the night her great-aunt was killed.

The psychologist concluded that Debra Shelden "felt the need to make things right." Presumably, she felt badly about her great-aunt's murder so admitting she was involved seemed like the right thing to do. Or perhaps she had killed Helen Wilson herself. You would have to make that conclusion, because I don't think I can.

A final suspect emerged as a result of the

interrogation of Debra Shelden. Kathy Gonzalez lived in an apartment above Helen Wilson's at the time of her murder. Debra Shelden believed she was also involved. Since Debra said that was the case, Gonzalez was located and arrested in Denver, Colorado. She told police she knew absolutely nothing about the murder of Helen Wilson. However, she agreed to return to Gage County, saying, "I figured I'd go home and tell them the truth, and the truth shall set me free." She continued to deny involvement in the murder, but was frustrated by the statements of others saying she was, in fact, involved. How she was involved was never clear, especially to her. But that didn't seem to matter to the prosecutor and investigating team. She, too, was taken into custody. Kathy Gonzalez was then interviewed by the same psychologist, said she didn't remember anything, and couldn't understand why she'd block out something she wasn't even involved in. She went on to say, "I don't think I was there, but they seem to have evidence or they wouldn't have arrested me."

The psychologist concluded it was "enough evidence to convince the judge."

In a statement after the case was resolved years later, Gonzalez said, "They just found a bunch of suckers. They weren't getting anywhere, so they found a bunch of disposable people, and that was us."

At that point in 1989, there were six defendants in a case only one could have committed. Four years after Helen Wilson was buried, the investigative team had all six people behind bars.

CHAPTER FIFTY FIVE

"If I Dreamed About It, I Musta Done It"

The role of a prosecutor in a criminal case is equally as important as the evidence he's presented with. He can look at a multi-defendant case much like a pride of lions would look at a herd of zebras. The lions will pick out the most vulnerable and go after that zebra, exclusive of the others they probably can't catch. My involvement in many multi-defendant cases over the years, proved the same to be true. We'd simply go after the "weakest link," explaining to them that the train was leaving the station, and they had one chance to get on board. In prosecutor and investigator terms, that was another way of saying, "If you plead guilty and admit what you did, then give us some other people, you'll get a break." Sometimes it worked. In this case it did, because six people were potentially facing the death penalty.

But a prosecutor's job is not only to convict people of crimes, it is also to assure the rights of a defendant are protected. He or she is also responsible for dismissing the charges against a person if the evidence conclusively proves that person is not guilty of a crime. The latter part of that responsibility did not seem to hold much importance in this case.

By now there were clearly two, if not three, vulnerable people in custody. The primary leverage a prosecutor can use in a murder case is the ominous threat of the death penalty. That's a daunting, if not terrifying, prospect to wrap your mind around. Debra Shelden and Ada Taylor were the most obvious for the investigative team to lean on at this juncture. James Dean was on the short list. And so it began.

Getting two marginally-competent women to believe

they were *probably* guilty of *something*, but had repressed the memories of that event in the intervening four years, might not have been that difficult when faced with a seemingly competent and convincing psychologist. Someone who just happened to be a part of the investigation and had an obvious stake in the case. The nature of those conversations is not known or available to the general public. However, it's not difficult to extrapolate from what had already happened during the so-called investigation. A whole group of innocent people were being railroaded in the name of "justice."

With six defendants in custody, the prosecutor started negotiations with their attorneys. The prosecutor would later say, "I was trying to show a distinction between the ones who did the crime and the idiots who came along for the ride." But the prosecutor needed some of those *idiots* to be witnesses. Aside from a match of blood types, he had no useful physical evidence to put any of the six suspects in the victim's apartment. The case was built on word of mouth statements, and the principal investigator would later say he had little interest in proving the case with forensic evidence.

The case was to rely heavily on eyewitness testimony from people who claimed they were participants in the murder of Helen Wilson. When it came to convincing these witnesses to testify, the prosecutor had a sledgehammer: the threat of execution. Like all county attorneys, he knew the possibility of being cooked in the electric chair was not palatable, and tended to motivate cooperation. Realizing this, all but Joseph White elected to roll over. White knew he had admitted to nothing since his arrest in Alabama, and had nothing to admit to. He'd done nothing wrong. Why admit to something you hadn't done?

Motions to suppress statements and various items of evidence were filed by defense attorneys for the defendants. Some of them had tried to recant the statements they had made against their own interests. Mental and physical coercion were alleged in the motions, as were promises of leniency. Even the prosecutor didn't like or completely understand how the two primary investigators had interrogated Ada Taylor. All he knew was that her statement more or less fit the facts of the case. That was apparently good enough to proceed. Attorneys noted there were interruptions in the taped *confessions*, but the prosecutor didn't believe that violated the law. He presented forms in court showing that Taylor had been advised of her rights, had waived them, and said there had been no threats made in her talking about the crime.

Following arguments before the court, the judge ruled that "No force, fear, oppression, or coercion were used against the defendant (Ada Taylor)." Thus, her statement would be allowed as evidence in court. That ruling by the court made the dominoes start to fall even faster. Attorneys for the remaining defendants in the case saw the futility of proceeding further. Except for Joseph White, who continued to maintain his innocence. It seemed there was nothing that could inspire him to plead guilty.

While sitting in the Gage County jail charged with first-degree murder, Joseph White struggled to understand how the case had gone this far. Months earlier, when he agreed to come to Nebraska, he thought his innocence would quickly surface. Surely police would see his accusers were liars. It was all a big mistake. He'd be back in Alabama before he knew it. Instead, he waited. If convicted, he knew he could be sautéed in a wooden chair, or at best spend the rest of his days in prison. But White put his faith in the system. He read books as the days slowly crawled past. He wrote short stories and poetry. But in court, things weren't going quite so well for Joseph White.

The judge denied every significant motion that was made on White's behalf, with one exception. He ruled the primary investigators had improperly continued their interrogation in an Alabama police station after White made it clear he wanted an attorney. That was a small victory. He still had a horde of other people lined up to testify against him.

Debra Shelden, who White said he didn't even know, had already pled guilty to aiding and abetting second-degree murder. She told authorities she saw White beat and rape her great-aunt, Helen Wilson.

James Dean was next. Initially, he said he had no involvement in the crime. But he panicked after he failed his polygraph test. "I knew I was screwed at that point," Dean would say twenty years later. So he started talking. His first recollections were fragmentary, but he said he was with a group of people who broke into the apartment and attacked Wilson.

The county attorney, who sat in on several of Dean's interrogations, interrupted with a question. "Prior to this time...you denied you were there," he said. "Can you tell me now why you were saying you were not there?"

"Well, I feel I remembered it in my sleep," Dean said. "I obviously had some kind of subconscious block or something. I don't know what it was for sure. I couldn't remember and I thought I was telling the truth." At about the same time, the county attorney and Dean's lawyer began discussing a plea bargain.

In due time, and under extreme pressure, Dean transformed himself from a reluctant suspect into a cooperative chatterbox. Over the course of two months, he gave authorities five more statements, for a grand total of nine since his arrest. Each statement was different. That didn't seem to matter. With Dean essentially saying, "If I dreamed it, I must have done it," the prosecution was ready to use his statement at trial. One would think the problem would be *which* statement to use.

Nothing seemed to have a greater effect on Dean than the crime scene video that he saw on May 17, 1989. When Dean saw Wilson's lifeless body, he buried his head in his attorney's coat, sobbed, and said he was ready to plead guilty to aiding and abetting second-degree murder. In so doing, he agreed to "give total cooperation to the state of Nebraska regarding the homicide of Helen Wilson."

The plea bargains reduced the possible punishment for Dean and Shelden from death to a maximum of ten years in prison.

During depositions presided over by both prosecution and defense lawyers, Dean and Shelden both said much of what they recalled about the murder came from dreams. Dean estimated ninety percent of his memories were revealed to him as he slept. But the stories they told were devastating for White. They said a group of six—White, Taylor, Shelden, Dean, Tom Winslow, and Kathy Gonzalez—had broken into the apartment with a plan to rob the woman. White and

Winslow took turns raping Wilson. Taylor helped hold her
down and put a pillow over her face. The fact that the
intent of the crime was ostensibly robbery, that money
was readily visible and was not taken, apparently was of
little importance.

"Is there any part of it that you remember from
actually being there?" White's attorney, Toney Redman,
asked Dean during a pretrial deposition.

"Oh, well, when you dream about something that
you did, you're actually there." Dean also credited the
crime scene video with jogging his memory. And he
mentioned conversations with his attorney in which they
developed "a scenario as to what happened in the
apartment." His ability to recall supposed details from a
four-year-old crime, yet to be unable to keep straight
what he told authorities a day before, left lawyers for the
other defendants scratching their collective heads. When
asked to physically describe Joseph White, the man Dean
claimed he saw commit a rape, he could not.

"I wouldn't know him if I seen him," Dean said
during a deposition.

Faced with the testimonial evidence of other co-
conspirators, Ada Taylor pleaded guilty. Her deal with
the prosecution convicted her of second-degree murder
and kept her from becoming the first woman on
Nebraska's death row. It also meant she would testify for
the state.

Then White got his own shot at a deal. On
September 28, 1989, the prosecutor offered him a plea
of guilty to second-degree murder and twenty-five years
to life. White refused it.

A few days later, Gonzalez pleaded no contest to
aiding and abetting second-degree murder. The state
now had four potential witnesses. All of them were liars,
White contended. And he knew he was right. All he could
do now was hope a jury would agree.

CHAPTER FIFTY SIX

America's Worst Miscarriage of Justice

There were surprising outcomes for five of the six defendants in the case who made plea deals in exchange for reduced charges and sentences. Kathy Gonzalez, James Dean, and Debra Shelden pled guilty to aiding and abetting second-degree murder in exchange for ten-year sentences. Eventually those three served five and a half years in prison before being released in 1994. Thomas Winslow confessed to raping Mrs. Wilson. He was sentenced to a term of ten to fifty years in prison. Ada JoAnn Taylor confessed to smothering Mrs. Wilson while Winslow and Joseph White raped her. She received a sentence of ten to forty years in prison. Taylor would later say her statement and testimony were the result of "brainwashing" and, coupled with the threat of the death penalty, she decided to cut her losses and enter a plea. The daunting specter of dying in the electric chair tipped the balance for her.

Only Joseph White continued to maintain his innocence, opting to take his chances before a jury. During White's trial in 1989, James Dean, Ada Taylor, and Debra Shelden testified that the six were in Mrs. Wilson's apartment during her rape and murder. Taylor testified it was she who smothered Mrs. Wilson while White raped her. The jury convicted White of first-degree murder. He could have been sentenced to death, but the jury instead chose a penalty of life in prison.

White's conviction was appealed to a higher court, but that effort proved unsuccessful. While he, Thomas Winslow, and Ada Taylor languished in prison for years, White continued his quest to have the physical evidence re-examined using DNA testing. He knew if this was done, as it should have been in 1989, he would be exonerated. But his appeals fell on deaf ears until 2007, seventeen years after he began his term in the Nebraska State Prison.

Finally, the Nebraska Supreme Court ordered DNA testing on some of the evidence. Body fluid samples were obtained from all six defendants and compared with both known and unknown samples found in Helen Wilson's apartment. In the summer of 2008, the relevant evidence was tested. A comparison showed that, without a shadow of a doubt, none of the defendants could have been involved in the crime. That resulted in complete exoneration of the "Beatrice Six." By the time all of the testing had been completed and legal motions were filed, considered, and re-filed, Smith, Winslow, and Taylor had each spent eighteen years behind bars. In sum total, six people had spent nearly seventy years in prison for a crime they didn't commit.

But then came the question: If these six people didn't commit the crime, who did?

A twenty-two year old Oklahoma native, Bruce Allen Smith, had initially been identified by police as one of about ten potential suspects. Several days after the murder, Smith left Beatrice and returned to Oklahoma. In the early stages of the investigation, officers located Smith and traveled to Oklahoma to interview him and to obtain blood, saliva, and pubic hair samples. The Oklahoma State Crime Lab made comparisons with blood and semen samples found at the Wilson crime scene. Because of testing methods available at the time of the murder, Smith was deemed to not be a match and was excluded as a suspect. The method of blood testing in the 1980s was serology. That science could only tell that a person matched a blood type. It wasn't possible to exclude millions of other people in the world who had the same type, thus it was a very inexact science for forensic purposes. The advent of DNA profiling would change all of that. Unfortunately in 1985, that technology had not developed to the point of being functional in criminal cases.

Investigators would learn Smith had been drinking heavily in a Beatrice bar on the night of the murder. He was then driven to a party in a nearby town. Statements taken from people at the party revealed Smith was told to leave. Not only had he been drunk and obnoxious, he threatened to rape one of the women at the party. When he left he made more threats, saying he was going to "get even" for being thrown out. He was driven back to Beatrice and dropped off a couple of blocks from Helen Wilson's apartment building. The time was approximately three-thirty a.m. He was last seen walking in the direction of the apartment building where Helen Wilson lived. Early the following morning, Smith went into a nearby convenience store. The store clerk would later tell police he saw blood on Smith and the clothing he was wearing.

In 1992, Smith died of AIDS in Oklahoma City. By then, all six of the defendants had been convicted and were serving prison terms. Smith was no longer a suspect since the case was "solved." But he went to his grave knowing what he'd done, and probably knew six people had been wrongfully convicted for a crime he committed.

Finally, the wheels of justice began to turn. In 2008, DNA testing done on Smith's blood revealed a positive match with blood found in Helen Wilson's bedroom, blood on a pair of her panties found near her body, and also matched the semen found inside her body. Smith was conclusively identified as the sole suspect in the murder to the exclusion of any other person. Police would also learn Smith had an arrest for rape in 1981. However, it could not be determined if he had been convicted because a flood had destroyed the criminal files. Records from Oklahoma showed he served just over two years in the Oklahoma State Penitentiary from 1987 to 1989 for burglary.

In 2009, a deputy attorney general for the State of Nebraska would say in reference to Smith, "Nobody has any doubt this was the killer." While the attorney general's office was pleased to announce they had identified the true killer of Helen Wilson, they said they were saddened by the unethical actions of former prosecutors that led to the convictions of six innocent people. In their statement, they noted the record clearly showed prosecutors and investigators on the case "bullied" the six suspects, and "fed them evidence to get them to plead guilty."

Since I had told the reporter from Omaha that I would "stand by" the accuracy of my profile, I decided to do some research on Bruce Allen Smith, then compare that information with notes I had made back in 1985, which I still maintained.

Point-by-point, nearly everything pertinent in my assessment matched the official profile:

1. Suspect will be a white male in his late teens or early twenties. Correct. Smith was twenty-two when he committed the crime.

2. The crime was committed by a single person. Correct.

3. He would be described as a nice, quiet, and shy young man. True, except when he was drinking.

4. The suspect lives close to Wilson's apartment. He had once lived in the same apartment building with an older aunt.

5. He is dependent on this mother figure and has been dominated by her throughout his life. That was also correct. His aunt was a very demanding and domineering woman, and they apparently had considerable conflict.

6. He has poor self-esteem and wouldn't be comfortable in a relationship with a woman of his own age. Correct as well. He seemed incapable of maintaining a relationship with women. Plus, the issue of AIDS might indicate a tendency toward homosexual behavior.

7. It's possible he knew Mrs. Wilson and may have been in her apartment before. Not confirmed, although the fact he lived in the same apartment building would indicate some previous familiarity. In addition to that, on the night of the murder he apparently knew exactly which apartment to break into, and that there would be a victim there living alone.

8. May have been interviewed early in the investigation. Correct.

9. May have approached police, or provided information to divert attention from himself. Apparently not true, as he left town shortly after the murder.

10. The suspect was motivated by rape. His actions that night make it clear that was the case. (My notes also reflect that I thought he was an anger-retaliatory rapist. Roy Hazelwood gets credit for an assist on this assertion.)

11. It is likely he will have a past record of sexual assault. He was arrested for rape in 1981.

12. May have visited her grave. Probably not, since he most likely left town before the services were conducted for Mrs. Wilson.

The other personality traits listed on a previous page could also have proven instructive to the investigators. However it all came together in their minds, the fact that they believed six people were involved is simply astonishing in the worst possible way. At some point, one could assume common sense would prevail. But it certainly didn't.

On reflection, I suppose I felt satisfied in knowing I had given investigators accurate information that should have helped them in their search for a killer. But I couldn't help but feel a sense of remorse about the manner in which a seemingly cut-and-dried case could spiral so far out of control

It is still beyond my comprehension how all of this could and did transpire, but I now have an answer when asked, "What was the most interesting (or strange) case you ever worked on?"

"I did a profile on a murder case in which I was sure the crime was committed by a single male suspect acting alone. The profile was accurate, but six innocent people, including three women, spent nearly seventy years in

prison."
    "How did that happen?"
    "I'm still not quite sure."

EPILOGUE

In July of 2013, the first edition of this book was published. I will readily admit that my primary motivation behind writing this book was to bring publicity to what I felt was the greatest travesty of justice I had ever heard of in over forty years in law enforcement—the Helen Wilson case.

It is now June of 2014 as I add what I suppose will be called an "Epilogue" for this book, but in reality is more of an "Update." Why? Because after nearly thirty years, this case is *still not* resolved. Justice has not, and probably never will be served for Helen Wilson, or the six people who were unjustly convicted. However, the case is now out of the criminal courts and onto the civil side of the ledger. The six people who served over seventy years in prison have already and will have yet another day in court. Possibly *many* days in court.

Let me explain what I'm trying to say here, because it's difficult for me, as I will have a hard time not thinking about this case every day of my life. I'm going to put it in bullet points, because it will make it easier for me to organize and explain, and hopefully for you to understand. I know a book needs narration, but in this case I will have to make an exception. This should still tell the story:

The Nebraska Attorney General reopened the investigation in 2008. The goal was to tie the true killer, Bruce Smith, to the original six people already convicted of the crime. Instead, the task force investigating the case developed conclusive evidence to completely exonerate the six people who had been wrongfully convicted.

Upon conclusion of the investigation, the Attorney General for the State of Nebraska said, "I believe without a doubt that these six people are completely innocent." The label "Beatrice Six" was attached to the group.

Following their post-conviction exoneration, the criminal defendants, now civil plaintiffs, filed a suit in the United States District Court for the State of Nebraska – Lincoln Division. Among other defendants, Gage County and the State of Nebraska were named in the civil filing. The investigators and district attorney who prosecuted the case (who is no longer in office) were also named as defendants.

In 2012, Ada JoAnn Taylor was awarded the maximum amount permissible under state law: $500,000. James Dean was awarded $300,000. This money was awarded from the Nebraska Claims for Wrongful Conviction and Imprisonment Act of 2009. The difference in amounts is due to Taylor spending nearly twenty years in prison, while Dean spent just over five. The Wrongful Convictions Act was passed after the six defendants were exonerated. These awards have nothing to do with the civil case in federal court.

In a court ruling, the judge wrote that he was surprised the Nebraska Legislature placed a cap on damages in such cases. "To try to attempt to place any value on one's liberty to be free is a Herculean task," he said.

The follow-up investigation and examination of more than five thousand pages of documents from the original case revealed evidence that Gage County investigators used questionable interrogation techniques. It was also determined that Sheriff's Deputy Burdette Searcey was so eager to solve the cold case he hounded his top suspect—Joseph White—and either missed or ignored evidence that supported his innocence. (Author's comment: *"Form a theory and build a set of facts around the theory. Throw any facts that don't advance the theory out the window."*)

The investigation revealed psychologist Wayne Price worked both as a sheriff's deputy and a mental health counselor who provided therapy for two of the six before they were arrested, and then met with five of them as a deputy. This was deemed by the State of Nebraska to be a violation of professional standards. It was also highly unethical for law enforcement officers to so aggressively work both sides of the fence in this manner. (Author's comment: *"Even if they're not guilty, figure out a way to show they are. Guilt or innocence is less important than a conviction."*)

The state's position in defense against the claims was that Taylor and Dean provided false testimony in court, thus committing the crime of perjury. As a result, their claim for reparation from the state should be denied. In considering the nature of their original statements, the court ruled the statements were not perjury. The court essentially scalded the investigators and district attorney for every step they took to further a completely flawed investigation.

Joseph White returned to Alabama after he was released from prison. In 2011, White died in a workplace accident at a steel mill. His name is still a part of the civil filing and any awards will be paid to his estate. His estate received $500,000 from the state after his death. This was from the Wrongful Convictions Act, and is not a part of the federal civil suit.

Under the same act, the state has paid an additional $500,000 each to Thomas Winslow and Kathy Gonzalez. This is also not a part of the pending civil action. Debra Shelden has a claim pending against the state of Nebraska. She remains a party in the federal civil suit.

The estate of White and the surviving five were seeking at least $14 million in damages, claiming their civil rights were violated during the investigation. They also claimed that they were coerced into making damaging statements. The result of these actions brought about a total of over seventy years of undue confinement.

In August of 2013, about a month after the first edition of this book was published, I was contacted by Joe Duggan from the Omaha World Herald. Duggan had become aware of the book, and wanted to do an article about my role in the Wilson case. I agreed to be interviewed and we talked for about an hour on the phone. Following the interview, an article was published in the paper on September 3, 2013. Duggan did an excellent job of reviewing the facts and bringing the status up to date in the article. I particularly enjoyed a statement he made, and I will quote directly from the article: "The turns and twists in a murder case Klismet briefly reviewed 28 years ago couldn't have been dreamed up by a fiction writer. And they were enough to shock an old FBI agent."

I called Duggan back after he sent me the link for the article. We both had a good laugh talking about the last comment, "...an old FBI agent." Of course, I chided him about the comment, but he's right. I never dreamed I could still be involved in a case that is now thirty years old. I was in my thirties when I was first called to assist in the investigation. I'm not in my thirties any longer!

Several days after the article went public, my phone rang at home. The person calling was an attorney in Lincoln who told me he was representing one of the parties in the civil suit. He explained that he had read the article in the paper, and he wanted to know if I would be willing to be a witness for the plaintiffs in the civil suit. He said, "I didn't know you were still around." (I'm not that old if you're implying I had died!)

I told him I would have to think about it. When I did over the next couple of days, I felt I had no choice. The research I had done told me the investigators had made one huge failure, among many others, and that was taking a four-year old cold case and not looking back at the file. Had they done that and found my profile on the murder, the words "ONE SUSPECT ONLY" should have jumped off the page at them. You simply don't open a cold case on spurious information and run with it before you look back to see what happened years before. It was this failure that ultimately led to the tragic events that unfolded in 1989.

My son is a practicing attorney in Denver and I will occasionally seek his advice on various things. In this instance, my concern was the possibility of libel. Kary is familiar with the case and I updated him and refreshed his memory. The most instructive comment I received from him was, "Dad, there is one absolute defense to libel. The truth." That tipped the balance for me and I called the attorney in Lincoln, telling him I would be glad to testify. He told me the date the trial was set to begin was January 6, 2014 in federal court in Lincoln. I then decided I might not be so pleased about my decision, because I know what the winters are like in Nebraska. But he said he was going to buy a book as a reference.

That made points.

I received a subpoena and followed the developments through online articles in the Lincoln Star Journal. There were motions to delay the trial, of course, but U.S. District Court Judge Richard Kopf held the attorneys' feet to the fire and denied those motions. The civil suit went to trial as scheduled.

About a week into the trial, several defendants, including the State of Nebraska and the former Gage County District Attorney, were dismissed from the suit. I still don't understand the latter, but I wasn't there listening to the testimony and presentation of evidence. The trial proceeded and was submitted to the jury. On February 6th, after three days of deliberation, the jury informed Judge Kopf they were hopelessly deadlocked. It was an exact split, six for the plaintiffs and six believing the plaintiffs had not proven their case. Judge Kopf declared a mistrial.

Shortly after the ruling of the judge, the plaintiffs' attorneys said they would proceed ahead to a second trial. The date for that trial has yet to be announced that I am aware of as of this writing. I have yet to receive a subpoena. An attorney for the plaintiffs called me and said I still might be called as a witness in the second trial. I'm inclined to believe if he'd called me for the first trial, there wouldn't have been a second one.

I don't know if my testimony would have tipped the balance, but when one suspect becomes six, it seems to me a jury might pay attention to "an old FBI agent."

ABOUT THE AUTHOR

      Pete Klismet served his country with two separate tours on submarines during the Vietnam War. After an Honorable Discharge from the U.S. Navy, Pete finished college and was hired as a police officer in Ventura, California. He continued his education and earned two Master's Degrees. Appointed as a Special Agent of the FBI, he received numerous awards and commendations while serving in three FBI Field Offices. He was named 1999 Law Enforcement officer of the year by a multi-national organization. After retirement, he became the Department Chair of Criminal Justice programs at a college in Colorado. Since his retirement as a college professor, Pete and his wife Nancy enjoy life in Colorado Springs, Colorado.

Look for more exciting books soon from this fabulous author.

www.fountainbluepublishing.com

If you would like to be notified by email when new books are released from Fountain Blue Publishing by this author or other authors, send an email to info@fountainbluepublishing.com with SUBSCRIBE in the subject line.

Made in the USA
Middletown, DE
23 December 2016